From Purdah to Parliament

From Purdah to Parliament

Shaista Suhrawardy Ikramullah

Karachi
Oxford University Press
Oxford New York Delhi
1998

Oxford University Press, Walton Street, Oxford OX2 6DP

Oxford   New York
Athens   Auckland   Bangkok   Bombay
Calcutta   Cape Town   Dar es Salaam   Delhi
Florence   Hong Kong   Istanbul   Karachi
Kuala Lumpur   Madras   Madrid   Melbourne
Mexico City   Nairobi   Paris   Singapore
Taipei   Tokyo   Toronto
and associated companies in
Berlin   Ibadan

Oxford is a trade mark of Oxford University Press

© Oxford University Press, 1998

All rights reserved. No part of this publication may be reproduced, stored in a retrieval system, or transmitted, in any form or by any means, without the prior permission in writing of Oxford University Press.

This book is sold subject to the condition that it shall not, by way of trade or otherwise, be lent, re-sold, hired out or otherwise circulated without the publisher's prior consent in any form of binding or cover other than that in which it is published and without a similar condition including this condition being imposed on the subsequent purchaser.

First Edition by Cresset Press, London, 1963
This Revised Edition by Oxford University Press

ISBN 0 19 577804 9

Printed in Pakistan at
Mueid Packages, Karachi.
Published by
Ameena Saiyid, Oxford University Press
5-Bangalore Town, Sharae Faisal
PO Box 13033, Karachi-75350, Pakistan.

*To my husband
who took me out of purdah and has
regretted it ever since.*

CONTENTS

	page
List of Photographs	ix
Foreword to the First Edition	xi
Preface	xiii
Introduction	xvii

1. An Old-Fashioned House (1915)	1
2. In a Modern Home (1919–22)	12
3. Childhood (1922–24)	18
4. Early Education	27
5. Political Background	38
6. My Marriage	47
7. Adjustment	61
8. Twilight of an Empire (1933–36)	68
9. Years in England (1937–40)	77
10. The Return Home	83
11. The Shadow of Coming Events	90
12. History in the Making	100
13. Heading Towards a Crisis	111
14. The Gathering Storm	120
15. Under the Darkening Sky	126
16. The Storm Breaks	135
17. The Year Between	148
18. Arriving in Pakistan—The Promised Land	156
19. Inside Parliament	164
20. Plight of the Refugees	173
21. Third Session of the UN (1948)	182
22. Prophetic Words	193
23. Eleventh Session of the UN (1956)	202
24. The Years in Morocco	209

Appendix 1	228
Appendix 2	231
Appendix 3	237
Appendix 4	248
Appendix 5	250
Glossary	253

LIST OF PHOTOGRAPHS

Between pp. 142–143
1. Nawab Syud Muhammad.
2. Hasan Masud Suhrawardy.
3. Hasan Masud (aged 18).
4. Begum Ikramullah (aged 12) with her father, Sir Hassan Suhrawardy.
5. Receiving Ph.D. from the University of London.
6. Muslim Women's Students' Federation, 1941.
7. With the Quaid-i-Azam at Simla, 1945.
8. A family portrait.
9. Mohammad Ikramullah, Sarvath, Salma, Begum Ikramullah, Naz, and Inam at their Clifton home, December 1947.
10. Mohammad Ikramullah.
11. With her *Mamoo*, Syud Hussain, the first Indian Ambassador to Egypt, 1949.
12. Begum Ikramullah, Fatima Jinnah, Naz, Salma, and Inam at Flagstaff House, September 1949.
13. With her husband and Mr and Mrs Alva Warren, US Ambassador.
14. Inter-Parliamentary Conference, Dublin, 1951.
15. With Begum Raana Liaquat Ali Khan and wives of diplomats at a lunch at PM House.
16. Huseyn Shaheed Suhrawardy, Hasan Shahid Suhrawardy (Pakistan's Ambassador to Spain), Mohammad Ikramullah (Pakistan's Ambassador to France), and Begum Ikramullah, 1953.
17. With Queen Elizabeth II at the Pakistan Stall, British Trade Fair, 1956.
18. With Vijaya Lakshmi Pandit (sister of Jawaharlal Nehru) at the UN, 1956.

19. With Prince Wan (left) at the UN, 1956.
20. Deputy Chairman of the Pakistan Delegation, UN 1956–57.
21. Security Council meeting, 1956. *Front*: Feroze Khan Noon. *Second row*: Begum Ikramullah and Mohammad Ali Bogra. *Third row*: Aftab Ahmed Khan and Rahat Said Chhatari.
22. With President Ayub Khan and Zulfikar Ali Bhutto.
23. Presenting her credentials to King Hassan Thani of Morocco, 1964.
24. Leaving the royal palace with Siddi Mameri (left) and the Protocol Officer (right).
25. With her daughters and staff at her house in Morocco.
26. Sarvath greeting Lalla Aisha, the first Moroccan woman to be appointed Ambassador to England.
27. With Lalla Aisha.
28. Tying the *imam zamin* on Lalla Aisha's arm.
29. Begum Shaista Suhrawardy Ikramullah.

FOREWORD TO THE FIRST EDITION

I consider it a privilege to write the foreword to the book of Begum Shaista Ikramullah. Very close relations have existed between our two families for the last four generations. The grandfather of Begum Ikramullah, Maulana Obaidullah Al-Obaidi Suhrawardy, who was the Principal of the Madrassa Alia and one of the great Schahero of Dhaka, was a personal friend of my great-grandfather, Nawab Sir Abdul Ghani; and my maternal grandfather, Nawab Sir Ahsanullah. Her maternal grandfather, Nawab Syud Muhammad was also a great friend of my family. He belonged to one of the old aristocratic families of Dhaka. He was a brilliant conversationalist and wit, and an Urdu writer and author of great repute. His essays in the well-known journal, the *Oudh Punch,* had the same satirical humour as Akbar Alahabadi's poems. Sir Hassan Suhrawardy, father of Begum Ikramullah, materially helped me in the start of my public career. Begum Ikramullah, in spite of the official position of her husband, was a comrade in the struggle for the achievement of Pakistan.

The book, *From Purdah to Parliament,* is an extremely interesting account of a Muslim lady brought up under old Islamic traditions and culture, acquiring modern education at the same time, and gradually emerging as a modern, educated woman taking not only a prominent part in the social life of pre-Partition India, but starting with political propaganda at social parties and finishing up as a member of the Constituent Assembly of Pakistan. At Delhi, her house was a place of rendezvous for Muslim leaders and at her dinner parties one met politicians belonging to various schools of thought where brilliant conversation was an additional treat to the excellent cuisine. I remember one such dinner at Delhi where half a dozen of the most important conversationalists were gathered together and it was one occasion when I enjoyed the conversation even more than the food.

I remember the author as a young girl in school who was allowed to appear before me at her father's house because of the relationship between the families and because of her extreme youth. I have thus really seen her coming out from Purdah to Parliament.

Khawaja Nazimuddin
Second Governor-General of Pakistan
and President of the Muslim League

PREFACE

It was in early 1963 when I finished writing *From Purdah to Parliament*. The book launching ceremony was scheduled for 22 September but a personal tragedy prevented this. My husband's sudden death on 12 September left me completely shattered, and my intellectual and political activities came to a complete standstill, for it was his support and encouragement which had made this possible, just as it was my father's wish and the education that he had given me that had made me enter politics. With both of them gone, I felt that I could not face the strains and stresses inherent in practical life.

The launching was of course cancelled. Some sporadic reviews appeared in the press but I had lost all interest in everything and did not do the necessary follow up. I also did not have the time for writing because the day to day mechanics of mundane life and its attendant irritations had to be faced and resolved. So it came as a pleasant surprise when after nearly two years of the book's publication, I got a letter from the Cresset Press saying that the book was almost sold out. There were a dozen or so copies left and what did I want to do with them? I wrote back saying that they should be sent to my eldest daughter Salma who happened to be in England at that time. It never occured to me to ask if they would consider bringing out a second edition. After some time the Cresset Press itself closed down and I did not think that any other publisher would be interested in publishing it again.

Therefore it never ceased to surprise me that even after several years after its publication, the demand for *From Purdah to Parliament* continued and I was occasionally asked if I could spare a copy for interested readers. Suggestions were made that I bring out a second edition but no concrete proposals were ever made. It was only when Mrs Ameena Saiyid, Managing Director of the Oxford University Press, very kindly offered to publish a second edition of the book, if I could bring it up-to-date, that I seriously began considering the proposal. I had myself felt at times that the book was incomplete. It stops at my taking oath in Parliament. This understandably raises some questions in the reader's mind as to how I fared in Parliament. Therefore, when the offer of re-publication was made I thought of bringing my book up to the secession of East Pakistan, showing how the seeds of that tragic event were to be found as early as in the deliberations of the First Constituent Assembly; but, on consideration I realized that my knowledge of events that occurred after I resigned from Parliament in November 1953, was no more than that of any concerned citizen of Pakistan and therefore, I would undoubtedly be treading on very controversial ground, it would be like the opening of Pandora's Box and I did not feel competent to deal with this.

Therefore I decided to end my book on 23 October 1954. I felt that this made the book more compact and its veracity easier to substantiate as I was myself a witness to the events mentioned. Of course my interpretation of the events may be questioned but the factual details are as accurate as I can remember them.

The Constituent Assembly was dissolved by the Governor-General, Mr Ghulam Muhammad, exactly a year after my resignation and my apprehension regarding the delaying of the Constitution came true but it makes me sad that it did. It is one of those occasions when one wishes one had not been proved right.

As I began writing extra chapters I realized that some of the political events I had been concerned with happened after my resignation but they may be of interest to the readers for example the United Nations Session of 1956 at which I led the Pakistan delegation and my appointment as

Ambassador to Morocco—in a way these are extensions of my having entered Parliament, so I have included these as well.

As a final postscript I wish to add that the dedication at the front was phrased by my husband in his typical irreverent manner.

Ikram had a delightful sense of humour. Jilly Cooper who was editing my book for the Cresset Press, asked me, 'and what about a dedication?'

I replied, 'I want to dedicate it to my husband,' and then we began discussing the wording. Ikram who was listening said, *'To my husband who took me out of purdah and has regretted it ever since'*

We all laughed. 'But I can't say that,' I protested, 'goodness knows what people will think. But Jilly liked it and insisted I have it as a dedication. I gave in.

Shaista Suhrawardy Ikramullah,
January 1997.

INTRODUCTION

I often feel that I have lived through three distinct eras. This may sound impossible, but the fact is that I was born before the last vestige of Mughal civilization had quite disappeared from the Indian subcontinent. My childhood was spent in the heyday of British Imperialism and the early years of my youth coincided with the period when the struggle for independence was gathering momentum. I had the privilege of getting into the arena as the struggle progressed and of witnessing the liquidation of an empire and the heralding in of a new state, a state born out of the dreams and desires of one hundred million people, welded into a nation by their spiritual need and economic necessity.

These years are crammed with events and crowded with personalities. Memory cannot hold that picture for very long. I feel a great desire, an urge, to put it all down on paper, to sort things out and to see them in perspective. And, if while doing so, I can catch and convey a fraction of the colour and movement of the great panorama I have been privileged to witness, I shall be very happy.

Chapter 1

AN OLD-FASHIONED HOUSE (1915)

I was born in Calcutta in my maternal grandfather's house. It was a very old-fashioned house, built in the style of Muslim houses of the nineteenth century. It was sold when I was only eight years old and my mother, Shaherbano, had not lived in it continuously after I was two, but she visited it a good deal and so I can remember it very clearly and can describe it almost room by room.

It stood in a narrow lane off the main road. (It was considered in very bad taste to have a house from which the main thoroughfares of the city could be seen.) There was a small unpretentious gate which opened into a long gallery. At the end of the gallery at the left was a door. This opened into yet another uncovered gallery which turned into a courtyard. All around the courtyard were the various living-rooms. These rooms were grouped together with a deep verandah running the entire length of them and each group formed a separate unit. In a large house there would be a dozen or so such self-contained units, but as my grandfather's house was not very big there were only four or five of them. To the right of the courtyard was the largest. It had a very large, deep verandah, which consisted of small living-rooms. These verandahs were the equivalent of drawing-rooms in a Western house. The rooms were quite small and were used more or less as dressing-rooms or for storage purposes.

One sat and did one's sewing and reading, ate *paan* and received visitors on the verandah. The most important piece of furniture here would be a large *takhat*. These were raised wooden platforms, covered with an embroidered or woven material, or only with clean white sheets. They had elaborately carved or lacquered legs, very often of silver. On special occasions *masnads* would be placed over them. *Takhats* were always placed against a wall and had several bolsters scattered over them for one to recline on. A *paandaan* was always to be found on one side of the *takhat* from which every member of the family helped themselves to *paan*. Of course, every member had her own small *paandaan* and several of these would be found dotted on the *takhat* throughout the day.

The *takhat* was, literally, the stage of all household activities. Ladies sat there making and eating *paan*, cutting *chalia* and gossiping. The more industrious ones brought their sewing or embroidery and stitched their daughters' trousseaux while listening to the gossip. Even shopping was carried on from there, for women vendors brought their goods and spread them at the foot of the *takhat*. Children also had a corner for themselves and their toys would be found littered all over it.

Besides *takhats*, there would hardly be any other piece of furniture on the verandah; Muslim houses did not begin having furniture in the English style until much later. Wardrobes had only just begun making an appearance and, if there were any, they would be found in the small living-rooms. English-style trunks, were also coming into fashion, but were still a novelty. Most belongings, therefore, were still kept in large wooden chests.

Besides the large *takhat* for sitting on, there would be a *choki* on one side of the verandah for saying one's prayers. Quite near it would be placed the shining, pot-bellied goblets in which water for ablution before prayer was kept. As most of the ladies said their prayers five times a day, it was necessary to have the water at hand. Keeping these vessels filled was the duty of the innumerable maidservants.

Drinking water was also kept in earthenware jars on a lacquered and carved wooden stand in another part of the verandah. In a hot country, the convenience of having drinking water at hand need not be emphasized. So it came about that vessels containing water for drinking and washing were to be found in what was the equivalent of a sitting-room.

The smaller verandahs were arranged more or less in the same manner. There was one used exclusively by young girls as their sitting-room, for they were not supposed to make themselves too conspicuous even inside their own home and would not be found in the large verandah but in one at the side. There was a verandah for the servants alongside the kitchen and a long gallery where all the old pensioned-off servants lived. I remember at least half a dozen or so such old servants living in my grandfather's house when I was a child. It was because we looked after our old servants that the need for old-age pensions and old people's homes did not begin to be felt in our country until recently.

There was an upper storey and another completely self-contained apartment with courtyard, kitchens and servants' rooms leading from the main part of the house. But, as the windows of some of the rooms opened upon the lane, only young married couples were allowed to live in this part of the house. It was not even considered suitable for young unmarried girls to go there. The young matrons would come to the main part of the house after their housework was done if they wanted company; but they were rarely visited in their own domain for it was not customary for the elders to visit the young. It was the duty of the young to come and pay their respects, while young unmarried girls were not allowed to go visiting on their own at all.

The house was old-fashioned and behind the times and the life that was lived in it was no less out of date. My grandfather, Nawab Syud Muhammad, belonged to an old aristocratic family and he never came to terms with the new rulers or the way of life they brought with them. His ancestors had come from Iran and settled down in Dhaka at the time of the Mughal Emperor, Faruk Saiyar. They were men of wealth and position and are mentioned as such in standard works of that time like *Tarikh Nusrat Jangi* and Bishop Heber's Memoirs. They prided themselves on the fact that, though they had lived for several generations in India, they had married only into families of birth and status similar to their own.

Dhaka had been one of the outposts of the Mughal court and had become a sort of enclave of Mughal culture in Bengal. On a small scale it had all the refinements of living that were to be found in Delhi and Lucknow. Families such as Nawab Syud Muhammad's regarded themselves as custodians of the Mughal culture and guarded it jealously as a precious possession. This made them rather isolated from the rest of the people in the Province of Bengal and their social life was confined to a narrow circle, while for marriage they most often had to go to the families outside Bengal or to other enclaves of Muslim culture there, such as Murshidabad, Midnapur and Shaistabad. Nawab Syud Muhammad, or Nunne Syud as he was called in his youth, was married at the age of seventeen to his cousin, a beautiful girl of fifteen. After two or three years of blissfully happy marriage she died in childbirth. The family fortunes had also reached a very low ebb by then because Nunne Syud's oldest brother, who had come into the estate when a very young man, had, as is the wont of young men, picked his friends unwisely and, in consequence, lost his fortune rapidly. He died fairly young, but one of his daughters lived till I was fifteen. It was from her that I heard most of the family history and a good deal about the manners and customs of that period. She was a wonderful raconteuse and could make the past come to life. In the long winter evenings she used to sit with us children, cosily tucked under her warm soft *razai*, and tell us about her childhood and youth, of times when life was gay and colourful, how when she used to sleep ôn beds that were covered every evening with fresh flowers, how in the summer, in the moonlight, they went sailing in *bajaras* on the Padma river, how they celebrated *Eid* and with what ceremonies marriages were performed.

But Nawab Syud Muhammad had to forsake this way of life at the age of twenty-two and come to Calcutta with his maternal uncle, Muhammad Mirza. Calcutta was then the capital, the centre of progress and home of the newly prosperous. Nawab Syud Muhammad lived there for the rest of his life but I do not think he ever really felt at home in it. He was, however, almost immediately discovered by Nawab Abdul Latif.

Nawab Abdul Latif is to Bengal what Sir Syed Ahmed Khan is to the rest of Muslim India. He is the man who realized that the British had come to stay and the sooner the Muslims came to terms with them the better. Therefore, like Sir Syed, he entered Government service himself, sent his son to England to study for the Bar and did everything in his power to encourage education among the Muslims. Nawab Abdul Latif was charmed by my grandfather—this sad young man, scion of an old family, now so completely at sea. He married him off to his daughter and persuaded him to take up Government service. Nawab Syud Muhammad, though he had had the best possible education in the old style (he learned calligraphy alone for seven years), knew little English, but the passing of examinations was not then necessary to secure Government positions. The British were keen to encourage men of good families to enter their service and nominated them to high posts.

So Nawab Syud Muhammad became a Deputy Magistrate, the highest post open to Indians at that time. He later became head of a department, one of the first Indians to achieve that distinction. He was the recipient of many titles and honours from the British but he never really became reconciled to their way of life nor did he cease to regard his joining the Government service as almost an act of collaboration. He thought the 'WOG' was something ridiculous and in his essays in *Oudh Punch,* the well-known literary magazine of the time, gave vent to his real feelings. These essays are priceless specimens of ironic humour and are merciless and accurate portrayals of the times, which today take on an added significance since they show how the pendulum had swung from complete non-cooperative to abject and slavish imitation.

Nawab Syud Muhammad perforce had to accept certain things for himself and his sons, but he was determined not to accept them for his womenfolk. They were kept in the strictest purdah and even visits from women were restricted. The dressmakers, the bangle sellers and other women hawkers, who must necessarily be allowed in, were regularly vetted by the *derban*; no strange woman could gain entry. Nawab Syud Muhammad did not consider the womenfolk of the new-rich of Calcutta fit company for the ladies of his household, so they never went visiting or received any calls except from relatives. The people my mother and aunt knew best, outside their own home, were their two aunts, stepsisters of their mother, who were about the same age as themselves. Their father, my mother's grandfather, Nawab Abdul Latif, was dead and their mother was not so strict with them. Coming in contact with these girls was the nearest my mother and aunt came to seeing anything outside their own extremely secluded existence.

My mother's education followed the orthodox pattern. She was taught to read the Koran by one of the many distant relatives who lived in the house. In a household like my grandfather's these ladies occupied the position of super governesses or seamstresses. They did the same sort of work as governesses in European households, but enjoyed a slightly better status. The fact that they were related was never forgotten; they had their meals with the family and were consulted, at least formally, on all family matters. They made one or two of the children of the family their special charge and became responsible for everything pertaining to their welfare and education. The children, in their turn, became very fond of their special aunts and, when they grew up and had a household of their own, their favourite aunts were assured of a place of honour in it and, in due course, took charge of the children of the children they had brought up. It was a very graceful way of solving the problem of well-born women with no income.

After learning to read the Koran, girls were taught to read and write in Urdu but were not encouraged to delve very deeply into literature; but such was the atmosphere that they picked up a good deal of literary appreciation from their brothers. Cooking and sewing were considered the important items of a girl's education and, here again, one of the aunts was put in charge. Music was not taught for unfortunately it had fallen into disrepute, but girls picked up a great deal because it played such a part in everyday life and no ceremonial or festive occasion was complete without it.

Nawab Syud Muhammad had seven children, two daughters and five sons. His eldest daughter-in-law was his wife's niece and had been brought up in his house. The daughter of his eldest brother also stayed with his family. My mother and aunt said that he was fonder of them than of his own daughters, and at least they enjoyed many more privileges and favours. Their dress allowances were larger, they received more costly presents, were privileged to give their opinion on matters of family concern and had a greater say in everything than his own daughters. On his daily visits it was to them that he addressed himself first. But in this, as in everything else, Nawab Syud Muhammad was being true to the tradition of his time and class. Those who were dependent should be treated with greater courtesy and kindness so that they should never feel their position. He believed that the guests should not have anything less than the best even if it meant curtailing the privileges of his own children. This rule was extended not only to guests who came for a short time but to those who came and made their home with the family for good.

Though Nawab Syud Muhammad's fortunes had dwindled to nothing, there was not a time when there were not three or four such guests in his house. Some of them were old and ill, needing a lot of attention. Nawab Syud Muhammad saw that they got it, for it was the tradition of the house that they should be waited upon with all courtesy. My mother was his favourite child and the most beautiful of his children. Although a girl, she was not only like him in features but in build and carriage as well, but even she was not allowed any latitude. It used to amaze us when she told us how it took her father quite a long time to get over the fact that she had once cooked a dish which needed sixteen pints of milk with only eight and then served that 'mess' to him as *muz'afar*. He was horrified that a daughter of his should not know the difference between *muz'afar* and porridge. He always said that such bad taste, such lack of appreciation in a child of his was truly appalling, for Nawab Syud Muhammad regarded a breach of good taste in matters of dress and food of almost equal importance as breaches of good conduct. He was shocked if he heard one of his sons had not paid his debts, but it shocked him no less if one of them could not distinguish between various flavours in mangoes.

It was said that one of his sons actually plucked up sufficient courage to refuse a marriage suggested by his father and that he wrote his refusal. His father exploded, as was to be expected, but he was not much more furious at his son's audacity in having refused an alliance suggested by him than at the sight of the writing paper (on which this 'piece of impudence' was written) which had been torn off so carelessly as to have a jagged edge. If the children sought permission to do something and were told, 'This is not done in our family', they knew that their case was hopeless. To his children, not only the family tradition but he, himself, was the law. 'That a son of mine should do this' or 'that a daughter of mine should fail to do that' was, to his mind, the greatest reproach he could administer to any of his children, and they themselves regarded it as such. He judged every action by the yardstick of his family tradition, which took precedence over every other code of conduct. He worshipped at no other shrine and paid homage to no other gods than the god of his own family tradition.

Nawab Syud Muhammad lived by the values of a vanished age and, what is more, he so impressed these virtues on his children that they all clung to it and thus failed to come to terms with their world and, because of this, became, by worldly standards, failures. All of them, that is, except the youngest, Syud Hussain, who reached great eminence as a fiery young writer and politician and who, after India's independence, became Ambassador to Egypt.

Those who saw Nawab Syud Muhammad when young are now old themselves, but they remember him as the 'last of the Barons', a grand old man, white-haired but still extraordinarily handsome. As it was not customary to be on intimate terms with one's elders, they knew him only very slightly but they remember him as an extremely gracious person, full of old-world courtesy. These young men were sons of old friends so he was extremely nice to them and showed great concern for their comfort and saw that they were entertained and taken great care of when they were visiting him. They recall many acts of real consideration and thoughtfulness. Nawab Syud Muhammad might appear unbending and autocratic, but he was not really so. He belonged to an age that had vanished and the civilization he was bred in had crumpled to dust before his eyes. He loved that civilization and clung to it, desperately, and to be able to do so he had to be uncompromising.

My cousins, that is to say his grandchildren, who were old enough to have been taken notice of by him, still remember him as somebody who, though rather awe-inspiring, was extremely interesting and who always made them laugh. His personality had left such an impression, not only on my mother but on all his other children, that I feel I know him very well. When my mother talked about him I felt that I could almost see him and hear him admonishing his children in measured phrases. His conversation with them seemed to consist entirely of admonitions; but, since he was always ironically witty, sarcastic and clever, although, they withered under it, they could not say that it was boring.

His children not only respected and admired but loved him very deeply. I have often wondered at this, as the relationship between them seems to have been on such a formal basis. He visited the *zenana* once a day at a stated time, and his entry into the *deorhi* was announced as ceremoniously as any other visitor. When he had taken his seat, the ladies presented themselves one by one. *Dupattas* well over their heads, eyes downcast, they sat and spoke only when spoken to. Still, I cannot help feeling that they enjoyed his visits very much and looked forward to them as the peak event of the day. Stern and uncompromising on principles though he was, yet he had a great tenderness for his children, especially for his daughters and nieces. If they were not well and happy it perturbed him greatly. Though he saw them so little he knew exactly what they were like, which one had inherited his temper and who was of a gentle nature, who was ambitious and who had a contented disposition. My mother said that it used to surprise them very much when, by a casual remark, he showed that he had guessed at their innermost thoughts. He not only had an ironic wit but a delightful sense of humour as well, which showed itself in dealing with small children.

To compromise on principles was a great sin, according to Nawab Syud Muhammad, and so it remained a cardinal sin for all his children. They rejected adjustment and discarded 'give and take' as compromise and so they continued to live in a changing world by the values of one that had vanished.

I do not think I have ever met a woman like my mother. I know that is what every daughter feels but, quite objectively, I have never met a woman like her, for she did not belong to her own age—she belonged to the age that her father had seen vanish. On the other hand, my father belonged not only to the present but to the future. While she looked back, he looked forward. And so it was that I was brought up in a home which was at the same time a very modern one and yet one in which the values of an older world still held sway.

CHAPTER 2

IN A MODERN HOME (1919–22)

My father was one of those visionaries who always see ahead of their contemporaries. He was born and brought up at a time when the old-established customs were crumbling away and a new concept of life and a new mode of thought were beginning to find favour amongst his countrymen. His family traditions and background also contributed towards giving him a reformist outlook. His father, Obaidullah-Al-Obaidi Suhrawardy, was a pre-eminent scholar of Arabic and Persian, known and respected throughout the Indian subcontinent. But while most scholars of that time were extremely antagonistic towards English education, he was an advocate of it. He went to the length of learning English rather late in life and was amongst the founders and the first Principal of Dhaka Madrassa, a boys' school of the type of the English grammar school.

He died comparatively young, leaving a large family. My grandmother, however, had been so imbued with his ideas of education that, despite many handicaps, she decided to continue to educate her children. She had to return to her village, Midnapur, but she decided to send all her four boys as boarders to Dhaka. It was still a very rare thing to do this and my grandmother was subjected to much adverse criticism by friends and relations.

It was also an expensive undertaking for an inexperienced woman behind the purdah and with very slender means. But my grandmother must have really believed in education for she sold her jewels and most of the few pieces of land that she possessed to be able to educate her sons. Her courage nearly broke when her eldest boy died at the end of a brilliant academic career and after securing a Government scholarship to Oxford. But her sacrifices were finally rewarded and her other three sons lived to achieve distinction. My father and his brothers revered their mother greatly and were extremely mindful of what she had suffered and sacrificed for them. In their attitude to her there was something almost akin to worship. I was almost ten when my grandmother died so I remember her quite well and remember a number of little incidents which firmly implanted this impression in my young mind.

The other person who had a great influence on my father's life was his eldest sister, Khujista Akhtar Bano Begum. She was a pioneer of women's education in India, founder of two girls' schools and author of several books. The story of her education is rather interesting. She was only eleven when her father died but he had implanted such a love of learning in her heart by teaching her Urdu and Persian himself that, as there were no girls' schools as yet, she got her young brothers to continue her lessons in Persian and in English. She acquired great proficiency in both these languages. She could speak and read and write English fluently and translated several novels into Urdu from English. In Persian, as far as I am aware, she is the only woman to have been given a Degree of honour by Calcutta University and to have been the examiner in Persian for MA in the same university.

Besides her intellectual attainments, truly remarkable for that time, she possessed great sweetness of character and disposition. Everyone I have met who knew her seems to have loved her. Her home was a haven for my father and uncles, and she gave them encouragement, advice and help. Her husband, who became a High Court judge later on, was a struggling young lawyer at that time and she had young children of her own; but her brothers' welfare was and always remained her chief concern. They, on their part, absolutely adored her and even after her death she remained the most important person in their lives, a sort of guardian angel of the family whose conduct and behaviour had established the standards for the family for all time. To this day, all the girls in our family are given her name as their second name as a mark of respect to her memory.

And so it was that my father grew up in an atmosphere of puritanical austerity and high idealism. But this did not make him rigid and narrow; he had a temperament and gift for friendship, a liking for and appreciation of the good things in life and this made him a very warm, likeable and humane person.

He was married fairly young as was the custom in those days. He was still a medical student and he completed his studies after marriage, then went to England for postgraduate work. He stayed over two years taking the degrees of MD, FRCS, and LM; he was the second Muslim from the subcontinent to receive the degree of FRCS and amongst the very few Indians. On his return he was given a lecturership in the Calcutta Medical College and soon established a flourishing practice, for, even before proceeding to England, he had gained a reputation as a brilliant surgeon and many years afterwards, when he had abandoned medicine for politics, his colleagues never ceased regretting the loss of one who was considered a genius in his own profession.

At this time other Higher Services were just opening their doors to admit Indians, and my father was persuaded by his family to accept a post of District Medical Officer in the East India Railway. So it came about that I spent most of my early childhood in the pseudo-English railway colonies. I do not remember going there, but my earliest recollections begin with our house in Lilloah. Lilloah was a small residential suburb seven miles from Calcutta, of the type that was to be found outside every big city in India. The English did not like living in the congested parts of cities; therefore, outside every large city there would be open areas known as the *chaoni* or Civil Lines. Here there would be no bazaars, hardly any traffic, in fact none of the bustling, colourful activity that characterizes the cities of the East. The quiet lanes, well-trimmed hedges and well-kept gardens with wicket gates, all helped to create the illusion of an English garden suburb, and the mentality and attitude of those who lived in these parts were also suburbanly correct; but, of course, I was not aware of this till much later.

We had a very nice house and a really lovely garden, both of which my father kept in very good condition. This was the stage when Indians went in for extreme Westernization in every way, particularly those who joined the Service, which so far had been reserved for the English. They felt that it was their incumbent duty to prove to the Englishman that they could emulate him to perfection. This attitude may sound absurd now but at that time it did not seem so; it was considered to be synonymous with progress. Our house, therefore, was furnished to look exactly like an English house. In the drawing-room there were the heavy sofas, fender stool drawn near the fire, lace curtains looped up and tied with corded silk, gleaming brass and silver and various other knick-knacks displayed in cabinets. The dining-room had a fairly massive sideboard on which was displayed a lot of heavy silver. The hall and study were also furnished in the typical English style of the times and so were our bedrooms. The servants wore uniforms similar to those worn by the servants of English people, complete with gloves, cummerbund and monogrammed *pughris*. We had afternoon tea with hot buttered toast and even at other meals we ate what was called 'English' food which I now realize was a mixture of English, French, Portuguese and Indian culinary efforts. My mother did not like English food, so there would always be Indian dishes at the table cooked by her personal maid and these we ate with much greater relish than the so-called 'English' food.

In a house such as my grandfather's there would be a full complement of men as well as women servants and the men of the family would be in charge of the male staff. But in a modern house like ours there were no separate apartments for ladies and it was not possible to have a duplicate establishment, besides which my mother could not get any of her maidservants from her old home to come out to Lilloah. They considered it unseemly to go and live where only the *ferangis* lived. 'Poor Chhoti Begum,' they said. (That is what they called my mother. It means 'younger lady'.) She had married a young man with strange ideas and he had taken her to live among outlandish people. They felt very sorry for her. 'How dull it must be', but they regretted they could not share her exile. The only one to agree to defy convention and come was our nurse. She did so because she loved my brother and me far too much to be separated from us, and after we were grown up and did not need her as a nurse, she stayed on as my mother's personal maid.

Despite the fact that she kept strict purdah from the menservants, my mother ran the house very well. She gave all her orders through two small boys called the *chhokras*. They brought her the account books to see, and through them she ordered the menu for the day. She saw to it that the food purchased was fresh and handed out the stores, in each case the boys bringing and taking things to and fro. It sounds difficult but it worked, and worked fairly smoothly.

My brother, Hasan Masud, and I both spoke English even as very small children for we had nursery governesses from the time we were babies. We dressed like English children, my brother in shorts and shirts and what is known as 'Eton suits', I in frilly muslin frocks and starched pinafores with my hair tied with ribbons. We played with English children who introduced us to Beatrix Potter and Mother Goose Nursery Rhymes.

Each year at Christmas time we went to a children's party at the 'Club'. There would be a huge, glittering

Christmas tree and a resplendent Father Christmas to hand us out our presents.

I began going to school at Lilloah. I went to a small private school which was run by a middle-aged English lady with two other ladies to help her. It was run exclusively for English and Anglo-Indian children and I was the only Indian child in it. Miss Gasper, the headmistress, and both the other teachers belonged to the old-fashioned school. Our studies were essentially English; I learnt about Alfred and the Cakes, of the Hundred Years War, of Good Queen Bess and of the Iron Duke. I did sums with English money and English weights and measures and learnt to read through books written for English children. But I was not an exception in this matter; many of my generation were being educated in this way. What was unusual in my case was that alongside this anglicized life the orthodox pattern continued, and though I went to an English kindergarten I also started to read the Arabic Primer with a view to learning to read the Koran at the traditional age of four years and four months. There are thirty chapters in the Koran and it took me three and a half years to finish it. This was about the usual time. One is not taught to read Urdu separately but, as the alphabet is the same, by the time one finishes the Koran one has learnt to read Urdu also. Thus, by the time I was eight, I could read both Urdu and English.

CHAPTER 3

CHILDHOOD (1922–24)

Most of my childhood we lived in places similar to Lilloah; that is to say, in artificial English colonies where we followed the outward pattern of the English way of life. But, because of my mother, naturally the core of our home remained essentially orthodox and excursions into the old world were sufficiently frequent for me to come to know and love it. Whenever I visited my mother's family I stepped into the nineteenth or the eighteenth century. For though my grandfather had died, no change whatsoever had come over the lives of the members of his family for many years. Whenever we were staying in Calcutta my mother visited her sister and aunts frequently.

There was not then the glut of social life that there is now, and so even an ordinary call was looked forward to with eagerness and undertaken with a certain amount of formality. The intention to visit was sent a day before through a maid. Use of telephones had not yet been accepted or become common, and although we had one, my mother never used it.

The usual time for the call was about three in the afternoon. Lunch would be early that day, after which my mother and I would dress very leisurely; the servants would be given careful instructions regarding their work during our absence and the *doli* sent for. A *doli* was equivalent to the sedan chair. It was customary for ladies to travel in *dolis* as it was carried right inside the courtyard and so there was no chance of even a glimpse of them being seen by outsiders while getting in and out of it. Travelling in cars was considered unladylike and, therefore, my mother, though we had a car, always went by *doli*. One could not see anything at all while travelling in one. There was a bit of coloured glass on one side for light, and even if it had not been at an angle from which one could neither see nor be seen, it was not much use, for the *doli* was always covered with a most attractively embroidered curtain. It was absolutely essential that it should be so and even those who could not rise to a *ghata-toap*, put just a plain sheet over it; but a lady never went out without one.

I enjoyed these visits very much for I was very friendly with my younger cousins and with the one nearest my age I had cemented my friendship in the usual fashion by arranging a dolls' wedding together. This was always an elaborate affair at which all the ceremonies performed in a real wedding were meticulously observed. The idea was to teach girls social etiquette and household arts, particularly sewing, for the doll's trousseau had to be entirely stitched by the girls themselves. I, being no good at sewing, wisely chose a boy doll. Our dolls had a long engagement and we had a lot of fun during that period.

There could not have been longer discussions about an actual marriage than we had about our dolls. Painstakingly over the year we collected household furniture, china and linen and as soon as we had acquired a new item we would beg our mothers to go and pay a visit so that we could show our new possession and talk it over; for, though we lived within walking distance of each other, we were never allowed to visit each other by just walking over. My cousins already observed purdah, and, though to my mother's great mortification my father still did not allow me to be put 'behind the veil', I certainly could not be allowed to walk on the road. Nor was it customary for girls to go visiting without their mothers, not even amongst their relatives, so we had to wait until our mothers felt like seeing each other. Luckily for us, they did want to see each other fairly frequently.

But I enjoyed these visits even apart from the pleasure of meeting my cousins, because the atmosphere in my aunt's house was so different from that in my own. Our home had been reduced to the manageable proportions of a Western home, but my aunt's household consisted of the usual large number of dependants, relatives and old servants which meant that there was always a great deal of noisy activity going on all the time.

There were so many things happening at the same time but on different levels. One could join the children who would be avidly listening to the story told by an old aunt with such a wealth of detail that it gave it an intimate personal quality. Then there would always be some minor domestic crisis brewing in which everybody was taking an inordinate amount of interest.

The maidservants played a considerable part in contributing to the liveliness of such households, and brought a touch of reality into this otherwise unreal world. They had been with the family for years and were as jealous of its honour and traditions as members of the family themselves. There was a well-established hierarchy amongst servants at the lowest rung of which came the servant girls. These gradually rose to a position of trust and responsibility and having been brought up by and amongst ladies acquired their manner of speech and had a surface polish and veneer. Such a person was Muna Buwa. She had come as a servant girl in the time of my great-grandfather and so now regarded herself as the doyen of all the maids. She was what one usually describes as a character. She had a crisp and terse style of speech and did not mince matters when speaking her mind. She did not hold with any of the newfangled notions, such as speaking English, reading magazines, going to school, etc. She disapproved not only of us girls, but even ticked off our mothers. They had just recently taken to visiting outside the family circle. This Muna Buwa considered absolutely *infra dig*. 'Imagine,' she would say, 'Nawab Abdul Latif's granddaughter's *doli* being hawked round from door to door. Who would have thought it possible?' Besides Muna Buwa there were several others, who had all given a lifetime of devoted service to the family and whose staunch loyalty was so touching that at times it became almost ridiculous. There was an old maidservant called Allah-Rakhi. She had also begun life as a servant girl in my great-grandfather's house. She had never graduated to the status of Muna Buwa, but she was mindful of family traditions in her own way. She never went shopping for even a trifling thing without recounting the whole genealogical table of the family for the edification of the shopkeeper.

Besides these old servants, who were an institution and an indispensable part of households such as my aunt's and great-aunt's, there were the women vendors, the *choori-wali*, the *bisatin*. They came all day bringing a hundred and one attractive little things, perfume, *kajal, surma,* embroidered slippers, coloured powder for dyeing one's *dupattas*. But the selling of their wares was the least part of these women's jobs. Their most important role was that of purveyors of news. They were, in reality, the news carriers of the women's world. And so accurate and detailed were the accounts these women gave that, though visiting outside the family circle was not done until recently, my mother and aunts knew a great deal about other well-known families, such as which of their contemporaries had married and to whom, how many children they had, whether they got on with their in-laws or not and which of the daughters were of a marriageable age.

Because, these women knew so much about a family's private affairs, only the ones that were very well known and reliable were allowed to come to the house. In fact, most of them were ex-maids and some of them did not even make a pretence of buying or selling anything but just came over frankly to bring and collect gossip. They had all the time in the world and stayed a whole day or half a day at their ex-mistress's house giving a hand in any household task which needed some extra help.

And there were numerous tasks for which any extra help was more than welcome. Hand dyeing and hand printing were still carried on in homes. Gossamer *dupattas* of ladies and fine muslin *kurtas* of men were never worn unless *chunoard,* that is to say crimped. This sort of crimping was not done by tongs, but by pulling out a half-inch of material at a time between thumb and forefinger and twisting it. The use of sweet-smelling herbs was still in fashion. The sorting, pounding and preparation of them to be used as a base for cosmetics, shampoo, hair-oil and to be put as a sachet to scent one's clothes and linen took a lot of time. One of the sophistications of our life was having newly made, freshly filled quilts each winter. These were, of course, stitched at home. Hand-printed satin quilts, lined with silken soft muslin, which were dyed and herb-scented, smelt delicious. They were filled with beaten-up cotton to a snowy lightness and then held in place with most attractive stitching. For all these tasks, an extra pair of hands was more than welcome and in the midst of it news was gathered.

My mother, living in 'English Colonies', was brought up to date as to the latest news by my aunts when she went to visit them. In fact, my mother would ask the *choori-wali,* the *bisatins* or *silai-wali* to come on the day she would be visiting Chhoti Nani so that she could buy whatever she needed and also hear all the news although she was temperamentally not very fond of gossip.

Besides these informal calls, there were a number of occasions for visiting in connection with innumerable ceremonies with which ladies 'behind the veil' seemed to while away their time. There was a ceremony to mark each stage of a child's life, for the ladies wanted any occasion for celebration so as to give them something to do.

Apart from the ceremonies connected with specific occasions, the most popular occasion for ladies to get together was for *milad*. *Milad* is a ceremonious recitation of the story of the Birth of the Prophet (PBUH). During the month of his birth (Rabi-ul-awwal), it is held as often as two or three times in the same day. But all through the year, every auspicious occasion is marked with the holding of a *milad*. It was particularly popular amongst the ladies of my mother's family, both because they were of a religious turn of mind, and because several of them were good at reading *milad*.

Like every other ceremony, *milad* had its own form and tradition. The room in which it was to be held was cleared of all furniture and the floors covered with *durees*. In the centre, preferably on a raised dais, *masnad* would be spread for those who would be reciting the *milad*. Silver stands with burning incense would be placed in front of them as well as vases of roses or other sweet-smelling flowers. During the recitations of a certain portion, corresponding to the singing of Hallelujah in *The Messiah,* everyone would stand up and rose-water would be sprinkled and *ittar* sprayed on the assembly so that the air would be heavily laden with scent. The whole ceremony was charged with emotion—hence its great popularity.

The highlights of the lives of women in purdah, however, were marriages. These were deliberately made into elaborate affairs to provide occupation and amusement for weeks. My mother and I, having been away from Calcutta a great deal, missed several weddings, but we happened to be present at R's wedding, the cousin who was my particular friend, and with whom I had the dolls' marriage when we were children. She was marrying another cousin, so it meant a double wedding in the family, and an occasion for still greater festivity, and numerous meetings amongst the ladies of the family. Clothes, jewellery, the dates for various ceremonies, would be the topics of conversation on these occasions.

These family gatherings before the marriage were of help in choosing the trousseau and jewellery and other wedding presents which the girl was to receive from her other relations. Then the jewellers would be called and various ornaments ordered, and the aunts and cousins present would say what they were going to give as a present so there would be no duplication and the expense of that particular piece of jewellery or silver would be saved for the parents. The girl received at least one or two dresses as presents from her near-relatives and this was made known during the time the trousseau was being gathered together. An aunt would mention casually, 'No, do not get this green brocade. I am giving her a *jora* of this material.' Another cousin would tell the mother, 'I am giving her a bracelet in the same style you liked the other day.' In this way the arrangements would proceed.

During these meetings there would be lively discussions as to the style and fashion of the bride's dresses. The younger ladies, particularly a young cousin of mine, who had a delightfully happy temperament and was all in favour of trying everything new, would suggest more pastel shades, or a new style in trimmings. Her suggestions would be indignantly repudiated by the other ladies. 'For goodness sake,' they would say, 'you girls are becoming absolute *mems*; even for a wedding dress you do not want to have bright colours and rich trimmings. If you had your way I dare say you would like to get a white gown.'

Azimi Apa would giggle and say, 'Phupi Jan, the girl would never wear this dress if you made it so gaudy', and eventually they would come to some compromise.

This was the time when we were going through what was called the modernization of our dress and jewellery. This was a great error in taste for we discarded dresses of beautiful material and exquisite embroidery, and gave away or sold beautiful old jewellery we would now give anything to have back again.

One of the mistaken notions women of the West have about our women is that 'the poor things' missed all the fun of shopping, but that was not so. Our women did not miss any of that great joy of Eve's life; only they had all the fun of shopping without having to push and jostle in a crowd and stand for hours waiting their turn to be served. For they did not go to the shops, the shops came to them. On *Eid* and the other festive occasions and whenever there was a wedding in the offing, jewellers, silk and cloth merchants and *gotay-walas* were all sent for to bring their goods. Our shops did not go in for window dressing and, therefore, the ladies missed nothing by not going to the shops. The attraction lies in the beauty of the wares and not in the art of displaying them. These were brought to the house and the *takhat* on the ladies' verandah was turned into the most attractive of counters. It was fascinating to watch the process.

The silk merchant would come with two or three large bundles tied in white coarse cloth and carried on the heads of coolies. A mat would be spread for him on which he would dump the bundles and deftly begin to undo the knots. Still smaller bundles, tied this time in coarse muslin, would tumble out of the larger bundles. These were also securely knotted. In a matter of seconds these would be undone and the most gorgeous sarees would spill out— sarees in ruby red, emerald green, peacock blue and saffron yellow; sarees with rich borders and *pallus;* sarees with designs worked all over; sarees stiff with embroidery; sarees so soft that one could well believe that they could be passed through a ring—rolls of brightly coloured slipper satin would open out and fall in rich cascades at a few deft flicks of the wrist. Lengths of rich *kamkhab* would glisten and yards of gold and silver tissues would gleam. Such a feast of colour, such a profusion of richness, the eye could not take it all in, and, quite honestly, no shop window in later life has given me quite the thrill I got watching those heaped piles of silks and satins, nor can going and buying *chooris* from a shop where they are kept in neat rows be compared to the joy of peering into a *choori-wali's* basket where strings and strings of *chooris* were heaped and one could not keep one's fingers from touching them. I feel sad to think that my children have never seen the magic of that sheer feast of colour.

Maidservants would stagger in with piles of these gorgeous stuffs. My aunts and mother would put exploring fingers on them, feeling the quality, placing them against each other's cheeks for texture. Trimmings would be tried and matched, silks, tissue and *kamkhab* for pyjamas would be selected. At last the choice would be made and the rejected things would be sent back. Then while the *saree-wala* packed up his goods, the ladies would refresh themselves with tea after the exertion of 'shopping'. Pushing my way in department stores, I now often sigh for that leisurely shopping of 'behind the veil'.

All the sewing and stitching was done at home. Seamstresses were engaged for it, and the lady's maids knew how to sew, but the ladies themselves did a great deal of really fine sewing. Great ingenuity was shown in stitching the sachet of sweet-smelling herbs called *sohagpura* for the bride. This was made by an old aunt of mine who was really a beautiful needlewoman and I do not remember ever seeing a more exquisite piece of embroidery. The wedding preparations continued, and finally the wedding took place—the last one in our family in which the guests were confined exclusively to relatives, and so a much more intimate and enjoyable affair than the weddings of today.

And so I spent my childhood and early girlhood between the Arabian Nights world of my mother's family, and my ultra-Westernized home, and the English school. This dual existence did not seem to have worried me, and I used to slip easily from one to the other, as I can still, only that Arabian Nights world of my childhood has all but disappeared.

Chapter 4

EARLY EDUCATION

My education, like everything else in my life, followed a dual pattern. As a child I began attending an English kindergarten, and was learning to read the Koran at the same time. After this, for some years I followed the usual pattern of a girl's education in my country in those days. That is to say the formal education of a girl being given actual lessons by teachers at set times, stopped after she had learnt to read the Koran and read and write Urdu. She received instruction in religious matters and, would perhaps have been taught the rudiments of Persian, but she was supposed to concentrate on homecraft and needlework. Although the girls didn't go in for higher studies as such, those who had a literary bent, and wanted to, did acquire a wide knowledge of poetry, literature and history. This was possible because their homes possessed such an atmosphere that they learnt by just living in the midst of it.

For poetry is the breath of life in our society and literary discussions were the accepted and established way of spending one's leisure hours amongst the educated. In fact, the word 'educated' was, and is still, synonymous with being literary. Not only was it a mark of a gentlemen to be able to read and write poetry, the ladies also did so. In every family there would be at least one or two women poets. Fathers, brothers and other male relatives were always ready to encourage by explaining a difficult passage or lending the latest book of poems or criticism, so it was not very difficult for girls to develop their literary taste.

It was in this manner that I myself pursued my studies, and though it may seem rather haphazard my generation of girls taught in this way did seem to know as much about our language and literature as those who now receive a more systematic education. In fact, we knew, and certainly had read, a great deal more thoroughly than the young people do now, because reading is no longer the sole recreation of children. Radio and the cinema now claim much of their leisure and even those who do read do not get the same mastery over literature, whether Urdu or English, because they rarely read a book twice, while we chewed and digested it so it became part of our thinking and our imagination, and we lived for days and months in the world created by the magic of the author's pen.

Most of the reading I did on my own; but whenever my father had time, he asked me to read aloud while he and my mother listened. I remember those evenings so well. We would all be sitting out in the garden, the air would be filled with scent, the heavy fragrance of Mogra flowers mixing with the clean, fresh smell of new earthenware *surahis* and *khas*. My mother would be reclining on a *charpai* twisting Mogra flowers to wear round her hair and on her wrists, my father and brother sitting on wicker chairs. There would be enough light to read, and as the shadows fell, an oil lamp would be placed on a table which would throw sufficient light on the book and yet not break the magic of the twilight. My father would be listening carefully, correcting my pronunciation and explaining the meaning of words I did not know. A lively discussion would follow as to the merits of the book and the point of view of the author and whether or not he had been successful in the portrayal of his character. Such quiet and happy evenings are almost a thing of the past. Addiction to radio and cinema on the part of the children and the much heavier round of social activities on the part of the parents have put an end to it.

During this time I received hardly any regular teaching in English because the places we were posted to were hardly better than villages, and it was not possible to get good teachers there. I used to have lessons from my brother's tutors until I was put in purdah and after that had a succession of English or Anglo-Indian governesses, none of whom was very satisfactory from the scholastic point of view. The obvious solution would have been a boarding school, but this was an unheard of thing, and even a person as modern as my father would not have considered it. The only people who would consider doing such a thing were those who had no tradition at all and my father was certainly not one of those, for though modern in outlook he had a very deep respect for our own tradition.

But when we came for a fairly long stay in Calcutta in 1927 my father decided to put me in an English school. He chose a convent, Loreta House, which was considered one of the best English schools in Calcutta. I was delighted, for I had yearned to go to school. How satisfactory it was to be really learning at last. 'How good it is to have proper textbooks and not to be made to read from anything at hand,' I thought, as I hugged my lovely new pile of books with affection. But while I was revelling in being allowed to go to school, a storm of criticism assailed my poor mother, for the idea of a grown-up girl (I was twelve) going to an English school was considered outrageous.

All her relatives came to see her on a sort of condolence visit and commiserated with her for her misfortune in having got married to a man with such strange ideas. 'Honestly,' they said 'we did not think that even he would go so far.' 'What will he do next?' 'Oh, you never know, he might take the girl to England,' one of them would add, making my mother turn pale with apprehension.

After several hours of this sort of conversation and much clicking of tongues, they would leave. It was, after all, not their affair. The discredit of my going to school, reflected, according to our way of thinking, mostly on my father's side of the family.

Nor were my father's family unaware of this situation. My father's eldest cousin, who since the death of his sister had been regarded as more or less the most senior lady in our family, on hearing the news immediately came over to try and rectify the situation.

She first put me through a questionnaire about the school. 'Are there any men teachers?' she asked. 'Oh, no,' I said, 'none at all. They are all women and most of them are nuns.'

'But there must be menservants, are there not?' asked my aunt.

'Yes, there are but we do not see any. You see, they do not come into the classrooms at all. The only place they come into is the refectory and as Mother Superior, on father's request, has given me permission to eat in the parlour, they do not see me and my car is allowed to go right up to the entrance hall. I do not have to get out at the gate like the other girls,' I added to reassure her further.

Having failed to find any shortcomings from the purdah point of view, she turned her attack towards another direction. 'It is a Christian school, is it not?' she asked. 'Yes,' I admitted, 'it is.'

'Well, then, do they not teach you their religion?' she asked.

'Well, not really,' I explained, 'non-Christians do not have to do Catechism, only the life of Christ.' I knew enough of my religion to know that it was not a sin, according to it, to learn about the life of Christ, for we regarded him as a prophet ourselves and I had learnt all that we were being taught on the subject in school already as part of my own religious instruction.

'But they make you say their prayers, do they not?'

I hedged. 'They do not make you say their prayers, but we all have to go to the hall where prayers are said.'

'Well, there you are. That is attending prayers, is it not?'

'Of course it is,' agreed my mother. 'The place is full of statues.' (Idols is the word she used.)

'Well,' said my aunt, 'I will have to speak to your husband about it. When does he come home?'

'Well,' said my mother, 'he is staying in Lilloah still, you know, but he generally comes in just before dinner.'

'Oh dear, that is a bit late for me. You ask him to come and see me,' she told my mother.

'Oh, I wish you would stay and see him,' pleaded my mother, 'you see, he is due to sail for England very soon and he is very busy and might not find time to go over.'

'Ah well, I shall stay and see him, then,' said my aunt. She realized it was a case of saving the family name.

My father came in the evening and was very pleased to see my aunt and went up and paid his respects to her and she gave him her blessings. After mutual inquiries as to health and other formal conversation was over, my aunt came to the point.

'What is this I hear, Brother,' she said in tones as if loath to believe anything so evil, 'that you are sending your girl to an English school?' She put a world of meaning in the word English.

'Well, yes, I am,' said my father. 'What is the harm?'

'For goodness sake, do you not realize what a lot of talk that is causing?'

'I do not care for ignorant people's talk. You see, Sister, I am only doing what everybody else will do in another twenty years' time. Those who begin something new are always criticized, but if nobody had the courage to begin something new the world would never progress.'

My aunt had to get a fresh set of arguments. 'What about the religious influence on the girl? Is it not dangerous to expose a child of tender years to such dangerous teachings?'

'My girl is too well instructed in her own religion by now for it to do harm to her,' said my father, fondly pulling me on his knee and stroking my hair.

'Oh yes, I am sure she is,' said my aunt, looking at me benevolently. 'May God bless her and make her take her aunt's place. But, Brother, we must think of her future,' she said in a meaningful way.

My father immediately understood what she was hinting at. 'Go and do your lessons, darling,' he told me, giving me an affectionate shove. I went to my room which was next door and glued my ear to the door.

'Brother, how will you ever get anyone to marry her off if you persist in sending her to school?'

'I am not going to marry her off to a *mulla* or a *maulvi,* Sister,' replied my father, 'and the boys of today want an educated wife. That is an added reason, if anything, for educating girls. But, Sister, it is getting very late, come along, let us have dinner.'

'Oh no, I think I will go home now.'

'I would not dream of letting you go without having dinner with us. It is ages since you have been to my house,' said my father; and he really meant it, for father was most courteous and respectful towards his older relatives.

My aunt, somewhat mollified, agreed to stay.

In 1927, my going to an English school was looked upon with much disfavour and yet by 1947 every girl of good family was going to school. What my father had said had come to pass and in another twenty years' time women were taking part in processions, had been to gaol, worked in refugee camps and were sitting in legislatures and participating in international delegations. It seems incredible, but it has happened.

But to get back to 1927 again. The criticisms continued without a break. My mother received visits of protest from every relation of ours. Even my father's youngest sister, a sweet, gentle, non-interfering person, was goaded by the criticisms of the in-laws of her daughter into coming over and seeing my mother. She told my mother of all the talk that was going on. Ordinarily my mother would have replied in a spirited fashion, for she could not bear my cousin's in-laws, but by now she was reduced to such a state of nervous exhaustion that she even agreed to my cousin's husband coming and speaking to my father about it.

So, one evening, he came. My mother observed purdah from him but she had a sumptuous tea served to him, after which he waited looking solemn and disapproving, for, though a young man, he was very pompous. My father came just before dinner, as was his wont, and was rather taken aback at seeing this young man, for he very rarely visited us.

'Oh, hello!' he said, not too enthusiastically. 'Nice to see you. Will you have some tea?'

'Oh no,' my cousin's husband replied. 'I have had tea.'

My father sat down, concealing his impatience without much success, and tried making polite conversation. At last my cousin came to the point. He had heard news he could hardly believe.

'Really,' said my father, pretending not to understand him. 'What is it?'

'Oh, that your daughter is attending an English school; if true, this is a matter of disgrace for the family.'

My father's patience was at an end. He had put up with criticism from his seniors and members of his own family, for he felt they had a right to it, but having an outsider, and a much younger man than himself, criticizing him was a bit too much.

'Well, my dear young man,' said my father, 'I do not see why it should bother you; it will be a disgrace for my family, you know,'—putting an emphasis on 'my' which implied that he was not a member of the family and so it was presumptuous of him to interfere—'and now, if you will excuse me, I have only a few days left before I leave for England and I have a lot of things to do and, believe me,' he said before getting up, 'in ten years' time every one of you will be sending your girls to school. I am only a little ahead of my time and therefore I have to put up with all this criticism.'

This was the last of the visits we had; at least till my father left for England.

After my father's departure I was left to face all the criticism, and it began to wear me out. After all, I was only twelve, and at this age one is not certain of one's values. I began to feel that I was doing something that was unseemly and injurious and was disgracing the family, that it was due to my keenness for studies that father had taken these steps and that if I myself gave up the idea he would not mind my leaving school. I therefore stipulated that I would leave school provided arrangements were made for me to study at home. My mother promised that she would see that this was done. She was not at all averse to the idea of my studying, even though she did not understand my longing to do so, and though it was no use for a girl, she realized that it meant a great deal to me and was prepared to humour me in whatsoever I wanted even if it was something as unconventional as studying. Besides, women's education was not looked upon with disfavour in my family. What was objected to was going to an English school, and it was decided that I should study at home, but as things turned out, I did not resume studying for a long period, in fact I did not do anything very much for the next year or so as tragedy struck at us.

My only brother, who was now nearly eighteen, a handsome, intelligent and charming boy, developed tuberculosis and died within a few months. What his death meant to my parents no words can express. Light went out of their lives from that day and only my mother's deep religious faith and my father's deliberate plunging into work carried them through their ordeal. On my life it had many and far-reaching effects. My brother was not only an only son but an only son among four brothers and the responsibilities and burdens of family traditions which should have been his had to be shouldered by me alone in future years. It had the immediate effect on my mother and other members of the family of withdrawing their objection to my going to school. They realized that, as my father now had no son, they had to agree to his educating me as one. It also resulted in my getting married comparatively early. My father would never have consented to that otherwise, but, as he felt that it was the one thing that would give my mother some happiness and bring some interest back into her life, he agreed.

When our lives had taken on an outward semblance of normality I went back to school and this time stayed on for nearly five years, though not without long intervals of absence. That I could complete my studies in school and even go on to college was due to the encouragement, help and understanding which I got from Mother Joseph Agatha. Under her guidance my mind seemed to open out and my knowledge widened. Mother Joseph Agatha taught me so much. Many of the values I hold today I learnt from her. She educated me in the real sense of the word and at the same time taught me the meaning of education. She made me travel in the 'realms of gold' and introduced me to the treasures of English literature and to the proud history of its people.

No better teacher of history, no better disciplinarian and educationist, no greater lady have I yet met than Mother Joseph Agatha. She came from a very distinguished English family. She had been born a Protestant and had adopted the Catholic faith at the age of nineteen. But the nun's habit did not succeed in hiding the proud carriage of an aristocrat, nor did twenty-five years in religion succeed in quelling the fierce pride of class and race.

But besides enjoying my studies, I enjoyed my school in other ways also. It was very pleasant to have daily companionship of girls of my own age and I gossiped and talked with them on the same subjects and in the same way as they did themselves. Film stars, cinemas, and the Royal Family were favourite topics of conversation, and though these subjects were completely remote from my personal experience and knowledge, it did not prevent me from airing my views on them with as much confidence as my companions.

When in school I wore a school uniform of blue skirt, white blouse and navy blue tie, but the moment I got home I changed into *kurta-pyjama-dupatta*. In fact if my mother had visitors, I was not allowed to appear for one single moment before them in what she considered 'half-naked dress', but had to come up the back stairs and creep into my room and change into my own costume. This was typical of my dual existence. I talked, behaved, and felt like an ordinary English schoolgirl while within the four walls of the school, but at home with my mother and amongst my other relations I was expected to behave as a traditionally well-brought-up Muslim girl.

I stopped wearing English clothes because my eldest uncle Sir Abdullah Suhrawardy accidentally saw me in them, and expressed disapproval. This was sufficient for my father to ask me to discontinue wearing English clothes in the future. It may seem strange that my father should have deferred so much to the wishes of his brother, who was, after all, not so very much older than himself, but family ties were still very strong, and though we lived apart from the rest of the members of the family, and my father was in no way dependent upon my uncle, it would have never occurred to him to question his authority. Not only my parents but even I as a child knew that not only the opinion of my eldest uncle mattered, but the opinion of every single member of the family had to be considered in everything.

The children of today have no such feeling and acknowledge no authority beyond that of their parents, if that. But when I was a child, the idea of the joint family still persisted, and though each unit lived separately and was financially independent of the others, together they formed a single larger unit, the acknowledged head of which in our family was my father's eldest cousin, Sir Zahid Suhrawardy, whom we called Chacha Jan. He was the sweetest and gentlest of persons, but despite his gentleness he had such a quiet dignity that I do not think that anyone ever had the courage to be impertinent to him. His presence was like the shade of an old and venerable tree which sheltered us all. We knew and admitted the fact that his opinion was final in any matter of family dispute, and, therefore, when my mother was worried that I had reached the age of nine without being put in purdah, she appealed to Chacha Jan to speak to my father, which he did. I do not know what he said to my father, but after his departure my father sent for me and told me that now I was grown up it was time I started observing purdah.

This formal stepping into purdah made very little difference in my life. I did not go out of the house anyway, so all that it meant was that I did not now appear before the menservants and did not go to that part of the house where my father received his friends and that I now watched functions held there through *chiks;* these are pieces of bamboo curtain which are put up for ladies to see through without being seen. Ladies also watch through Venetian blinds. There is an art in opening it at the right angle so that one can see but not be seen. I never got the knack. According to my mother it was because I had been put in purdah too late. She said I never really learnt the art of living in purdah properly, and it is a fact that it is an art and it consists of many things besides knowing how to look without being seen yourself.

Chapter 5

POLITICAL BACKGROUND

The storm that was to sweep away the pattern of life that I knew as a child was already brewing. Its rumblings could be heard and even my child's mind could sense the tension though it could not comprehend the reason for it.

The First World War (1914–18) had just ended and there was general unrest in India caused by frustration and disappointment because the promises made and hopes held out during the war had not been fulfilled. Two things contributed to intensifying this after-war malaise. The advent of Gandhi with his dynamic philosophy of non-violence and non-cooperation was one, and the burning indignation that the Muslims in India felt at what was happening in Turkey was another. It was impossible for anyone who is not personally aware of the peculiar attachment the Muslims of India had for the Muslims in other parts of the world to understand this. The revival of the Pan-Islamic movement in the early part of the century had given this an added fillip and so, after the war, the attempted dismemberment of Turkey by Greece with the connivance and half-hearted support of the British was sufficient to inflame Muslim feeling in India. This sympathy for Turkey was no mere pale sentiment, but took a real and tangible form. The students showed their sympathy by boycotting universities, men by giving up Government jobs, women by eschewing foreign cloth, and children by reciting passionate songs in praise of Turkish valour.

I myself still remember learning such poems and the emotional hysteria which swept over us in this connection.

Gandhi was quick to take advantage of this. By sympathizing with the Muslims over the question of the Caliphate, as this movement was called, he won their whole-hearted support. It was the first time in the history of the Indian struggle for independence that Hindu and Muslim unity was achieved. It was the time when the Hindus shouted 'Allah-o-Akbar' and the Muslims shouted 'Gandhi-ji-ki-Jai'. These were the days of high resolve and great emotional fervour but not of clear thinking or the formulation of definite objectives. The British, usually wise in such matters, made a terrific blunder at this time—the notorious massacre at Jallianwala Bagh in Amritsar. General Dyer, the British Commandant, in order to disperse a mob, ordered the shooting of 20,000 unarmed people who had assembled in defiance of an order which prohibited political gatherings, and, as the meeting was in a walled-garden, when the shooting began, the people were completely trapped. How many were actually killed will never be really known; the official figures put the number down as very small, but the Indians believe them to be very high indeed. Whatever the actual number, there is no doubt that the massacre in Jallianwala Bagh sounded the death-knell of the British Empire in India. The wave of indignation that swept the country was tremendous and, for the first time, the British began to be hated in a way they had never been hated before.

Jallianwala Bagh Massacre occurred in 1919. In 1922, I could still feel the reverberations of it and it remained a trigger word for the Indians ever after; the name of General Dyer, coupled with that of General Hudson, who during the Mutiny of 1857 had the infamous task of executing the sons of the Mughal Emperor in cold blood and without trial, have become the two most hated British names for the people of the Indian subcontinent. Because of this wave of hatred the visit of the Prince of Wales, which should have been an occasion for rejoicing, was greeted with a sullen resentment by the Indians and with grave apprehension by the British. I remember seeing the procession on his arrival and, full of colour and pageantry though it was, even my child's mind could sense the tension in the air.

There was a feeling of apprehension and not all the trappings and gaiety could hide the underlying feeling of gloom. I can still clearly remember the awful feeling of unspoken fear and not understanding why it should be so, and why something that outwardly was so gay should make people look and feel so mournful.

As always when political agitation reached a certain point, efforts were made by the British to ease the situation by granting some measures of self-government. This was done now and what are known as the Montagu-Chelmsford Reforms were introduced. While considering them inadequate, a large section of the Indian people availed themselves of the opportunity and contested the elections. In Bengal it was mainly due to the far-reaching policy of my uncle, Sir Abdullah Suhrawardy, that the Muslims used this chance, thereby laying the foundation of future independence. My uncle was a remarkable man. His brilliance amounted to genius. At nineteen he had written a book for which he received an appreciation from Tolstoy. As a student in England he became a leader of the Pan-Islamic movement. The first public prayers to be held by Muslims in Britain were led by him. He sacrificed a lucrative career at the Bar and the certainty of a High Court judgeship to the task of creating political consciousness among the Muslims of Bengal; and the debt they owe him cannot be over-estimated. Their objective, so far, had been securing a place in the Government services. The young men who came to my uncle for a recommendation for this purpose could not understand his remark 'I want you to become one who gives jobs to others'; for it had not occurred to them that they could have a say in the very act of governing the country. So my uncle trained and drilled hundreds of students in the way of politics. His large house in Mirzapur Street looked like a seminar for young men. Many of those responsible in guiding the destinies of their people today are men whom my uncle persuaded to give up the secure path of Government Service for the hazards of a political career. He also prevailed upon as many members of our family as he could, to abandon their well-paid jobs and enter politics. Our house therefore became the centre of intense political activity.

I could no more understand the reason for the excitement and exaltation of these elections than I did the cause of the tension earlier on, but just as I had sensed the tension, I shared the feeling of excitement. I liked talking to people who were working for the elections. They seemed to express very gratifying sentiments about my father and other members of the family, and I entirely agreed and thought that anyone opposing them was acting in the height of bad taste. The political significance of it all dawned on me much later. I do not think that the people who voted for my father and my uncles, and got others to vote for them, understood about the political situation either. Their support was based on personal loyalty and personal likes and dislikes. Parties and party alignment had not become clear and were not to become so for a few years yet. I do not remember hearing anything about Congress or the League, but very often I heard people speak about Gandhi, Muhammad Ali and Shaukat Ali. They probably knew nothing about the Montagu-Chelmsford Reforms and what these had given them, but they did sense that something was happening; something that meant change for them and that what they were doing was in some way connected with the attainment of *Swaraj* and that it was right that *Swaraj* should be attained.

'Of course it should,' I agreed without understanding a thing, and held forth on the subject at length. They listened to me with an amused tolerance. I think I flattered their vanity by being such an avid listener, so they put up with me. My mother, however, strongly disapproved of my being in the company of strange men and often, just as I was in the midst of a very heated discussion, I would be sent for and scolded.

I remember the day my father was elected, the wild excitement, the procession and the congratulations. Later on this feeling of partisanship shifted from a person to a party, from an individual to a cause.

There was an easing of tension for a few years after the election during which my father resigned from the Legislature and we were away in places in the north of India, and far from Calcutta, which was at that time the nerve-centre of political agitation. Our return coincided with a fresh wave of unrest sweeping the country. My father was appointed Vice-Chancellor of Calcutta University, which is the oldest in the Indian subcontinent and justifiably proud of its traditions. Its students were also the most politically conscious, for Bengal has always been in the forefront of the struggle for independence, and my father was therefore stepping right into the arena of political unrest.

Unrest had begun to grow since the Simon Commission had come to India in 1927 to examine the progress made in self-government since 1919. The fact that no Indian was included in it caused it to be boycotted, and the subsequent formation of the Indian Statutory Commission to advise it had not succeeded in placating public opinion. Nor did the succeeding Round Table Conference meet with much approval from extremist opinion in India. The feeling of frustration was being given vent to in a wave of terrorism, particularly in Bengal; three successive magistrates were shot in Midnapur and in many other districts there had been successful or unsuccessful attempts on the lives of British officials. Hunger strikes were being carried on in gaol by Indian prisoners, and the death in prison of Jatin Das and the execution of Bhagat Singh caused further tension. Students, the most emotional and vulnerable section of the people, reacted to all this and I remember delegations and counter-delegations of them coming to see my father continuously. It was in connection with one of the student riots that Miss Mary Slade, the famous disciple of Gandhi, came to see him. I remember her talking to my father and mother and being struck by her obvious sincerity, but I could not help feeling there was something rather incongruous about an Englishwoman adopting the way of life that she had.

Terrorism was at its height when the time for the annual Convocation came round. The Governor of Bengal was always the *ex officio* Chancellor of the University of Calcutta, and at this time the Governor was Sir Stanley Jackson, a kind and liberal-minded man who must have disliked the atmosphere in which he found himself. My father was advised not to hold the Convocation or to hold it without the Governor presiding, but he considered this would be bad for discipline and would make the controlling of the students still more difficult and decided to hold the Convocation as usual. It took place on 6 February 1932, and during the giving of degrees Bina Das, a girl student, twenty-three years of age, attempted to shoot the Governor. Luckily the first shot missed its target and my father was able to get to her and stop her. This caused a great stir and much comment in the Press. As Hindu-Muslim differences were already growing, the fact that my father was a Muslim and the girl a Hindu was played up by the Press a great deal. On the other hand, as my father was knighted by a special communiqué 'for conspicuous gallantry in the face of personal danger' it brought him back to the forefront of political life and got him involved in many controversial matters of the time.

During these years, there were many currents and cross-currents in Indian political life. The Hindu and Muslim objectives had not yet become separate and clear-cut but the gulf was getting wider and wider. Individual action by narrow-minded and bigoted people was adding fuel to the fire. One of these was the writing of obscene and malicious things about Islam and the Prophet of Islam (PBUH) by certain Hindus. There was quite an epidemic of such obnoxious writing and indignation amongst Muslims was mounting high.

Since terrorism and killing were in the air it was not surprising when two young Muslim boys, Amir Ali and Abdullah, aged sixteen and nineteen years, killed the Hindu author of a particularly revolting book called *Rangila Rasul*. These boys were caught almost red-handed and condemned to death and a wave of sympathy for the young culprits swept over the Muslims. It was argued that all the terrorists who had attempted to murder British officials had got off with a sentence of imprisonment due to their extreme youth, and therefore these young boys should also be let off. My cousin, Huseyn Shaheed Suhrawady, who had gained a great reputation in 1926 by securing a reprieve for men condemned during the Calcutta riots, was one of the lawyers in charge of the case, and when the Governor's life was saved, as it was thought, mainly because of my father's presence of mind he began receiving deputation after deputation from Muslims to use his influence with the British Governor in trying to secure clemency for Amir Ali and Abdullah.

One afternoon a procession of at least 10,000 came marching up to our house. This was my first experience of crowd charged with emotion and almost drunk with fanatical faith, though later I was to see many such. The impact that mass emotion like this has on one is something one cannot convey to another unless that person has himself, or herself, witnessed it. Shakespeare alone has succeeded in describing it in *Julius Caesar*. What happens is that for the duration, while the mass emotion holds sway, one ceases to be an individual with any individual judgement of feeling and becomes part of the mass, sharing the one predominant emotion which is for the moment swaying it. Though I watched that surging mass of humanity from a balcony in the second storey of our house, I felt enveloped in it. The cries of 'Allah-o-Akbar', 'Islam Zindabad', 'Namus-ai-paimbar Zindabad', 'Dushman-ai-

Islam Murdabad', rent the air, and as each slogan was raised and echoed by the thousands I felt a tingle of emotion pass through my whole body.

The mother of these two unfortunate boys also came and saw my mother and asked her to speak to my father to try and get the death sentence repealed. She was a simple village woman from the Punjab who understood very little of what political repercussions her sons' action was causing and only felt the pain all mothers feel. I thus quite early in life saw both the tragic and spectacular side of political strife.

I have mentioned this incident in some detail because it did have a most profound effect on my young mind and imagination. It can almost be said that my political career dates from this time, for I made my first speech proposing a motion of censure on the execution of these two young men whom I regarded as martyrs. It was a highly emotional speech ending with a stirring verse of the Koran which asks for God's help for the Muslims and prays to him to smite all enemies of the true religion. Everyone was deeply stirred and a resolution was passed with all the ladies standing and a prayer was said for the souls of the two boys. Making this speech was a great act of daring on my part. It was tantamount to a criticism and condemnation of the Government and this ladies' meeting was sponsored by a group of women who had nothing farther from their minds than criticism of the Government, but this aspect of the matter had not struck my young egotistical mind at that stage.

What had needed the screwing up of every ounce of courage I could muster was the fact that I was making a speech in public, a bold and unheard-of thing for a young girl to do and I had done this without seeking my mother's permission but merely by giving my name to the secretary. As I have said earlier, girls were not taken to any house other than to those of relations and very close friends. My mother had taken me to this meeting as a special concession and only because it was being held in the house of a very special friend and the ladies present at the meeting were almost all personal friends, but even in such a small and exclusive circle for a young girl to get up and make a speech was unheard of. I knew full well that it would shock and displease my mother very much and that I dared to do so was a proof of the extent I had begun to be swayed by political emotion.

At the conclusion of the meeting many people went up and congratulated my mother on my speech. She accepted the congratulations with a suitable show of pleasure but during the rest of the time we were there I dared not meet her eyes.

When we got into our car to go home, she told me just this: 'It is the last time I ever take you out'; and she kept her word. This was early in 1931. I was married early in 1933, so my sentence of punishment did not last for a very long period.

Chapter 6

MY MARRIAGE

One of the things all my Western friends ask is, 'Did you not object to your marriage being arranged?' And they are surprised when I say, 'No, I did not.' Yet it should not be a matter of surprise because it is not so very long ago that marriages were arranged in every country in Europe and even today, in Spain, France and Italy, arranged marriages are quite common. So are they in Latin American countries, and in North America, in pioneering days, marriages were arranged with a view to convenience, and 'King's girls', who came from France to be brides of Canadian pioneers, had little, if any, say in the choice of their husbands. What is new is the idea of the love-match rather than the arranged marriage. Amongst the older nations marriages were looked upon as social institutions and as such were not to be entrusted to the fleeting fancy of youth but to the mature judgement of elders. If you are brought up in a milieu which regards love-matches as something that is just not done, you accept this as the only and correct point of view.

At this juncture my Western friends say, 'Yes, we understand that it would be so with girls who were brought up entirely with that point of view, but you, who went to an English school and knew that girls of your age had more freedom in this matter, did you not resent it?' Here again the answer is no. I cannot explain why, but the fact is that it never occurred to me that I should have a say in my marriage, and this was not because I was not affected by my English education. I was—particularly just at this period of my life—very much affected by it and by all the movement and talk of women's emancipation and women's rights which was then common. I used to cause my mother many an awkward moment by blurting out a remark which, according to orthodox opinion, was an extremely bold one and which was always imputed to my unfortunate English education. I was always getting into trouble for expression of views which were shocking, not only because of their unorthodoxy but doubly so because they were voiced by a young unmarried girl who was not supposed to think of these matters, much less express a viewpoint on them. And yet where the question of marriage was concerned, I held absolutely orthodox views; in this matter tradition had won over experiment, and so it has continued throughout my life and has puzzled others and has made life difficult if perhaps more interesting for me.

I would like to give some idea here of how a girl was schooled in tradition. It was not that I was ever made to sit down and listen to long lectures on the subject, but from my mother, from my aunts, from older cousins, from the maidservants, from the general atmosphere in the family and the house, one somehow gleaned what was expected of one, what was right and what was done and what was not done.

We—that is girls of my generation—accepted the fact that marriages would be arranged for us, that we would have no say in them, and that getting married was inevitable. There was, of course, no question of a career and also no question of not getting married. One was born, one eventually got married also. Mrs Naidu, that wonderful and witty woman, had once replied to a query 'What is your unmarried women's problem?' in these words: 'We do not have any. Our women are born married!'

That marriage was our destination and that we were being trained for it was brought home to us in many ways. Every time we did something we should not have done we were reprimanded by these words, 'What will "They" think of you? Is that how you are going to behave there?' We knew that 'they' meant the in-laws and 'there' meant the *susral,* that, in our language, is the word for your husband's family. (I have not been able to find an English word which corresponds to it or which indicates even any conception of a *susral* existing in the English mind.)

Girls in my days were brought up with the one and only view of doing credit to their mother in *susral.* Here again I want to say that the hold this sort of conditioned reflex takes on one's mind is very strong. I have never been able to rid myself of the feeling of awe for in-laws even though, because of the rapid social changes that have taken place in the last twenty years, they now have very little, if any, say in the lives of their daughters-in-law.

So it was that, trained to accept marriage as the eventual goal of one's existence and the arranging of it as the absolute right of one's parents, when the time came for me to get married, I had no feeling of resentment about it. As I have said, the question of my marriage had begun to be discussed from the time I was eleven years old. The first definite proposal had come when I was thirteen and the same family had persisted for several years. But my father considered me too young and had always refused—and had it not been for the fact that my mother's health had begun to fail very rapidly his answer to their latest proposal would have been the same. But fate had decreed that I was to marry this particular person and therefore my father sent for Chacha Jan, as he was the head of the family and no marriage could be arranged without his formal consent. Once he had agreed my father decided to accept. Amongst us, once a proposal is accepted one does not go back on it without very grave reason. All the preliminary inquiries are done before the acceptance and my father had gone into it two years before when a tentative proposal had been made. This also is customary. Definite proposals are not sent till enough time has elapsed after the tentative proposal for inquiries to be made on either side and there is a reasonable chance of acceptance. This was some time at the end of July 1932. My husband, Mohammad Ikramullah, however, came down in September and was seen by all the male members of the family and, before he left, my father tied *imam zamin* on his arm; this is a golden embroidered armlet which is ordinarily tied on when one is going on a journey but also signifies formal engagement. Feverish preparations for the marriage then began.

As I have said, our marriages are like a pageant and, since I was the only girl among four brothers, arrangements for mine were even more elaborate than usual. Not only my parents' wishes but those of my aunts and uncles counted on every score: how many dresses I was going to have, what sort of jewellery, where would the garden party take place, how many days the wedding ceremonies should last, where would the wedding banquet be held, and so forth. The house was full of women all the time discussing and making clothes. I was being sent for constantly to be measured and fitted, though I was not allowed to say whether I liked or disliked any of the things that were being made for me. This I think was really extremely silly and carried things too far for it resulted in my giving away masses of clothes because I did not like them and I am glad that now, arranged marriages or not, girls have a say in the choosing of their trousseau. Luckily for me I had a room on the third floor of the house where I could study undisturbed but even so it was very difficult to concentrate with such a hullabaloo going on.

Each stage of the preparation was marked by a ceremony. The day the scissors were put to the cloth all the ladies of the family gathered. There was singing and music till late in the evening. Then the day the *dupattas* and sarees were to be dyed there was again a great gathering of ladies to the accompaniment of music and singing. When the dresses were all stitched and ready to be packed, all the young girls of the family came over. It is really incredible the amount of work that is put into the preparation of a bridal trousseau amongst us. Each set of dresses, complete with lingerie, is wrapped separately with fine gold threads and then six or eight sets are put in a square cloth of silk which is folded over. This silk square is in itself a work of art, being elaborately embroidered and edged with gold lace. In fact, every article made for the bride's use is a masterpiece of handwork. Marriages in our society were so elaborate because they provided our women with amusement and work, for in those days they otherwise had very little of either.

Besides the ladies who came almost daily to help in the preparation of the trousseau, my cousins would descend on me in a bunch practically every other day for the sole purpose of teasing me and talking about my would-be husband. This was also customary and was the only way in which a girl could learn about her future in-laws and obtain other pieces of information regarding her marriage. It helped to make one familiar with some of the aspects of one's future life and it built up a sort of pseudo-romantic atmosphere about the whole thing. This, too, was a conventional behaviour pattern and I and my cousins conformed to it. I always maintained an air of complete indifference to any information that they might have collected, while they gave every bit of important or unimportant news with an air of doing me the greatest of favours. The day they got hold of my husband's picture they came looking extremely smug and self-satisfied and began dropping hints, saying to each other, 'Do you think she will be interested in what we have got or will she not?' 'Just look at her...she is all ears!'

'I certainly am not.' I replied with a great show of unconcern and fixed my eyes securely on *The Tempest*.

'All right. If you are not interested we won't show it to you. Isn't it a pity? We went to so much trouble in getting it from Khala Amma's box.'

'Yes, we had better go and put it back before she misses it,' said Raisi Apa, the eldest, who was trying to put on a responsible and reliable air. After this announcement, she pulled out a photograph, waved it under my nose and pretended to go downstairs to put it away. Halfway down, they all stopped and Rehmat Khala said, 'Oh, no, really we can't do this to her. It will break her little heart and she won't be able to study one bit. I think we will be kind to her though she doesn't deserve it.' Saying this, she flicked the photograph from where they were standing so that it fell in front of me, hitting me on the way, at which there were further giggles. The photograph was one of my husband with his two younger brothers. It was most tantalizing to have it under my nose and not know which of the three young men was supposed to be destined for me. Anyway I was not going to give in. So, after a while, they all came and bent over my shoulders and began teasing me again. 'Now, which of the three do you like? Which do you think it is or aren't you interested? What do we get if we tell you?'—and so forth.

'Oh, I am not interested at all,' I said, 'and get off my shoulders, you people, and let me get on with my work.' I pretended to be very cross.

Not a bit abashed, they continued their banter, and in the end I was told which was the one that was going to be my husband.

In this same way I learned that I was going to get married in April after completing my examination and not in December before I had taken it, as at one time seemed probable. This bit of information was not given to me in a straightforward manner but after a great deal of mild torturing. I remember the incident very well. Rehmat Khala came bouncing up the stairs, snatched the book I was trying to read and flung it to the other end of the room, announcing,

'Hi, why do you bother with this any more?'

'Yes, why do you?' came a chorus from the others, bounding in after her.

'Well, I have got an exam to do in five months. You may have heard of it,' I replied with what I considered heavy sarcasm.

'Hum, that's what you think. You have got to do another exam, my girl,' they replied in unison.

I ignored the remark.

'Honestly,' one of them said, 'it is a pure waste of time because you are never going to be allowed to take the exam. Your in-laws are insisting that the marriage take place in December.'

'What!' I exclaimed, jolted out of my feigned indifference.

'Yes, they are insisting,' they replied.

'Oh, no! Oh goodness me!' I said, almost on the point of tears.

'Ah well,' they replied, 'it seems that the dearest wish of your heart is known to your lord and master. He has very kindly and graciously agreed that you should be allowed to take the exam and he will compose his soul in patience till April.'

'You horrible creatures,' I said, 'what a scare you gave me.'

'Hum, that's all she has to say to us! Aren't you pleased that your would-be husband is showing so much consideration already?'

'Of course, she means to have him toe the line and she is beginning now,' one of them replied—I do not remember which.

And so the teasing and bantering went on right till the day of the marriage.

My examinations were completed on 10 April 1933 and the wedding ceremonies started from 14 April. That morning the bridal party arrived from Nagpur and that afternoon the *Mayun* ceremony took place. This occurs three days before the wedding and for it perfumed oils, perfumes and all toilet accessories and a set of clothes in yellow comes as a present from the husband's family. As soon as these things had arrived and had been arranged in the drawing-room, I was taken out of my room and made to sit in the centre of the drawing-room on a *masnad*.

Seven ladies of the family put the perfumed oil and the *ubatna* on my forehead with their fingers. The ladies chosen for this ceremony are those considered to be especially happy and fortunate in their marriage and children. After they had put the token *ubatna* on my forehead I was again taken back to my room where, amidst much joking and laughing, I was rubbed thoroughly with *ubatna*. This is a perfumed paste made by pounding all sorts of herbs together. Rubbing it on the skin is supposed to be very good for the complexion. Those three days before the wedding, I was rubbed with it twice a day at least and I must say my skin never felt so satiny smooth as it did then. After *ubatna* has been rubbed on, it is taken off with perfumed oil. It is altogether a very messy affair, and therefore, for those three days one is dressed in the simplest yellow-coloured muslin so as not to show the stain, for *ubatna* stains yellow.

From the day of the *Mayun* practically the whole family had moved into our house, to say nothing of dozens and dozens of servants. The pandemonium was something indescribable, but all that is so much a part of our weddings and ceremonies that, if it had not taken place, I suppose one would have thought that there was something wrong. After the *Mayun* ceremony, the bride-to-be never leaves her room and one or the other of her friends always stays with her to keep her company.

The last two days passed in the last-minute hustle of getting everything ready. Eventually the day of the wedding arrived. At about ten in the morning I was taken into the bathroom and made to sit on a low silver stool while I had a final rub-down with *ubatna* and my hair was washed with perfumed herbs, after which the maids and my cousins left and I had a bath. My hair was tied and left loosely plaited to be done in a more elaborate style later in the evening.

After that I had a light lunch and *mehndi* was put on my hands and feet.

Mehndi is a henna paste which we use to colour our nails, but on the wedding day the entire palm of the hands and the feet are coloured with it. After they had finished that I was told to try and go to sleep, which I obediently tried to do, but it was impossible because of all the noise and rush that was going on. I do not know why it is that in my country we cannot do anything without shouting a great deal and making a terrific amount of noise. I have lived abroad and have had occasion to arrange fairly large receptions, but there is never quite that commotion in connection with them as there is at home. I believe the only people who get as excited and noisy as we are the Italians.

Our house, like all houses in Calcutta, did not have much of a garden but just a narrow strip at the back. And it was from there that all the shouting and the noise came.

'Here, you fool, how do you think I am going to get this ready by eight o'clock if you keep working at that pace? I have been cooking for every wedding in this family for generations. Do you want to disgrace me? For goodness sake get me some more large *daigchees*, otherwise I will not be responsible for anything.' ...And so it went on. It was a way of showing self-importance and personal interest. There was a great deal to be done between then and the evening; there were no less than fourteen hundred people coming to dinner.

Barat, that is the bridegroom's arrival, was scheduled for seven o'clock in the evening. *Sachakh*, that means the bride's dresses and jewellery and other presents, are sent beforehand. There was plenty of time yet, but my cousins, out of sheer nervousness, began grumbling.

'Goodness me, it is nearly five o'clock! How are we going to get her dressed in time? *Sachakh* has not arrived yet!'

'Oh yes and Uncle (that was my father) said that the ceremony should finish by ten o'clock at the latest!'

Just then my aunt came in and heard this remark.

'What! Whoever heard of weddings finishing at ten o'clock!' The tone in which she said it implied that to do so would not be quite decent.

'Oh, Uncle said it,' replied one of my cousins.

'Hum,' said my aunt, 'he would. One of these newfangled ideas of his. It is time he learnt to get over them. Other people are concerned in this matter and not only he. What do you think the bridegroom's people will say if we hustle them off at ten? The ceremonies will go on as they always go on right till the early hours of the morning and that's that.'

Well, between my father's attempt at modernization and the rest of the family's determination to forestall him in his efforts, a compromise was reached. The ceremonies did not go on quite till the early hours of the morning, nor did they finish at ten o'clock. They finished, I believe, somewhere near half past one.

The *sachakh* arrived in due course. It consisted of seven beautiful sarees, complete with all accessories, a complete set of jewellery, further toilet accessories, *sehra* and mounds and mounds of *ladoos,* a particular kind of sweetmeat shaped like a ball especially made for weddings. Three of my cousins were in charge of dressing me, while other younger girls hovered around.

The bride's hair, as I have said, is done in a most elaborate style. It is parted in the middle and about a dozen very fine plaits are made, twined with gold thread, and all these dozen plaits are again plaited together with a great deal of gold lace and tassels. The hair in front is also done in elaborate curls and sprinkled with gold dust and gold stars. When my cousins were about halfway through doing my hair, the band struck up, heralding the approach of the *Barat.* Everyone rushed out to see it and I was left all alone in the room. At that moment I was seized with a terrible feeling of panic.

All the months that the wedding preparations had been going on I had been preoccupied with my exam and had not really had time to think much about the impending change in my life. It was only in the last week that I had had time and the more I thought of it, the more apprehensive I became and the lonelier I felt. In all my nearly eighteen years I had never left my mother except for that one trip to Delhi and a short stay in a school in Aligarh. I had never really been away from home and now I was to go to a completely strange household where I did not know a soul and begin making a new life for myself. Most of my cousins had married into families in Calcutta, or at least in Bengal, and had known some member of the family before, but I was going to complete strangers. This feeling had been growing on me for the last week and the band heralding the *Barat* sounded to me like the trumpet of doom. I had a terrible feeling of being left alone and abandoned during these moments when everybody had gone away and left me.

Soon, however, I heard my mother's and aunts' voices scolding my cousins and directing them back to their duty, namely that of dressing me in time. They came tripping in, chattering all the time, saying how wonderful the procession had looked, how the electric arches had gleamed, how they had or had not got a glimpse of the bridegroom, how so and so had posed and how impossible somebody else was always getting in first! All this petty talk grated on my ears. I was feeling dreadful, but my cousins, oblivious of my feelings, took up their half-finished task.

They had not made much progress when it was announced that the men were coming in to receive the bride's consent. Our marriages are done by proxy, that is to say the girl appoints someone as her representative in the presence of two male witnesses and this representative then acts as her proxy at the actual signing of the wedding contract. The person chosen is always a near relation of the bride; in my case it was Chacha Jan. The witnesses were my cousin, Huseyn, and my mother's cousin, Nawabzada Latifur Rehman. As their coming was announced, a veil was hastily thrown over my shoulders and a purdah held up from behind which these gentlemen were going to ask me for my consent to the marriage; though they were close relatives, this also is customary.

This is one of the most poignant moments in our weddings. My mother came over and sat holding me throughout the ordeal. Every bride always cried at this moment but I could not stop crying for a long while afterwards. My cousins looked aghast at my tear-stained face, not knowing what to do to hide the ravages. They bathed my face with cold water and put foundation cream on, only for it to be washed away by another avalanche of tears. At last they began to get desperate and ran to the older ladies for assistance. My aunt, whose word had great weight with all of us, immediately ticked me off in a few crisp sentences.

'My dear girl, you are not the first girl in the world to be getting married and leaving your parents. Every girl, once she has grown up, has to go through this ordeal. It is a woman's lot and there is no use making a scene and a fuss.'

I realized that what she said was true and, as I have said, she had a great influence on me; but the tears would not stop.

The ladies from my husband's family had arrived and had been greeted with the traditional ceremonies and now the banquet began. Electricity nearly always fails in the midst of our weddings but at my wedding the water supply also gave out and my sister-in-law used to tease me by saying that she had to wash her hands by opening soda and lemonade bottles.

At last the dinner was over. Throughout its progress and after it, a sort of relay service was carried on by my men cousins outside and my girl cousins behind the purdah. This is how every bit of news of what was happening outside was passed on... So and so was sitting in such and such a place. So and so had come. So and so had not come. The bridegroom's brother had made this remark. His father was heard to say such and such a thing... Backwards and forwards they came, bringing bits of news and at the same time telling the girls to hurry as it was getting very late for the *Ru-nu-mai,* that is the ceremony when the bride and bridegroom see each other for the first time.

Just before I was taken out to the drawing-room for the *Ru-nu-mai, sehra* was tied on my forehead. This is very pretty to look at but very heavy to wear. I was again carried into the middle of the room and made to sit on a *masnad.* My cousins sat round me, adjusting my dress and *sehra.* After a few moments had passed my husband came and sat opposite me on the *masnad.* A gold and red gauze veil was thrown over us in the customary fashion and a copy of the Koran and a mirror put between us. The bridegroom reads a few verses from the Koran and then sees his bride's face in the mirror, after which he asks her to open her eyes. (By the way, I forgot to mention that ever since the girl's *Mayun* ceremony, the girl keeps her eyes shut or at least completely downcast for several days or, in olden times, a few weeks after the wedding.) After a great deal of coaxing, in which all her friends join in, the bride is supposed to flutter her eyelids for half a second and after this the *Ru-nu-mai* ceremony is over.

Now everybody gave the bridegroom *Salami,* that is a gold sovereign in a silk handkerchief as a present. This is, or I should say was, our way of giving a wedding present. Now most people give wedding presents in the European style. At my wedding there were both. I received from my father's English and Hindu friends hundreds of wedding presents and *Salami* from my own relations and the more orthodox Muslim friends of the family. After this was over *Sonpana* takes place. The bride's and the bridegroom's fathers come in; the bridegroom's father takes the hand of his son, and the bride's father takes the hand of his daughter and places it in the hand of the groom. This is another poignant moment in the wedding and is equivalent to giving away the bride in the English wedding ceremony.

While all these ceremonies were taking place, the wives of my father's English friends had been waiting impatiently to catch a glimpse of me, it was not the custom amongst us for anyone to see the bride before the *Ru-nu-mai* ceremony so they had to wait until it was over. Then I was taken out on to a verandah and made to sit on a sofa while they came in and shook hands with me and wished me happiness. I knew some of them very well and there were amongst them all my college friends and teachers, but I was not supposed to speak to anyone and had to keep my eyes closed lest my orthodox relatives, who were terribly shocked anyway that the *ferangi* women should be allowed to see me at all, would have been further horrified. Just when these ladies began to come to see me, the fireworks began. I believe they were very good but I could not see any of it though I felt sorely tempted to turn my head just a bit and have a look; but, amongst us, at your own wedding you are a sort of puppet who performs for the amusement of others.

At long last it was over. Ordinarily I should now have left for my husband's home, had it been in Calcutta, but as my husband's family were staying in a rented flat, it was considered best that I stay on at my father's house. The room that had been arranged for me had been beautifully done up with flowers all over and a sort of canopy of flowers on my bed.

The day after the wedding there were more ceremonies and further exchanges of presents and the day after that I left for Nagpur, where further elaborate and colourful ceremonies took place, for our weddings are long drawn out affairs, lasting days.

Chapter 7

ADJUSTMENT

The greatest change that marriage brings into the life of a girl in our society is that she has to adjust herself to the way of life of a completely new family. In some ways, her position is similar to that of an English girl going for the first time to a boarding school; only her ordeal is greater.

As I have said before, in my country a girl is trained from her childhood towards this end. She is prepared for it as for an examination. Her manners, her behaviour, her conduct in every respect are made to conform to the pattern which will be expected of her by her in-laws. Any sign of self-assertiveness is curbed with the remark: 'You will not be able to get your own way in *susral*.'

And it is true that one could not be very self-assertive and, therefore, it was wise to train girls to the sort of life that lay before them. It was a life which required above all things tact and ability to give and take, a power to endure and to be able to put the interest of others before oneself. It puts a premium on virtues such as obedience and self-sacrifice. Mothers laid the foundation of these qualities in a girl's character and mothers-in-law built on them, so that they could grow into wives and mothers possessed of these virtues which had been the hallmark of well-bred women in our society.

At first I found adjustment comparatively easy. My in-laws had expected me to be much worse, that is to say much more modern than I was. They knew that I had been to an English school and college and this had branded me as completely *outrée* in their eyes. They had asked for my hand in marriage because their English-educated son wanted an educated wife, but they were prepared for this wife to be an absolute *karanti,* as the few girls who did go to English schools were usually completely Westernized.

What they did not know was that I had a 100 per cent orthodox mother who was not relegated to the background as some Westernized men relegated their orthodox wives but who had as much say and influence on my education as my father, and whose personality was so strong as to dominate and subjugate the otherwise Westernized household. So, 'English-school educated' though I was, I had been drilled most rigidly to conform to the expected patterns of behaviour of a young bride at her in-laws. I kept my head down, my eyes shut and the veil well over my face. I did not move at all of my own accord but was taken from one place to another and on such occasions behaved more or less like a limp rag doll. I ate very little and that after a great deal of persuasion. This by the way, was not out of modesty but, being an active person and used to moving about a great deal in my home, I had lost my appetite completely now that I was confined to sitting in one place for hours. Though this was not intentional, it helped me to get another good mark, for it seemed that nicely brought up girls were never ravenously hungry.

In fact, I got good marks all round for I dressed in the orthodox bridal style, or rather I did not protest when I was so dressed up. I had *mehndi* on my hands, *kajal* in my eyes, *afshan* and *chamki* on my hair, the traditional cosmetic for brides, and *ittar* on my clothes, which, by the way, were always of very bright hues and richly embroidered, and I remained loaded with jewellery. I was absolutely the traditional bride.

It delighted my mother-in-law and all her family that they had found an 'English-educated' girl who was at the same time absolutely old-fashioned. That I was not so, at least not entirely, that my character would eventually reveal some unmistakable sign of Western influence, they were to discover later. But, all went well for the present.

My conforming to the traditional behaviour was not play-acting. My mother had succeeded in persuading me that it was the only correct behaviour of well-brought-up girls and those who did not conform to it were ill-bred. I had come to believe this and, therefore, conformed willingly. To this day I still believe in the traditional observances in a wedding, although perhaps not in all their rigidity; but I do believe that they should be observed for they are colourful and are characteristic of our way of life. Even if I had not believed in it, I would have conformed for I was not only fond of my mother but held her in great respect and, if I had not behaved according to tradition, it would have meant her losing face. This would have hurt her very much and I would not have dreamt of doing so. Anyway, had I attempted any deviation, I do not think I would have got away with it for amongst the maids who had come to look after me was Muna Buwa and I have described earlier what a stickler she was for discipline in tradition and therefore accompanied every girl of the family on her first visit to her in-laws. My mother had borrowed her from aunt. She was taking no chances with me.

My in-laws lived in Nagpur where my father-in-law Khan Bahadur Hafiz Mohammad Wilayatullah had retired and settled, but their family came from Bhopal, a Muslim Princely State, and had originally belonged to the United Provinces, that centre and cradle of Muslim culture. So, though they now lived in a predominantly Hindu province, they and a few more families like them maintained an enclave of Muslim culture in the same way as my family did in Bengal. There was no difference of background to overcome except that in some ways life at my in-laws was even more orthodox than at home. My father-in-law was less Westernized than my father. He had not been to England and he had not spent years of his service living in anglicized areas of Indian towns.

The house in which we lived in Nagpur was originally a bungalow but it had been modified and had taken on the look of the traditional Muslim house with the large enclosed courtyard and a verandah running the entire length of the house. On the verandah there was the usual large *takhat* with the inevitable *paan-daan*. Alongside the wall, *charpais* were stacked, which were taken out in the evening into the courtyard for sleeping. There were the *surahis* for drinking water and the samovar on one side for washing. All the living in the East is done on verandahs and, though we now build dining- and drawing-rooms in imitation of the West and have even taken to building suffocating little flats, we still go on living on verandahs and verandahs always have *takhats* which can be said to be the stage of all our activities. Though houses are now furnished with sofas and chairs and all modern European furniture, the *takhat* still holds its own as the most used piece of furniture in our households. It did not take me very long to feel quite at home on the large *takhat* on the verandah at Nagpur.

I have said that I found settling down in my new home easy because my in-laws were pleasantly surprised by my orthodoxy. It was also made easy by the fact that my mother-in-law was a most kindly person. She, like my mother, was in poor health and was soon to become a complete invalid, though she lived for some years after my marriage. Even the few weeks in which I saw her before she was struck down by illness, she left in my mind a great impression of her kind and mellow wisdom. She, like my mother, had a great influence over her whole household. Actually women in Muslim households invariably had great influence and a much greater say in household affairs than their menfolk. The fact that they observed purdah did not mean they were nonentities, though I know this is the general impression in the West and, like many other impressions, it is an erroneous one.

The relationship between father-in-law and daughter-in-law in our society is one of great formality. A daughter-in-law is never supposed to be seen by her father-in-law with her head uncovered or rushing round or speaking loudly, much less reclining or even sitting in a negligent manner. She is never supposed to speak to her husband before her father-in-law. During the seventeen years that my father-in-law lived after my marriage, I never once spoke to my husband in his presence, for it was not done. Despite this formality there generally is a great affection between father-in-law and daughter-in-law. As opposed to the mothers-in-law, whose attitude was traditionally critical, the fathers-in-law had an affectionate tenderness towards the young girls separated from their homes and brought under their roof. My father-in-law was wise and kind and loved his children deeply but unintrusively. He was happy if they did what he wanted them to do, but his love for them did not waver if they did not—a rare quality in a parent anywhere and still more rare in our country. His loving kindness to me throughout the years is amongst my most treasured memories.

But the person with whom I had most to do was my sister-in-law, my husband's widowed sister. Though she was only two years older than he, because she was a widow and because of my mother-in-law's frail health, she had been put more and more in charge of things and she had come to have a much greater importance in the house than her age warranted. In fact, after my mother-in-law's death, she had been virtually in the place of a mother to her brothers and a mother-in-law to all her brothers' wives.

Apa, as we all called her, was a typical product of purdah. She had all the good and bad points of the milieu she was brought up in and ruled over her household—consisting of a son and daughter-in-law, several grandchildren and twenty-two servants, not to say their families—in a truly matriarchal fashion. She was kind but firm with them, the firmness being more apparent than the kindness, though if one looked closely one would see that there was a lot of genuine kindness in her also. Her servants were those who had been with the family for years and she knew all about them, the exact number and the age of the youngest grandchildren of the *mali* and the latest development in the quarrel between the cook and her daughter-in-law. But she stood no nonsense from them and did not hold with the modern nonsense about everybody being equal. Even the school-going children of the servants, who entertained such ideas, showed her a feudal deference, for she would have no less. She was a remarkably intelligent person and her comments on current affairs were scathingly funny, though her outlook in many ways was narrow and she was not interested in anything that did not affect her small world.

Her rapier-sharp wit and sense of humour made her an excellent raconteuse and I fell under her spell from the beginning and, not having had a sister myself, lavished on her all my affection with the unsophisticated abandon of a schoolgirl. She, on the other hand, never forgot that I was a sister-in-law and there were set rules by which a sister-in-law's conduct should be judged and, measured by these standards, I fell very short in certain matters. A warm heart was, according to her way of thinking, no substitute for being ignorant about cooking and sewing and other household arts and crafts.

Besides this, when she came to know me better, she found in me what she regarded as some alarming tendencies towards modernity which, because of my conservative behaviour as a bride, she was not prepared for. My attitude regarding the furniture and furnishing of my first home shocked her very much, for I rejected, lock, stock, and barrel, all the things my husband had accumulated in the six years of his service, saying that they were 'awful' and so they were, for they were the typical furnishings of a district officer's bungalow, a hybrid mixture of the worst styles of the East and the West and whatever I may or may not have known about running a household, I did know something about furniture. But to give one's opinion so freely and to be so critical was not expected of a new bride and it was also considered extremely extravagant to get everything new. All this bordered on self-assertion and that is a quality which is not encouraged in the young in our society, particularly not in daughters-in-law. I began to feel an undercurrent of criticism, where so far there had been nothing but approval and there was more to come.

My sister-in-law was very orthodox but I was only partly so and the unorthodox side of me was to come in conflict over and over again with orthodoxy. Paradoxically, it was only because part of me was orthodox that the difficulty arose. Otherwise I could have ignored the tacit criticisms and implied disapproval and gone my own way as my other sisters-in-law did later on. But the traditional training that I had had ingrained into me could not ignore the disapproval of the *susral,* while the modern in me could not restrain me from doing what was disapproved of.

While I was struggling to come to terms with this new world which from now on was to be my home, my world, my own familiar world of childhood came to an end with a suddenness that left me benumbed with shock. For my mother died at the time I needed her most. When her advice and guidance would have been of the utmost value to me, I found myself without it, alone amongst strangers. To heighten the tragedy of it, I had been away in Nagpur at the time of her death, for, true to her traditions, to the last she had refused to send for me, refused even to let me know that she was ill. And when, having heard of it by accident, I had rushed down to Calcutta, she had sent me back after a few days for, according to her, a married daughter's place was with her in-laws, particularly in the first few months after her marriage.

Such utter unselfishness and complete adherence to tradition would not have been possible to an ordinary woman even in the East, but my mother was not an ordinary woman. She was a rare person, even amongst her generation and now we will not see any women of her calibre and personality, for the very mould that fashioned her is broken.

Chapter 8

TWILIGHT OF AN EMPIRE (1933-36)

My husband, belonged to the Indian Civil Service, commonly known as the ICS. This had acquired a prestige and a glamour which is not generally associated with the civil service in any other country. Its tradition of exclusiveness had made it into a caste and exposed its members to both criticism and envy. They were accused of narrow-mindedness and rigidity of outlook, but it was reluctantly conceded that their reputation for integrity and efficiency was justified. It was, at first, manned entirely by the English but at this time more and more Indians were being admitted to its charmed circle. The Indians conformed rigidly to the pattern of behaviour that had evolved over the years. This service was the backbone of the Indian Empire, the steel frame that held it up, and it was the administrative ability of the members of this service that helped the two new countries to tide over their first unusually difficult years.

Soon after we were married my husband was posted as Under Secretary to the Industries Department of the Government of India, and so I came to live in New Delhi. That was in 1933 and New Delhi was then the seat of the Empire, the Imperial Secretariat and the Central Assembly. But so much has happened since, so completely has the picture changed, had already changed even by March 1947, when I left, that it is difficult to believe that all this was so recent.

It was a wholly official city, and an English official city at that. For, though in less than fourteen years, power was to be transferred entirely to Indian hands, the number of Indian officials in New Delhi at this time was negligible, and in the dress, manner and speech of these few men there was nothing Indian at all. They might, or rather they must, have come from Indian homes but, in their New Delhi drawing-rooms there was nothing to tell you so.

While the men were more or less of a type, the veneer of Westernization covering up differences of province and caste, women tried to be as Westernized as their husbands and followed the code of official etiquette with meticulous care. They could not succeed in camouflaging the background from which they came. They all paid and returned calls with due formality, gave correct but dull little parties, knew the use of the right knives and forks and registered the same degree of disapproval as an English Memsahib if an unfortunate bearer made the slightest mistake in serving meals or announcing callers. This spectacle of their laboured Westernization was rather pathetic and ridiculous, as was their effort to give themselves the airs of 'grandes dames'.

Simple Indian women, mostly from villages, who had not been able to shed their orthodoxy to the extent of being able to eat meat and food cooked by a non-Brahman, had yet learnt the official snobbery well enough not to notice anybody below a Joint Secretary's wife. As I was on the lowest rung of official life, being the wife of an Under Secretary, I never came to know these, for by the time I had reached a sufficiently high status to be taken notice of, I had found for myself much more interesting things to do. But these were in a minority; in most their little affectations did not take away from their warm and kindly natures. They adopted the traditional Indian attitude of the older woman towards the young; that is an attitude of motherly affection. All these women were Hindus, for if the Indian officers in the Government were few, the Muslims were still fewer; in fact my husband was the only Muslim member of the ICS in Delhi. But in 1933 this did not matter and the happy relationship established then has continued in most cases despite the bitterness of Partition.

The English women could be similarly divided into two types. There were those whose efforts to assume Mayfair airs did not hide the fact of their suburban origin and others who had that graciousness without patronage which characterizes the best type of English woman in the East. Amongst these I made many friends and without making it obvious they gave me much valuable advice which was of great help. Even spending a morning knitting in their beautiful gardens helped me to sort out many of my problems. Friendships thus formed have endured throughout the years: have survived my participation in the struggle directed against the British, and are now being carried on into the second generation.

Though individually satisfying relationships were possible, the social pattern was a very rigid and dull one. The 'season', as it was called, started around November and went on till the end of March. The months before and after this period were taken up by the exodus from and to Simla. Its highlights were the Viceregal Ball, the Viceregal Garden Party, the Horse Show and polo. Next in importance to these came the garden parties given by executive counsellors. Each gave one in the season and innumerable little dinner parties. Strict precedence was observed and everything went according to established rules. One could not ask or be asked to dinner by anyone above or below a certain rank. Needless to say, I found these restrictions both boring and irksome.

It was at the garden party of one of the executive counsellors that I made my début. I was till then officially still in purdah though since my marriage its rigidity had been much relaxed.

I did not enjoy my first experience of being out of purdah at all. I felt embarrassed at being looked at by hundreds of men and my enjoyment of the party was further spoiled by my having to spend the entire evening trying to avoid

TWILIGHT OF AN EMPIRE (1933–36)

being seen by my uncle, who very strongly disapproved of my coming out of purdah.

My subsequent sallies into mixed society I found no more interesting than the first one. I had imagined that mixed society would be composed of intelligent people, who would talk of more interesting things than were talked of in the women's world to which I had so far been confined, but to my disappointment I found that this was not so, and all that they talked was a meaningless sort of official jargon.

What I enjoyed, however, because of their spectacular quality, were the functions at the Viceregal Lodge, where I had already attended the Investiture at which my father and uncle were knighted. It had an unreal fairy-like quality even then, and the memory of it has stayed with me as of something seen in a dream. I was still in purdah and my excursion from behind the veil into this dazzling spectacle was rather like Cinderella going to the ball.

That morning I had spent seeing the tombs of Humayun and Safdar Jung, one an example of early and one of late Mughal architecture. Humayun's tomb could be compared with Westminster Abbey. It is associated with the last scene of the tragic drama of the fall of the Mughal Empire, for it was here that Bahadur Shah, the last Mughal emperor, was taken prisoner by the notorious Major Hudson, and it was here that the two princes, sons of Bahadur Shah, were also taken prisoner and shot by Hudson while the aged emperor looked on. And that day, exactly seventy-five years after that tragedy, in the same city of Delhi was being held an Investiture by the power that had succeeded the Mughals. A few years only were to go by before this power itself was to disappear and the Empire, on which the sun never set, was to become a thing of the past.

But this did not seem possible that evening in March 1932, when our car drove up to the Viceregal Lodge. I shall always remember that evening. My father looking magnificent in his colonel's uniform; my uncle very dignified in a *jamawar chuga*.

As I was in purdah I could not go up with my father and uncle and sit near them. But, as my father was a member of the Viceregal staff, being the Honorary Surgeon to the Viceroy, he knew everybody and had arranged for me to be taken up separately and put in a seat not too far from him. All along the stairs and passages stood, as if carved in stone, the Viceroy's personal bodyguards, all of them at least six feet six inches in height, all wearing brilliant uniforms with black and gold turbans, holding rifles with fixed bayonets. They struck awe in my heart.

The Investiture was being held in the Mughal drawing-room of the Viceregal Lodge. This room has a magnificently painted ceiling and beautiful marble columns. It was ablaze with lights. At one end of the room was a raised dais upon which stood two thrones. In the seats facing it sat men in dazzling uniforms with medals and women in gorgeous evening gowns and jewels. Suddenly there was a sort of clinking noise and then my eyes saw a spectacle I have never forgotten. In a box at the side of the dais appeared the Indian princes, resplendent in the brocaded *sherwanis* and Benarasi turbans with jewels scintillating on their chests and swords strapped to their waists. They came, about ten or twelve of them, all at once and stood for a minute before taking their seats. It looked as if all the colour, the pageantry and chivalry that was India was symbolized in them. Barely a few minutes had passed when the Viceroy and Lady Willingdon came slowly up to the dais. Lord Willingdon was an extremely distinguished looking man and looked very elegant in Court Dress; many medals blazed on his chest and from his shoulders hung a blue cape, each corner held by two little page-boys. Lady Willingdon had on a magnificent evening gown and she too wore many medals. She had a diamond tiara on her head and ropes of pearls round her throat. Her cape was also held by two little page-boys, dressed in blue and white. ADCs, Military Secretaries and other members of the Viceregal staff led the procession, which slowly reached the dais. The Viceroy and Vicereine sat down. It all looked like a tableau.

Soon the Viceroy was standing up. The Investiture had begun. Men were going up to receive their honours from the representative of the King. The GCIEs, the KCIEs, the GCSIs, and the KCSIs came first. The recipients of these were members of the princely order. Then came the GCBs, and KCBs and, after them, the knights. My heart filled with pride as I saw, first my uncle and then my father go up to the dais and kneel on a velvet footstool. I watched the Viceroy touch their shoulders with his sword bidding them rise. After the knights came the Nawabs, the CIEs, and the CSIs, the MBEs, the OBEs, the *Kaiser-i-Hinds* and many other titles that I do not remember.

At last it was all over. Everybody was leaving. I again found myself being discreetly escorted out by an ADC.

Later on many of these titles were returned at the command of the Muslim League. When my father returned his knighthood, it was on a gloomy evening in Calcutta, with the dreadful scenes of the terrible riots still before our eyes and its echoes still ringing in our ears. My mind went back to this night of dazzling splendour. But all this was many years away and meanwhile I had to contend with the dull routine of society life in New Delhi. Fortunately, alongside New Delhi's narrow confines lay the wondrous historic city of Old Delhi, and soon I was to reach out to gather its richness. Delhi is one of those cities that is steeped in 'history, legend, tune and song', for it has been the heart of Indo-Muslim culture for two thousand years.

There have been eight Delhis in all, eight different dynasties had chosen it for their capital. Seven cities lie in ruin around it. In 1932, the eighth Delhi, which was called New Delhi, stood in radiant splendour encircled by the seven other cities, each one once the proud capital of an empire and still containing within its walls monuments of its past glory. Besides history Delhi is associated with our best poets and writers and in 1933, there still lived there men and women who were typical of its great culture. Mr Asaf Ali was one of them, Khawaja Hassan Nizami was another. Nawab Sirjuddin Khan Sael was still alive and so was Rashid-ul-Khairi. I had the privilege of meeting them and of listening to their talk. It was indeed a 'liberal education'.

Mr Asaf Ali, was not only one of the most prominent figures of the Indian National Movement but one of its most charming also. He belonged to Delhi, not only in the sense that he came from one of its oldest families, but because he was the quintessence of its culture. He had the courtesy and the charm, the grace, the elegance and the manner, that undefinable air of breeding which only those nurtured in the best tradition of our culture possess. I have never heard and never shall hear again Urdu spoken as Asaf Ali spoke it. Urdu is essentially a court language; it was born and bred in the court of the Mughal kings. It is capable of extremely subtle nuances. Stressing a single syllable the juxtaposition of a single word, can convey a world of meaning; only a few today know how to do this. Asaf Ali did. He was probably one of the last who knew how to use the language as if it were a musical instrument. It was becoming rare, even in my generation, to hear Urdu spoken in this manner. It makes me sad to think that my children have not even heard the full range of its musical cadence. I was indeed fortunate to have heard it, fortunate to have known persons of such rare quality as Asaf Ali and his young wife, Aruna.

When I met Aruna, she had a burning transparent sincerity and her subsequent revolutionary career did not surprise me. But I know that she was not the hard-headed revolutionary people imagined her to be but a woman with great sweetness and gentleness of character, capable of tender and deep affection. That is how she was when I met her and that was how she remained till she died.

As Asaf Ali was a great friend of my uncle, Syud Hussain, it did not take me long to come to know him and his wife very well. I was soon to be seen very frequently at Asaf Ali's house in Kuchai Chilan, meeting other interesting people and listening avidly to their conversation. Asaf Ali knew the history of every nook and corner, every inch and stone of Delhi, and I would listen spellbound as he told me about it. He knew so many forgotten anecdotes which made the stones live and speak again.

Bhabi, as we all called Mrs Asaf Ali, gave me my first taste of social service. She got me to become a member of the Delhi Women's League. I did not do anything very much, except attend various lectures given by well-known visitors. The most interesting amongst them and the one I remember the most clearly was by the famous Turkish writer, speaker and politician, Khalida Adeeb Khanum. It seems strange, when I look back on it all, to think that I, who eventually became such an ardent Muslim Leaguer, should have begun my apprenticeship under Aruna Asaf Ali. Little did she suspect the lines on which I would develop later. Little did I know myself.

I also saw a good deal of Mrs Sarojini Naidu. She was, without exaggeration, the most interesting, the most vivacious and the most charming person in India. She had a radiant personality which made even the staid and official drawing-rooms of Delhi pulsate with life. She was the most marvellous and interesting conversationalist that I have ever met. She had a fund of anecdotes which she told in her own inimitable manner. They all had more than a little soupçon of malice but her manner of telling them was such that one did not mind the malice, one only enjoyed the fun. She held court—no other word can describe it—at the house of Sir Siri Ram where she usually stayed when she was in Delhi. There would be anything up to thirty to forty people in the room every evening. She would be talking to all of them almost at the same time, calling them all by their first names and managing to make everyone feel absolutely and completely at home. Her memory was phenomenal; she knew almost everybody and she never forgot a face or a name. She was a great friend of my aunt as well as all the members of my family, but had seen me only when I was ten years old. So I had not expected her even to remember me, but she did. Not only that, when she met me the first time, she remembered that she had heard I had recently married and called out to my husband to come and sit next to her and get properly introduced.

She used to come to Delhi more or less every cold weather and everyone looked forward to her visit. She would ring me up directly that she had arrived, fix a date when she would come to dinner with me and order the menu herself. This she did with all her special friends. She liked food, as she liked all good things of life, and to any admonition to be careful, as her health was none too good and rich food was bad for her, she would reply 'Oh, be quiet! All the doctors that gave me six months have been dead for years.'

And so, before I realized it, our three years in Delhi were over and we were due for a transfer. We should ordinarily have gone back to the Central Province, but we were fortunate to get posted to London, one of the few foreign postings available to Indians at that time.

I had already been to England with my father the year before and had loved it. So I was delighted at the prospect of spending three years there. Though I did not realize it then, these were to be the last years of my life untouched by the stress and strain of politics.

CHAPTER 9

YEARS IN ENGLAND (1937–40)

Going to England for the first time had a strange charm for me, for it was like seeing something at once familiar and strange. History, legend, tune and song had made every historical and literary landmark familiar to me. I had in my mind's eye seen Westminster Abbey and the Tower, had wandered round Shakespeare's country and visualized Warwick Castle, all that had happened in Hampton Court and Windsor, and I knew every detail of life at Oxford and Cambridge as if I had actually studied there. So to see them all gave me a strange sensation, a feeling of 'I have been here before'. This was true not only of historical buildings but of every aspect of English life.

During the previous visit, I had lived most of the time in a small unspoilt English village, not far from London. I had loved going for long walks in the country, looking at old churches and stopping for tea on farms, eating home-made cakes and masses of bread and butter. I helped in picking salad and gathering strawberries and, as August came, took part in the haymaking and rode back home on a hay-cart. My father had come as a delegate to the British University Conference which was held in Cambridge. So, soon after our arrival in London, we went over to Cambridge where I spent a most interesting three weeks. I stayed at Newnham College, thus getting a taste of the sort of life I had so longed for. It was summer, so the colleges were closed but a number of students had stayed back and I quickly made friends with several.

There were many functions, the historical background of the University making them very impressive. But what I enjoyed most were the small parties which the Principals of the various Colleges gave to a few delegates at a time. One of these which I remember very clearly was given by the Provost of King's. With his snowy white hair and courtly manners, he looked as if he had stepped out of the eighteenth century. His setting was equally beautiful. We sat round his dinner table whose polished surface mirrored the silver candlesticks, and listened to conversation that sparkled and scintillated like diamonds.

During these weeks I heard more interesting and brilliant conversations than I had ever done before. Miss Strachey who was the Principal of Newnham had a great deal of her famous brother's (Giles Lytton Strachey) crisp and caustic wit. Other dons were equally amusing and in their casual remarks often laid open the heart of a matter. I had also made friends with several students and got asked to the famous 'cocoa' parties where all life's problems are discussed with an earnestness which would make an outsider think that the fate of the world depended on the conclusion that this particular group may reach.

Yes, I had thoroughly enjoyed my first visit to England and my glimpse of Europe, and therefore was very pleased indeed when we went to live there. My stay in England began with the Coronation of King George VI and ended soon after the Second World War had been declared. So I can say that I have seen the English people in their hour of triumph and in their hour of tragedy, and I can honestly say that I admired them in both. Anything as good-humoured or tolerant or disciplined as an English crowd is hard to find, and never have I seen a group of people face disaster with less panic and greater equanimity.

I am glad to have seen the Coronation. There are very few things left in this drab and modern world of ours that bring pageantry and colour into our lives and the coronation of a British King and Queen is one of these. It makes history a reality and tradition a living thing, and it satisfies that innate love which is in every human heart for show and pageantry.

I saw the Coronation procession from Hyde Park Corner where, like the rest of the crowd, we had collected from the early hours of the morning, armed with picnic basket and coffee. We heard the radio describe the ceremony and chatted and exchanged remarks with the crowds. The hours passed quickly and soon it was afternoon, and we heard that the procession had left the Abbey and was already winding its way back to Buckingham Palace. The excitement reached fever pitch as the procession came nearer and nearer Hyde Park. Now the sound of cheering could be heard, now we could see the beginning of the procession: the contingents from the Commonwealth countries resplendent in their varied uniforms, came in their serried ranks. They were followed by line upon line of British soldiers in colourful uniforms. The Highlanders, The Household Cavalry and many others whose regiments I do not know, but they all looked gorgeous as they came in an unending procession; then the cars of the Royal guests and finally, the gold and glass coach of the King and Queen, sceptre in hand, crowns on their heads, they looked like a picture from a book of fairy tales. Just as the procession had passed and even before it was out of sight, the rain which had threatened the whole morning came down. The route was still closed and so we sat and resigned ourselves to getting soaked. At last the road was opened, and for a few minutes the crowd became very disorderly in its efforts to get home. It took us ages to get to our flat which was just at Marble Arch, a few minutes' walk. Next evening I went to the Coronation Ball. I saw the King and Queen and another dozen or so crowned Heads of Europe, resplendent in their jewels and decorations. As usual, when attending a function of this sort, I felt I was watching a pageant. For several weeks after, there were garden parties, luncheons and receptions. At last it was all over, the coronation visitors left and England settled back to a normal pattern of life.

We found ourselves a small furnished house in Chelsea and settled down to living in England. It did not seem at all strange for I came from that small stratum of society that had adopted the English pattern of life to the minutest detail; cretonne curtains, fender stool, thinly cut bread and butter, cucumber sandwiches and all. Therefore, the inside of my house in Chelsea did not seem very different from my childhood home in Calcutta or my home in New Delhi. Even the food was not strange, for we always ate a typical English breakfast. Lunch and dinner were different only in having some Indian dishes added to a three-course English meal. Even the shops did not impress me as they should have done for I had lived in Calcutta where the department stores were as good as any in Oxford Street. Life in England was not different because it was strange to me, but it was different in being much less formal than the replica of it that I had known. Formal calls and stiff dinner parties were things of the past. I myself led a much freer life; even though compared with my English friends I had much more domestic help, I did little chores myself which in India I would not have thought of doing, such as buying my stamps, posting my letters, taking things to the dyers and cleaners, etc. But despite this, I found much more time than in Delhi for I had much less social life to cope with.

The years in London had a great formative influence on my mind and character. They gave me self-confidence and a broader outlook. My ideas began to form and my judgement to mature and in return I could see the hybrid society of New Delhi for what it was and I wondered why I had ever worried about not conforming to its standards. I could indulge to the full my new-found love of the theatre and ballet, and the pleasure of browsing in bookshops.

My eldest child Inam was nearly three years old when I arrived in England. Salma was born soon after, and Naz a bare fifteen months later. But despite this I was able to study for a Ph.D. By the time my thesis on the development of the Urdu novel and short story was completed and presented, war had broken out and the University of London had moved to somewhere in Wales, and it was from there that months after I left England I heard that it had been accepted and I had been given a Ph.D. for it.

Initially I had hoped to do a second BA but for the first two terms studying, with three small children to look after, presented difficulties. I decided to take journalism instead as it had an interesting syllabus of English. But even journalism meant regular attendance at lectures which I could not manage.

It was then my father suggested I do Ph.D. as for this I could prepare largely on my own. My supervisor Dr Graham Bailey was most kind and suited his time to mine and I was lucky enough to get an excellent Swedish nurse for my children. I owe her a debt of gratitude for without her I could not have done my work. Later on I was again lucky and found Helen, the nanny who stayed with me for thirty years. Her selfless devotion and complete reliability enabled me to carry on with my particular work without any guilty qualm.

At that time it was not acceptable for married woman to study and have a career. I therefore met with much criticism. I remember one particular instance. A family friend—a kind and gracious lady—dropped in one afternoon. The babies were sleeping contentedly in their cots in the garden. I was making some notes for my work. She put her arm on my back and said as if speaking to a wayward child, 'My dear you are now grown-up, give up all this' and she gestured towards my books and papers. I felt like saying, 'Your daughter-in-law spends her time playing bridge and tennis for much longer than I do in studying. Why is that acceptable and my studying not'. Of course I did not say it.

Though life moved peacefully and uneventfully, the menace of war came daily nearer. News in the papers began to become definitely alarming, and Hitler's speeches that one heard on the radio became more and more hysterical. The possibility of a war became the constant topic of conversation. Gas masks began to be distributed, trenches were dug and instructions about the blackout were given over the radio. And then, when war seemed a certainty, suddenly the cloud was lifted. Chamberlain came back from Munich with the promise of peace in our time. It was as if we had stood on the edge of a precipice, sure of being pushed over and miraculously had been saved at the last minute. But the respite was for a short while only. In less than a year from then the war came. I took my children and went to Paignton, where I had in any case arranged to go for my holidays. I remember the rush and the crowds at Waterloo station because London was expected to be bombed almost immediately, and therefore children were being evacuated by the thousands. The war was declared after I had been almost a week in Paignton, a week of hope and suspense, for it looked as if once again peace might be saved, but that was not to be. On 3 September 1939, at eleven o'clock in the morning, we all gathered in the hotel lounge and heard Chamberlain announce that a state of war existed between His Majesty's Government and Germany. It was a solemn moment, and all of us present felt the awful significance of it.

CHAPTER 10

THE RETURN HOME

I found the Delhi of 1940 much changed from the Delhi I had come to know in 1933. The tone and temper of society were so different that it was difficult to believe that only seven years had passed. In 1933 the pattern in New Delhi had been English; the efforts of the few Indians in the establishment had been to conform as closely as possible with that pattern. Now the number of Indian officials in the Imperial Secretariat had doubled and, as the war progressed and more and more Englishmen left to serve with the armed forces, and yet more officers were needed to cope with the vitally important and continuously increasing work of the War Supply Department, still more Indians found their way into the most coveted posts. So now the number of Indian officers in New Delhi was large enough for them to form a society of their own, and though in this society everything continued in the same manner only 'in a darker shade' to quote Pandit Jawaharlal Nehru, yet it existed on its own, separate from the English society, and members of the two groups met only at official functions. Since, due to wartime austerity measures, the Viceregal entertainment was cut down to a minimum, they met very rarely.

But it was not only the fact that there were more Indians in New Delhi that accounted for this separatist tendency; many things had happened during the intervening years to bring about the change. The Congress had gone a long way since the 1922 idyll of Hindu-Muslim harmony. The towering Muslim personalities in it were dead or had severed their connections with the Congress in bitter disappointment. Those who stayed, though remaining true to their ideals, did not carry sufficient weight. So the Congress that came into power in the eleven provinces in 1937 was, to all intents and purposes, a Hindu party and its first taste of power went to its head. In its twenty-seven months of rule (for the Congress Governments resigned in protest when war was declared) it rode roughshod over Muslim feelings and susceptibilities, thereby causing panic and alarm in their hearts.

The Muslim League had been reorganized in 1937 under the presidency of Mr Mohammad Ali Jinnah but it was still weak. It had not captured sufficient seats even in the Muslim majority provinces to form a 100 per cent Muslim League Government, but in each of the provincial legislatures it was the largest Muslim party; yet when the Congress Ministries were formed in the seven provinces not one League member found a place in any of them. A Muslim was taken here and there but the Muslims contended that the man thus chosen was a nominee of the Hindus and not their true representative. But weak though the Muslim League was in 1937 it was a mistake for the Congress to ignore it as completely as they did. Of course they did not know that the dynamic personality of Mohammad Ali Jinnah was going to transform that loosely organized ineffectual body into a well-knit, superbly disciplined, organization which in seven brief years was to formulate a demand, gain support for it and achieve what it set out to get. They cannot be blamed for not foreseeing this, one of the greatest miracles of modern times, but they were wrong to ignore the aspirations of the Muslims, because they were not then strong enough to present their case forcefully. In not a single province did Congress try to come to any understanding with the Muslim League Party. But that was not the only instance of their ignoring Muslim sentiments. The heady wine of power went to the head of the Congress Ministries. They passed laws forcing Muslim children to attend government schools which in their tone were completely Hindu, to salute the Congress flag, to sing the *Vande Mataram*. Petty Hindu officials harassed Muslims everywhere. A hundred and one small pin-pricks and irritations cropped up daily; unimportant in themselves, they were like the proverbial leaf which indicated the way the wind was blowing, and the indication in this case was that it was blowing towards Hindu imperialism and Hindu domination which would attempt to exterminate 800 years of Muslim influence and culture. Alarm and panic swept through the Muslims and resulted in the strengthening of the Muslim League. It also resulted in great bitterness, so that when the Congress Ministries resigned in September 1939, the Muslim League ordered a 'Deliverance-Day' to be celebrated throughout the length and breadth of India.

That is why New Delhi of 1940 was different from that of 1933. India had come a stage nearer independence and, because of that, Indians were less eager to ape their rulers. This difference I was to feel almost immediately on my arrival. The second change, namely the growing rift between the two communities, I was not to be aware of for some little while yet. In my three years' absence from India, though bits of news had come to me and every now and then I read an article in some Urdu magazine protesting against Congress attempts to stamp out Urdu or stating the injustices Muslims were suffering under Congress rule, I had not realized its extent.

It was a very trivial incident that brought home to me how Hindu communalism had grown in the last few years. A Hindu friend of mine objected to my using the word 'Begum' as it underlined the fact of my being Muslim. 'Begum' is a word of Turkish origin and was used by Muslim ladies with their first names as a title equivalent to 'Lady'. We had recently begun using it before our surnames as the equivalent of 'Mrs' and, if anything, it was an anti-English gesture or a simple expression of nationalism. It certainly had no communal intention, and Hindu objection to it showed the extent of their narrow-mindedness.

But the event that was to change the course of my life was yet to occur. In October 1941, my father came from England on leave and came to stay with me in my house in New Delhi. One morning he said to me, 'I am going to see Mr Jinnah. You come along with me.'

'Oh, I don't think I will,' said I. 'I believe he is very rude and snubs everybody.'

'Don't be silly,' said my father. 'That is just Hindu propaganda. I want you to meet him.'

So I went rather reluctantly and apprehensively.

Our house was less than ten minutes' walk from Mr Jinnah's and in the car it took even less so we arrived a little earlier than ten, which was the time for my father's appointment. We sat down in a small room leading from the hall prepared to wait, but the doorman who had taken in our cards came back and asked us to follow him. To our surprise we found ourselves being led into the dining-room where Quaid-i-Azam and Miss Jinnah, his sister, were still sitting as they had not yet finished breakfast. Thinking that the servant had made a mistake (probably he had), we tried to back out, but before we could do so Quaid-i-Azam got up with a welcoming smile and came towards my father with outstretched hands.

I remember that scene so clearly, the beautifully proportioned room, the early morning sun pouring through the windows, Miss Jinnah sitting looking most elegant at the head of the table that was laid with exquisite china and gleaming silver. Quaid-i-Azam pushing back his chair and getting up on seeing us, his snow-white napkin sliding from his knees as he did so, his quick gesture in stooping to pick it up and put it on the table, and then coming, hands outstretched, with a most radiant smile on his face. He smiled very rarely, but when he did his smile was the kind that lights up the whole face. That is how I first saw him—and that is how I see him over and over again in my mind's eye, each little detail as clear as if it had happened only yesterday.

My father had certain proposals which he wanted to discuss. He felt that, as Adviser to the Secretary of State for India, he might be able to bring about some sort of understanding between the British Government and the Muslim League. Quaid listened to what Father had to say very attentively and began to explain his point of view. And then, before I knew what I was doing, I was asking Quaid questions and he was answering them!—not impatiently or brusquely but kindly and in great detail. Quaid-i-Azam, Mohammad Ali Jinnah, the President of the All India Muslim League, the leader of the majority of the Muslims of the Indian subcontinent, reported to be arrogant and dictatorial, was allowing a completely inexperienced, unimportant young person to argue with him and was taking the trouble of meeting her arguments! The wonder of it did not strike me for the moment as I was carried away by the fascination of listening to Quaid.

Now, after nearly twenty years, during which I have met some very great statesmen, I still maintain that to listen to Quaid and not be convinced was not possible. It was not that he overruled you, it was not that he did not reply to your argument, but that he was so thoroughly, so single-mindedly, so intensely convinced of the truth of his point of view that you could not help but be convinced also. You felt that if a man with an intellect so much superior to yours believed this, then it must be right. Call it hypnotism or what you will, that is the effect he had on me; and I am not the only person on whom he had this effect—he had it on all who came in contact with him. Anyone whom he thought it worth his while to try and convince, he always succeeded in convincing. Even last-ditch opponents like Fazlul Haq and Khizar Hayat have admitted that while face-to-face with Quaid-i-Azam they never dared to disagree, and they were the premiers of two of the biggest provinces of India and Mohammad Ali Jinnah was only the president of the Muslim League—and the Muslim League, according to these gentlemen, was only a band of ragged ruffians!

That he should have thought it worth his while to try to convince me of the rightness of his cause I shall never cease to wonder at. But, because he did so, I am today in Pakistan.

It was ten o'clock when we had come. By one-fifteen Miss Jinnah appeared to remind Quaid that it was time for lunch and that after lunch he had other people coming. My father and I realized with a shock that we had stayed over three hours! It would be trite to say that the hours had flown like minutes.

We apologized profusely and began to take our leave. Both Quaid and Miss Jinnah were very kind and said that we must come again and this time to lunch. The day was fixed and Miss Jinnah very kindly asked me to bring my husband also.

The conversation at the luncheon next week was not as easy as on the morning of my first meeting with Quaid. I suppose the presence of my husband, a Government servant, must have had something to do with it. As a representative of the Government which would have loved to liquidate the Muslim League no less than Congress, it could not be expected that he would have much sympathy with, or understanding of, the Muslim League point of view. He, like all civil servants, had a sort of semi-cynical, semi-humorous attitude towards politics and politicians, and I remember his telling Quaid-i-Azam, 'I am sorry, Sir, but this idea of Pakistan does not appeal to me much. After all, I come from a Muslim minority province; we are only 3 per cent in the Central Provinces. What do we get out of backing Pakistan? Of course, if you were to plan to reconquer India, I would resign and join up with you immediately.'

Quaid-i-Azam, as is well known, had not much use for flippancy, especially where such serious matters were concerned. I remember his pausing for a minute, looking at my husband closely and saying, 'This is not a matter for joking, young man.' But my husband was not much abashed, and continued to enjoy his lunch. We left at about three o'clock and, though I did not know it, I had already taken the first step towards entering the tumultuous life of politics.

CHAPTER 11

THE SHADOW OF COMING EVENTS

A few days after my visit to Quaid-i-Azam, three girls from the Indian Parsat College for Girls in Delhi came to see me. They said Miss Jinnah had asked them to do so in connection with forming a Muslim Women Students' Federation. There was already an All India Students' Federation, but, a year or so ago a separate All India Muslim Students' Federation had been formed owing to the increasing divergencies of opinion and growing bitterness between the two communities, but there was no separate Muslim Women's Student Federation yet. These girls proposed to form one, because as they explained to me they found it increasingly difficult to see eye to eye on many questions with their Hindu fellow-students at college, and had to have a separate organization to be able to voice their point of view. They told me what I had been hearing over and over again in the year I had been back; stories of little pin-pricks, of petty persecutions, of things that in themselves were of no importance but in the tense political atmosphere took on special significance.

I now have only a hazy impression as to what these grievances were. A play had been staged by the Hindu girls that had shown the Muslim rulers to be cruel and intolerant. The Muslim girls had wanted to retaliate and stage a play but this had not been allowed by the Principal on the grounds that it was communal to do so. They had been made to take part in the Congress Independence Resolution Day celebrations, that is 26 January, but when they had wanted to celebrate 23 March, the Pakistan

Resolution Day, it had been forbidden. It seems incredible now to think that such petty and trifling matters could have caused all the heartburning and resentment and the tenseness and bitterness which resulted in the partition of the country, the uprooting of millions of human beings, the death of at least a million and destruction of property worth hundreds of thousands. And it all began because the Hindus, a nation with thousands of years of civilization behind them, were so petty, and because the Muslims, a people who had defied the might of empires and had won victory over armies many times their size, were afraid that they would be swamped and annihilated. And so, lack of generosity and fear combined to rend the country in two and bring misery to millions.

But in November 1941, I did not think that these girls' grievances were petty. I was as indignant as they, and agreed to help them to form a separate Muslim Girl Students' organization. I did not know much more than they did how one sets about forming an organization, especially a countrywide one. We had a great deal of enthusiasm, but no experience at all, so we decided that we would go and see Miss Jinnah and ask her how to set about it. She received us very kindly and told us that she had got the Secretary of the All India Muslim Students' Federation to come so that he could advise us how to form a Women's organization on the same lines. All three girls kept strict purdah and so they sat in another room while Miss Jinnah and I talked to Mr Noman. He told us that the Muslim Women Students' Federation would be a part of the All India Muslim Students' Federation in the same way as the Muslim League Women's sub-committee was part of the All India Muslim League, and that Raja Sahib Mahmudabad would be the President of the whole organization as Quaid-i-Azam was of the Muslim League. Raja Sahib Mahmudabad would appoint me convener (he did so by telegram a few days later) and I would then set about calling the Conference. He told me the procedure for doing so and of drawing up a Constitution etc. We decided when to hold the Conference and other details, after which Mr Noman left and Miss Jinnah and I came over and joined the girls. I remember that November afternoon so well. We sat on a hammock on Miss Jinnah's verandah, overlooking her beautiful garden. We sipped our orange juice and rocked ourselves gently, talking over our newly formed plans. It all seemed so easy and so wonderful. Little did I realize what it would lead to, how much bitterness it would cause, how many enemies it would make me, how many friends I would lose. That November afternoon it seemed just a thrilling adventure and nothing more.

I feel at this stage that I must say a little more about Miss Jinnah, for the great part that she played in bringing the Muslim women forward is not fully realized abroad. Quaid-i-Azam died just a year after the establishment of Pakistan, a year crowded with important work, and after his death she never sought publicity and limelight. But to those who had the privilege of knowing her, the part she played in this great drama is well known. So many women now doing very important work for Pakistan were given their first job to do by Miss Jinnah. She was an extremely good judge of character and capabilities and she had a quality especially rare in prominent people that she never got taken in by flattery. She could assess a person pretty shrewdly almost on the first meeting, but no amount of trying would get you an inch further with her unless she herself wished it. She was extremely reserved and made friends with great difficulty. It was my greatest privilege to have enjoyed her friendship until her death. Her kindness and advice to me in very difficult times were invaluable, and when she was a friend she was a real friend, putting her friend's welfare before her own personal interest. Many a time, after I had plunged into Muslim League work, she restrained my enthusiasm because she realized it was against my interests to go headlong into politics in this way. She never abused my enthusiasm, and always understood my difficulties. In short, she was truly a friend, philosopher and guide.

Finding and setting other women to do useful jobs was by no means Miss Jinnah's only work, though that in itself was no small achievement for not everybody has the knack of finding the right person for the right place or giving the right person an opportunity; wheresoever she went with Quaid-i-Azam she tried to start something useful. The first Women's Industrial Homes in Karachi, Lahore and Quetta were all begun by her in the brief and crowded year when he was Governor-General of Pakistan, or I should really say in the first few months, because towards the end he was ill and she spent her time nursing him in the quiet hill station of Ziarat. In those few months she started not only these Women's Industrial Homes, which have been a pattern and model for others since, but also a 'Women's Relief Committee', which was really the nucleus for the All Pakistan Women's Association (APWA) of today; most of the workers of the Women's Association got their first training in social work in the Women's Relief Committee. She had planned to convert this into a permanent organization for social service, but here again she did not have the time. She encouraged the Pakistan Women's National Guard; she formed the first women's Dramatic Committee in Karachi which produced an excellent play in aid of refugees within the first four months after the establishment of Pakistan. She had planned to bring out a woman's magazine, and my articles, which were later published as a separate book entitled *Behind the Veil,* were originally written for it.

The shattering blow of Quaid's death which made all Pakistan reel, was, naturally, for her a very great personal loss. It took her some time to get over it. Meanwhile her ideas were put into effect by others. Much happened in Pakistan after Quaid's death which saddened her, but she refrained from interfering. Her statements on important occasions, however, are a reminder of the ideals on which Pakistan was founded.

My acquaintance with Miss Jinnah more or less began that evening, but the appreciation of her character and personality came much later after years of association with her. That evening I was thrilled and elated at having met her because she was Quaid-i-Azam's sister and I considered it a great honour that she should have chosen to give me a job to do, and was determined to carry out the task she had entrusted to me to the very best of my ability.

I was, therefore, rather dashed when on going home and relating all this to my husband, he told me that he did not think it was advisable for me to involve myself in politics as I was a Government servant's wife. So far it had been considered wrong for Government servants or their wives to have anything to do with politics. This aloofness of the services constituted their strength as it retained their objectivity but lately this was breaking down and several wives of Indian civil servants were actively engaged in political work. These were however all Hindus. The Muslim women had so far refrained from doing so because the Muslim League was not yet strong enough, and they were afraid to associate themselves with an unpopular party. The very fact that this was the argument advanced to keep me from participating in the League activities made me more determined to do so. I was determined to prove that I at least was not afraid! In my youthful egoism I did not realize that it was not I but my husband who would have to face the attendant awkwardness, and strangely enough, though he objected to my taking part in politics at that stage, he did not do so later on, and I have often wondered at this, and have felt that it must be due to the fact that by that time he himself had begun to accept the inevitability of the old order changing completely. But this is only a presumption, I cannot say for certain what his thinking was. But what I can say is that but for his support, understanding and tolerance it would not have been possible for me to continue working actively in the Muslim League. As time passed, the atmosphere became increasingly tense and relationships turned bitter; fingers were pointed and malicious comments made. My husband took it all in his stride. When someone had the impertinence to say why does not Ikramullah control his wife. His reply was:

> My wife is an intelligent woman and comes from a political family. I will not and cannot control her. For myself I have nothing to do with politics. If the Government doesn't trust me I am prepared to resign.

How many men would have the self-confidence and courage to say this? Now that the heat of the battle is over and I can look back on events calmly, I feel that while in a time of national resistance to foreign domination it is right for all rules to be broken, it is not a good thing at other times for wives of Government servants to take part in politics. This rule should be enforced again, for Government servants' involvement in politics has been responsible for many administrative ills since the establishment of Pakistan.

For the next few weeks my energies were completely taken up in the task of organizing the Conference. Though it was not going to be a very large affair it was still on All India scale. I had issued invitations to Muslim Girls' Colleges of Lahore, Aligarh, Lucknow, Meerut and Nagpur, and expected about fifty delegates. My chief worry was to find accommodation for them, and as all the girls were in purdah and could not use buses or trams, transport also presented a great difficulty. A Girls' Conference was a completely new thing. It meant a great responsibility for me, as I was the only person who was not a student. If anything went wrong, the others would be excused on the score of their youth and inexperience, and I would get all the blame. I got no help from my friends in New Delhi. They were the wives of officials and did not want to get into trouble by taking part in politics. Nearly every one of these ladies today considers herself an ardent Muslim Leaguer and would have it believed that she has always been so. One who was now in the forefront of social and political activity in Pakistan on that occasion refused even to buy a Reception Committee ticket, saying—'I am sorry my husband is a Government servant. I do not want to have anything to do with Muslim League'. When her pretensions got on my nerves, I felt a malicious desire to remind her of this incident, but my better nature always prevailed.

Yes, in 1940-1, there were very few people who were prepared to associate themselves with the Muslim League and yet, though our numbers were few, there was amongst us such a spirit of comradeship, such an earnest desire to serve, that it more than made up for our lack of numbers. We worked with no feeling of rivalry, without any desire for 'kudos' or publicity, our one wish was to serve the Muslim cause which we felt was going by default.

As the day came nearer, I got more and more apprehensive, and it was with a great feeling of nervousness that I went to meet the train from Lahore which was bringing the first contingent of the delegates. Fortunately for me, this first delegation was led by Fatima Begum. Her warm and affectionate greeting and whole-hearted encouragement of what I was doing gave me great confidence. Fatima Begum was one of our veteran leaders of women's emancipation. She had known my aunt and other members of my family, and although this was the first time I had met her, she treated me as if she had known me all my life. I told her apologetically of my very inadequate arrangements but she waved my excuses aside and by her presence and encouragement immediately gave our effort, which so far was being looked upon merely as a piece of youthful folly, a much better status. I owe a great debt of gratitude to her for had this, my first venture, failed, I think I would not have gone on with my political career.

Throughout the day I kept meeting trains bringing delegates from all over India. We were very disappointed that Miss Jinnah, who had promised to open the Conference, was unable to come owing to ill health. The sessions of the Conference began at eleven o'clock with Fatima Begum reading a few verses from the Koran in her sonorous voice. It was followed by Begum Izaz Rasul's presidential address, the printed copies adding importance to our amateurish proceedings. The attendance was very poor and I was rather disappointed because we, that is to say the girls of my organizing committee and I, had gone practically from door to door asking ladies to come. If even those whom we had personally asked had done so there should have been enough to fill half the room. But, as it was, barely the first three rows were occupied. I always mention this, for it shows how little interest in politics there was amongst women in February 1942 and how quickly and rapidly political consciousness grew, for in March 1947, when in this self-same hall we organized a meeting of the Muslim League Women's Sub-Committee which Quaid-i-Azam honoured by coming and addressing, the hall was packed to capacity; there was no standing room in the corridors running around it and, though nothing could be seen from the garden, hundreds of women were standing there as well.

The Conference lasted three days and followed the usual procedure. Subject committee meetings were held, resolutions passed, and speeches made. Though it is quite a few years ago now, I can remember every detail of the proceedings very clearly and most of the speeches; I think they are a fair indication of what most of us at that time felt about the political situation. None of us had really pushed the idea of Pakistan to its logical conclusion. The demand for Pakistan was an assertion of our separate, independent, religious and cultural existence. We feared and objected to the assimilation being attempted, for we were proud of our culture and wanted to keep it intact. We wanted political power to enable us to preserve it. If we could have been assured that our religion, language and culture would be respected, that it would be possible for us to live our own way of life, then we would not have forged ahead and fought for political independence, which we did not originally seek. From the days of the Montagu-Chelmsford reforms to the Communal Award of 1947, we merely wanted safeguards. We wanted them because we were frightened that the economically superior and technically more advanced Hindus would swamp and over-rule us.

But it was dawning on our leaders that if we wished to preserve our culture, then we must have a country of our own to enable us to do so. And that is why, after only three years as President of the Muslim League, Quaid-i-Azam had already put forward the resolution that the Muslim majority contiguous areas should form a separate sovereign state of Pakistan. The Lahore Resolution, as this epoch-making resolution was called, had been passed in March 1940, that is six months after the Second World War had begun, and it was now February 1942.

However, to the majority of Muslims Pakistan was an idea rather than a reality, something they thought was their inviolable right but which they had not yet decided to exercise. The most ardent of Muslim leaders at this stage still hoped that it would be possible to come to a compromise which would enable Muslims to continue as a separate cultural entity within a wider political framework. Quaid-i-Azam himself favoured this. I definitely remember him telling me at that first meeting we had with him that the Canadian Constitution would probably be the best solution for us, and the fact that for seven years after the passing of the Pakistan Resolution he agreed to discuss and negotiate with the British and Congress and more than once almost came to agreement, is further proof. That an agreement was not reached is not because of Quaid-i-Azam's intransigence but because of the narrow-mindedness and bigotry of the Congress hierarchy.

Much of what I have just said may not have been very clear to us at this stage, but there was no doubt in our minds that we stood in danger of the annihilation of our culture and that if we wanted to preserve it and our separate entity we had to organize ourselves into an effective body. This the Muslim League was enabling us to do, and therefore was daily succeeding in getting more and more support.

The Conference came to an end after the passing of the resolution supporting the demand for the establishment of Pakistan and for the preservation and development of Urdu, and some other resolutions concerned exclusively with students' affairs. It had been a modest little affair, but it was the beginning of political consciousness amongst Muslim women, and, as such, was of great importance. For me personally it was an achievement. I had more or less single handed organized and called an All India Conference, and brought it successfully to a conclusion. I felt exhausted but very elated as I drove the delegates back to the station to catch their trains.

Chapter 12

HISTORY IN THE MAKING

In April 1943, the All India Muslim League held its annual session in Delhi. This was one of the most important sessions of the League since the passing of the Pakistan Resolution at its Lahore Session, three years before. Much had happened since. The Muslim League had grown tremendously in importance and had had to face many difficulties. It was only Quaid-i-Azam's leadership that had managed to steer it clear of pitfalls and dealt with each crisis in a manner which made it come out at the end stronger than before.

Congress had followed the resignation of its Ministries by launching a fully-fledged direct movement against the British.

The 1942 disturbances, as they were called, were really an abortive rebellion. They did not succeed because the British took prompt and drastic measures, but despite that they caused tremendous loss of life and property. So much has happened since August 1942, that it is now forgotten how widespread were the risings and what havoc they caused. Railroads were torn up, post offices burnt down, officers were burnt and injured. For at least three days the Government in several places came to a standstill and arson and looting took place everywhere. The British regarded this as a stab in the back; their somewhat amusingly tolerant attitude towards Congress changed to one of bitterness, at least for the time being. All the Congress leaders were clapped in gaol and kept there for almost the duration of the war. Congress regarded this as completely against the principles for which the war was supposedly being fought, namely the right of nations to be free.

The Muslim League kept itself aloof from this movement and was criticized by Congress, and by the Nationalist Muslims as well, for not taking part in what was, from their point of view, a war of liberation. Quaid-i-Azam kept the League aloof and prevented it from getting involved in violence because he did not think it was strong enough to withstand the repercussions that would have followed. Congress could and did; for it had been organized forty years ago. It was now sufficiently entrenched to risk taking direct action and its leaders being arrested without running the risk of completely going to pieces. But the League could not; it was still at the stage of being welded together. Had its leaders been put in gaol in 1942, or I should say its leader for it only had Quaid-i-Azam, it would have broken up. He realized that for the League to plunge into action before it was strong enough internally would be suicidal. The oft-flung accusation that he was frightened of going to gaol weighed nothing with him, for he was a man who was swayed neither by praise nor blame. I do know that this made him seem cold and aloof, but had he not been such a man he could not have done what he did, that is—to quote in his own words; 'make a disorganized mob into a disciplined nation'.

To achieve this end it was necessary not only to keep the Muslim League from precipitate action but also to restrain some of its prominent members from taking independent uncoordinated action. While he did not think the League was ready for direct action he was not in favour of wholehearted cooperation in the war effort because he felt that the Muslim point of view was not receiving the consideration it deserved from the British. This involved him in direct conflict with prominent Muslim Leaguers among whom was Mr Fazlul Haq, the Chief Minister of Bengal. His refusal to resign from the Defence Council when asked by the League to do so caused the first serious crisis in its ranks.

Bengal was the largest Muslim majority province and Fazlul Haq had a tremendous personal following there. He had a party of his own known as the Krishak-Proja Party, and after the 1937 elections when the League had captured a great number, but not the majority of the seats in Bengal he had made an alliance with the Muslim League and formed a coalition government. Later, as a reaction to the narrow-minded policy of Congress ministers in other provinces, he had declared himself to be a Muslim Leaguer and had become one of its staunchest supporters. In fact the first resolution demanding the establishment of Pakistan was moved by him in Lahore in March 1940. There were those who thought that if Fazlul Haq withdrew his support from the League it would collapse in Bengal, but not so Quaid-i-Azam. He took disciplinary action against Fazlul Haq by expelling him, which caused a terrific furore.

It is difficult to realize now what a tremendously bold and courageous step it was for Quaid-i-Azam to take. At that juncture, that is in 1941, the League was still a very small and unimportant organization, while Fazlul Haq was one of the giants of the Indian subcontinent. He maintained, and there were many then to support him, that he was every bit as good as Quaid-i-Azam himself and was not going to take orders from him. The same point of view was held by many other prominent men with the same personal vanity. Every one of them, pre-eminent in his own sphere, felt that they could not take orders from a man who, till very recently, had been a colleague of theirs. This was unfortunate as it deprived the League of the advice and counsel of men eminently fitted to give it, and accounts today for there being so few to carry on the work now that the Quaid is gone.

Quaid-i-Azam's point of view was that you could not have an effective organization unless it was disciplined and the organization could not be disciplined if its members, no matter how prominent they might be, refused to abide by its rules. It was in its trial of strength with Fazlul Haq that the League really proved its mettle.

This was the greatest crisis that it had had to face since it had been reorganized under the presidency of Quaid-i-Azam, and a similar situation could be seen looming up in Punjab. Sir Sikander Hayat Khan, the Premier of Punjab had belonged to the Unionist Party of the province but had become a member of the Muslim League though continuing to head a predominantly Unionist Cabinet. He had readily resigned from the Defence Council when asked by Quaid-i-Azam to do so. Unfortunately he died soon afterwards and his successor, Khizar Hayat Khan Tiwana, was completely under the sway of his Hindu colleagues in Punjab, and though not openly declaring himself against the League, would not commit himself to supporting it either. This boded trouble and Quaid-i-Azam knew it. He had paid several visits to Punjab since the momentous session of 1940 and had talked to Khizar, trying to make him see reason, but nothing decisive had yet happened. Because all these things had happened since the Lahore session the forthcoming session in Delhi was of great importance.

Since my meeting with Quaid-i-Azam, I had begun to get more and more involved in League activities. My cousin, Shaheed Suhrawardy, had taken the place of my uncle, Sir Abdullah Suhrawardy, in Muslim politics in Bengal. He was the general secretary of the Bengal branch of the League and it was mainly due to his organizational ability that, in 1937, it had been able to capture the number of seats that it had. When the coalition government had been formed with the Krishak-Proja Party of Fazlul Haq, he became the Finance Minister, and when the government was dissolved he resigned. He came to Delhi a great deal when he was a minister and also subsequently to discuss matters of policy with Quaid-i-Azam, and as he stayed at my house during his visits, my home became a sort of Muslim League committee room.

Important persons connected with the League's activities kept on dropping in and out and we never had less than ten or twenty for a meal. Press interviews, Press conferences, Press statements and other political activities went on there. It was very exciting and interesting to get a peep at the inside workings of great events and I even tried, now and then, to take a hand in them. One of my earliest efforts was an attempt to persuade Fazlul Haq to come back to the Muslim League. The most remarkable thing about this incident is that I was accompanied on this errand by Sardar Aurangzeb Khan. Sardar Aurangzeb Khan was a very old-fashioned person and came from the NWFP, which is noted for its orthodoxy and conservatism, and Fazlul Haq was staying at Dargah Nizamuddin Aulia, the citadel of conservatism, and yet my going there was not objected to. In fact, Sardar Aurangzeb Khan was very pleased that I should be doing this for he regarded it not as bold and unseemly but as an effort to help the community and so very creditable. It was this changed attitude that enabled women to come into public life so quickly.

By now the Muslim League had sufficient following amongst the people and had fired their imagination so that the forthcoming session of the Muslim League was being looked forward to with great eagerness and feverish preparations were being made days ahead for its reception. The excitement increased as it approached.

From early in the morning the day the session was to be held the people began gathering in the streets, for Quaid-i-Azam was to be taken in procession from his house in Aurangzeb Road, New Delhi, to where the session was to be held—a distance of five or six miles, and by the afternoon they were packed tight. We lost Delhi because it is said that more than half of its population was Hindu, but on that day it was difficult to believe that the entire population of Delhi was not only Muslim but Muslim Leaguers. The house of one of my friends was on the route of the procession and I had got there fairly early and had taken my children with me. It was April and, because of the crowding, very hot. I began to get worried that I had brought the children, but I am glad I did so, for that day was one worth remembering, and they do remember it. There was terrific excitement amongst the crowds and a feeling of elation and expectation. At least there was something to hope for and work for. Not only were the roads packed to capacity but the terraces of the houses were crowded and from the windows women threw rose petals as Quaid's lorry slowly wended its way. He was profusely garlanded and was sitting on a chair in the open lorry taking the salutes of the people with the characteristic gesture of raising his hand to a half salute. Alongside him sat the secretary of the Delhi provincial Muslim League, Hussain Malik.

As soon as the procession was out of sight, I slipped out of the house and after arranging for the children to be taken home, went off to where the conference was to be held. By dint of going through by-lanes and streets, I managed to arrive a few minutes before the procession got there. The huge *shamiana* was densely packed and the crowd waited in excited anticipation for Quaid to arrive. Deafening shouts of 'Allah-o-Akbar', 'Quaid-i-Azam Zindabad', 'Pakistan Zindabad' heralded his approach. For a while pandemonium nearly broke loose but almost immediately a hush fell. The crowd of its own accord divided into two allowing a passage for Quaid to walk through from the entrance of the *shamiana* to the *pandal*. I remember the scene clearly—Quaid coming in slow measured steps, followed and preceded by members of the Executive Committee, the crowd silent, tense and moved with deep emotion as he got to the dais. Cries of 'Allah-o-Akbar' and 'Quaid-i-Azam Zindabad' resounded once more. He raised his hand to accept the cheers and then after a couple of minutes made a gesture for the crowd to be silent, and in an instant they were silent. I was to see this happen over and over again. A tense, excited crowd charged with emotion, was, in the Quaid's presence, a controlled and disciplined crowd. A gesture, sometimes a mere look, would ensure silence and control. Quaid took his seat, and Maulana Akram stepped forward and read the verses of the Koran in a voice charged with emotion and then the League flag, white crescent and stars on a green ground, was unfurled and the strains of the popular song, 'This moon is not one that shall ever remain in eclipse' floated in the air. The crowd took up the refrain. The sixth session of the All India Muslim League had begun.

Next morning Quaid delivered his marathon Presidential address lasting for nearly three hours. The speech was not only eloquent but clear, well thought out and completely logical. Even today I can remember practically every point he made and several sentences by heart. He analysed the League's attitude towards the British; he explained his refusal to plunge it into direct action; he went over the difficulties that the League had to contend with since its last meeting.

The news that the Fazlul Haq Ministry in Bengal had fallen had come through that morning, and Hasan Ispahani had told me this a few seconds before Quaid arrived. This meant such a triumph for us that a person ordinarily as sober as Hasan Ispahani was beside himself with exultation, and when he told me the news I could hardly restrain myself from shouting with joy, but the crowds still did not know.

Quaid now announced it in a most dramatic way. He said: 'For the last sixteen months the Muslims of Bengal have been harassed and persecuted by a man who, I am sorry to say, is a Mussulman.' He went on to praise the discipline and endurance of the Muslims of Bengal and said: 'Today it has been rewarded. For I have just got the news that the Haq Ministry has been forced to dissolve because of a successful vote of no-confidence by the Muslim League.' This announcement was greeted by thunderous cheers and as they died down, Quaid hammered in the point, i.e., how by discipline and unity, by keeping our ranks unbroken we could defeat the biggest and the strongest of our opponents.

Then he went on to the question of the Punjab. I had noticed Khizar Hayat Tiwana quietly slipping into a seat soon after Quaid had started his Presidential address and he looked thoroughly deflated as Quaid said in a voice as clear and incisive as a razor's edge: 'Punjab is the cornerstone of Pakistan. It is destined to play a leading role in its affairs. It is not being allowed to do so by a handful of men. I have been very patient with Punjab's politicians;' but he warned, 'I cannot allow the wishes of the people to be flouted by a handful of men any longer and I want the politicians of Punjab not to go on ignoring their people's desire.'

And so, for two and a half hours and more we listened to Quaid's speech. He did not falter or stop once and did not even take a sip of the water which was often sent to him.

Most of the audience did not know English. As a matter of fact, it would be more correct to say that very few of them knew it, so they could not understand what Quaid was saying and yet, such was his personality that they listened spellbound for such a long time. I was to see this over and over again. At last the speech was over and limp and exhausted from so much emotion, we all went home.

That afternoon there was a dinner at Liaquat Ali Khan's house, followed by a *qawwali*. We all sat on the open terrace of that beautiful house. Quaid came out and sat amongst the guests, looking happy and relaxed. This was the first time I had seen him sitting on *farsh*, but he looked perfectly at ease; very rarely do I remember seeing him look as happy as he did that evening. The ladies were clustering round Miss Jinnah and I was amongst them. She caught a glimpse of me and asked me to come over and sit nearer to her. As I got up to pick my way towards her, she turned to Quaid, who was sitting not very far off, saying:

'You know this girl has done a wonderful job for the League. She has brought its message into official circles.'

Quaid looked at me and gave me a radiant smile of approval which made me feel I was in the seventh heaven. He asked me: 'Were you at the session today?'

'Oh yes', I replied, 'I thought you were wonderful. You did not even drink water once!'

'Is that all that impressed you?' he said, rather amused.

That was a happy evening. Soon the *qawwals* began strumming their instruments and the plaintive chorus of *shikwa* and *jawab-e-shikwa* floated in the air. This poem is an intensely intimate and personal appeal to God at the plight of the Muslim nation and God's reply, the most audacious and imaginative of all Iqbal's poems. The part that poetry has played in our national movement is considerable. Not only can it be said that we marched to our goal of Pakistan to the strains of Iqbal's poetry, but single poems such as the *'Shikwa'* and Mian Bashir Ahmad's *'Milat Ka Pasban Hai...'* have had greater influence on the minds of the people than any number of political pamphlets and speeches.

Two more days of the session were taken up by meetings of the Executive Committee (*in camera*) and open sessions at which most of the prominent members of the Muslim League spoke, some of them with great distinction, but the scene was dominated by Quaid and Quaid alone. On the last day there was an evening session which lasted well into the night. At this Bahadur Yar Jung spoke. He was a most eloquent and fiery speaker and once the audience had got a glimpse of him on the dais it was impatient to hear him. The crowd began to get restive and a slow murmur which sounded like the dull rumblings of thunder could be heard as speaker after speaker got to his feet and Bahadur Yar Jung was still not called. Quaid was well aware of all this and amusedly tolerant of it, but still would not give way. When the crowd's impatience seemed to grow, he smiled and said: 'Do not be impatient. You will hear him. Wait just a little longer.' At that one sentence the impatience of the crowd melted away and they cheerfully settled down to listening to the rest of the speakers. At last Quaid called Bahadur Yar Jung. He was a true orator and knew how to play on the emotions of his audience, and the Urdu language lends itself to this; he was its master and used every conceit and device in it for his purpose. He began by saying: 'I get up to speak only when the lady of the night has already opened her dark tresses, but tonight they are falling not only to her shoulders but to her knees.' In English translation it sounds like a forced artifice, but in Urdu it made a beautiful imagery. Then he went on to speak of the glorious past of the Mussulman and the glorious future that awaited him. Yet, unlike my clear recollection of Quaid's speech, my impression of Bahadur Yar Jung is rather a hazy one. One listened to him as if bewitched, but afterwards one could remember it only as something one had heard in a dream.

It was the early hours of the morning before the session was over, and as I drove back to my home in New Delhi its uniform rows of whitewashed houses, silent and symmetrical, presented a great contrast to the scene and excitement I had just left behind. I dropped two other ladies, also wives of officials, at their houses and slowly crept into mine.

My work during the session had mainly been in connection with the reception and accommodation of women delegates but this time I was not alone. The members of the Delhi branch of the All India Muslim League Women's sub-committee were with me. This had come into being as early as 1938 with the object of creating political consciousness amongst Muslim women. By a resolution passed by the Patna session in that year six women from various parts of the country had been nominated to form committees in their provinces. So far these had remained rather inactive, but now they were being galvanized into action. During this session there were executive committee meetings and an open session exclusively for women, presided by Lady Nusrat Haroon, at which representatives of the various branches submitted an account of their work. It was not very long or remarkably interesting for the work that was actually done, but it was significant as it showed how rapidly women were becoming politically conscious. This was being brought about not only by the stress of events but was directly encouraged by Quaid-i-Azam. He did it without saying much, but in little ways, such as making Miss Jinnah, his sister, always sit on the dais and, because she did, other ladies could also do so and Quaid's proximity protected them from any rude remarks by the audience, which gradually got used to the idea of women being present and participating in public meetings. Quaid believed in women's emancipation. At his memorial meeting at the Caxton Hall in September 1948, Miss Agatha Harrison said that when he was a student in England and the Suffrage Movement was at its height and very unpopular, young Jinnah was one of the few people who attended meetings and spoke in support of it. She added, 'Even then he was not afraid to support an unpopular cause'; and so remained throughout his life.

Chapter 13

HEADING TOWARDS A CRISIS

Events began to move very quickly from now onwards. The Muslim League had become a power to be reckoned with. Quaid had made good his claim that there were not two but three parties concerned with the Indian problem; the British, the Hindu and the Muslim. In less than five years he had so organized the Muslims and steered them past pitfalls that no decision could be taken regarding the future of India without the full consent and cooperation of the League. By this time, the war in Europe had also reached its last phase; an Allied victory seemed to be a certainty, which meant that the question of India's future must be decided soon. Lord Wavell flew over to London early in 1945 to discuss the question with the British Government and on his return called a conference in Simla. The Congress leaders, most of whom had been arrested after the terrible riots of 1942, were released to enable them to attend this conference. Mr Jinnah who had been recovering from a serious illness also went up to Simla.

The summer capital of the British Empire, which was usually the scene of nothing more exciting than Viceregal garden parties or other official functions, now suddenly became the stage on which the last critical acts of the Indo-British drama were being enacted. The whole place became alive. Journalists were the first to come, and they came by the dozen in anticipation of 'scoops' and stories. Then one by one the leaders arrived. Pandit Nehru, Maulana Abul Kalam Azad, Asaf Ali, Rajagopalacharya, Pandit G.V. Pant and other notables of the Congress all came and processions piled two or three times a day through the narrow streets of Simla to the station and back to the hotels in which they were staying. As they were Government guests, they were put up in either the Hotel Cecil or the Grand Hotel.

The excitement reached fever pitch as the time for Mr Jinnah and Gandhi's arrival drew near. How well I remember every single detail of the day of Quaid-i-Azam's arrival in Simla! The route which he was to pass on his way to the Hotel Cecil had been packed to capacity since the early hours of the morning, and it was with great difficulty that I somehow managed to secure a place at about nine-thirty. The Quaid arrived at about eleven o' clock, but the time that we waited did not seem long as a crowd bound together in common devotion or admiration is a very companionable one. As soon as Quaid's rickshaw had passed us, the crowd broke up, everyone trying to get to the entrance of Hotel Cecil and catch another glimpse of him there.

I had by this time become a complete political addict, and during the whole period of the Simla Conference went about drinking up political gossip with an avidity that would have done credit to a newspaper reporter. I was in a particularly fortunate position to do this. In the Grand Hotel, where I was staying, was also our dear friend Mr Asaf Ali, a prominent leader of the Congress; in fact one of the few prominent Muslims to be found in their ranks. Despite fundamental differences of opinion and outlook, he still had the same affection for us, and we for him. So we spent a great deal of time with him.

Begum Muhammad Ali, wife of that staunch fighter for the Muslims of India, Maulana Muhammad Ali, had also come to stay in the Grand Hotel. Mrs Sarojini Naidu had also arrived and was staying in the house of a friend, not far from there. As I knew all these people personally and each of them was a protagonist in the drama that was being enacted, I was certainly getting a cross-section of news and views.

Khawaja Nazimuddin, the Chief Minister of Bengal—where alone a Muslim League Ministry held sway—was staying with the President of the Assembly, who was a relative of mine and whose house, Hallcombe, was a few yards from Hotel Cecil where most of the members of the Muslim League Working Committee stayed. Lunches at Sir Abdur Rahim's house were almost informal meetings of the Muslim League Working Committee. I had the opportunity of gathering a lot of inside information and I found it very interesting to watch the reactions of people on whom so much depended. It was amazing to see how Quaid's personality dominated them even when he was not present. There were decisions of his which they disagreed with or did not agree with whole-heartedly, but not one of them had the courage to express his difference of opinion before him. It irritated me to see men in eminent positions, called in to give advice on momentous matters, hesitating to express their opinion honestly. With the audacity which goes with lack of experience, I could not refrain from saying this once, but of course my interruption was ignored, as it deserved to be. Looking back on these events, I realize that these men did not dare to express their differences, because none of them had the courage of their convictions, which Quaid possessed. Their motives were mixed and because of this they could not stand up to the single-minded conviction with which Quaid pursued his point of view.

It was during the Simla Conference that I managed to get the opportunity of seeing and talking to Quaid a great deal. I would go to his room almost every day, staying sometimes only for a brief period and leaving after making polite inquiries about his health, and other times staying for quite a while listening to him explaining his point of view on the controversial issues then at stake. This was a unique privilege and I am really very glad that I got this opportunity, though, looking back on it now, I am amazed at my audacity. To realize the extent of it, one has to know the awe and reverence in which Quaid was held. He had the reputation for being aloof, unapproachable and remote. Even the members of the Working Committee did not dare to see him without an appointment and that I should have the temerity to do so can only be explained by the *naïveté* of youth. I did so, in the first instance, on an impulse, impelled by my desire to see Quaid. After I had seen the procession of Quaid's arrival, I had rushed to the Hotel Cecil and thought that I had covered the distance in record time. I got to the lounge too late. He had already gone upstairs to his room, everybody was still standing around, and seeing me said: 'You only just missed him. He has just gone upstairs.' I was terribly disappointed, and I took my courage in both hands and decided to go upstairs. I hoped to see him in the passage, but he had already gone inside. The Pathan doorkeeper knew me from Delhi, he gave me a broad grin of welcome and allowed me to knock timidly at the door. Quaid opened it tentatively, wondering who was bothering him again so soon after the excitement of the reception. Seeing me, he very kindly held the door farther open and invited me in. I stayed a few moments only to make some inquiries about his health and about Miss Jinnah who had stayed behind because of illness.

The detractors of Quaid often say that he was arrogant, ungracious and rude. I can only say to this that I never found him so. He was aloof certainly and did not find it easy to make conversation, nor did he try to exercise the facile charm which so many political leaders put on. But I always found him extremely courteous, patient and kind, not only during the fortnight or so in Simla, when I saw him almost every day, but also later on in Delhi where I saw him fairly frequently whenever he came up.

I still continued to meet a number of prominent Congress leaders. I was constantly hearing their point of view, which raised doubts in my mind and I would say to them, 'I will go and ask Quaid' and I did. He always patiently explained the reason for his decision to me and I would go back convinced. So it became a joke and whenever I said, 'All right I shall ask Quaid', my husband would say, 'What is the use? He will say, "Begum Ikramullah, you do not understand", he will explain his point to you and you will come back convinced.'

He did not try to win people over by emotional appeal or cheap flattery. His appeal was always to the intellect and his reasoning was clear and logical. He expected people who joined the Muslim League to suffer for it. He did not consider that they were doing him a personal favour by it or were justified in taking a martyred or heroic attitude. Therefore, when the *Hindustan Times* printed an article attacking me, I went to Quaid seething with indignation. I did not find him very sympathetic. Even today I am extremely sensitive to criticism and this was my first taste of it. It had upset me greatly. Quaid sensed my uneasiness and asked what the matter was. 'Have you seen the *Hindustan Times?*' I asked. 'Yes,' he replied. 'There is a nasty article in it attacking me,' I said. There were always stacks of newspapers by Quaid's chair. He took the *Hindustan Times* from the pile, turned to the page I had mentioned and glanced over it. Then he carefully folded the paper and put it back, without saying anything to me for a moment or so. Then he said: 'Every day the newspapers say much worse things about me. What would happen if I let it upset me? This is to be expected.' I felt abashed and rather disappointed for I had expected lashings of sympathy, instead of which I had an astringent put on my wound. When I rose to leave, he added: 'You must not let small things upset you.' In later years, when I encountered meanness and malice, I remembered these words of Quaid.

Tension was growing daily and the communal feeling was even poisoning social relationships. Several of my Hindu friends dropped me completely, and the relationship with others also became rather strained and difficult. On one occasion at an after-dinner parlour game, disparaging remarks were made about Quaid-i-Azam which made me flare up and so cause a scene. Here, again, when I repeated the story to Quaid, he made me see what a trivial matter it was. I mention this because he has been accused of personal vanity. Had that charge been true he would not have considered even a silly attack on him as a trivial matter. It also shows his patience and forbearance in allowing me to discuss such trivialities, realizing that to me they did not appear as such and that I might need a training which he tried to provide. I think it was a rare privilege, almost a unique one and it has left its impact on my life forever. There are not many people who enjoyed this privilege, but those few who did, became, like me, staunch adherents, and their faith in him was unshakable.

My husband had not seen Quaid for two years, when we had all lunched at his place. But at the end of the Simla Conference, when I went to say goodbye to Quaid, he came to pick me up and met Quaid again. He discussed the cause that had led to the failure of the Simla Conference, and I remember his looking very thoughtful and preoccupied as we stood at the door of the Hotel Cecil waiting for our rickshaw to be called. Then looking at the hills, remote and silent witnesses to human conflict and turmoil, he said: 'You're right. He really means to have Pakistan.' 'Of course, he does,' I said indignantly.

That was so but it was not because Quaid disregarded other people's points of view or forced his opinion on them, he did not. Not even on anyone as unimportant as myself. Only he had what few people possess in this world, an absolutely single-minded conviction. It somehow had the effect of removing all one's doubts. To say that he was a dictator and forced Mussulmans to accept his idea of Pakistan is ridiculous because he had no arbitrary powers—only the force of his own personality.

He never made an emotional appeal to one's loyalty. He appealed to one's reason and put the case down in a clear and logical manner. I was to experience this when later he refused to let me accept the Government's nomination to the Pacific Relations Conference, but after he had succeeded in convincing me by cold reasoning, and I got up to leave, he said: 'One day you will go as the League's representative with honour and with the right to speak on their behalf.'

He kept his promise. Within six weeks of establishment of Pakistan he appointed me a delegate to the UN. I could not go then as my youngest daughter Sarvath was only a few weeks old, so he sent me the next year. It is one of my greatest regrets that he did not live to tell me whether he thought his choice was justified, but all this was to come much later.

This was summer 1945 and the proposals Lord Wavell had put forward were under consideration. The proposals were that the power should be transferred immediately to Indian hands even before the war was over, and that other details should be worked out later. There were two hurdles to be overcome before it could be put into practice. The proposals had suggested that the entire personnel of the Viceroy's Council, except the Commander-in-Chief, should be Indians; and the Indians, were not to be chosen by the Viceroy but nominated by their own political organizations. The Viceroy, however, was still to keep some arbitrary powers, particularly in connexion with defence, law and order. It was on this question that there was an acute difference of opinion between the British and the Indian political parties; both the Congress and the Muslim League objecting to the Viceroy's retention of arbitrary powers. The second hurdle, and the one which really caused the breakdown of the negotiations was the division of seats between the Congress and the Muslim League. The Muslim League claimed that it alone had the right to nominate the Muslim members of the Viceroy's Council, while the Congress maintained that the Muslim League could not claim to be the sole representative of the Muslims, as it, the Congress, also had Muslim members in its ranks and therefore should also have the right to nominate at least one or two Muslim members in the forthcoming cabinet.

Long and lengthy discussions were carried on, hours turning into days, and days into weeks, with no agreement being reached and the atmosphere becoming daily more tense and bitter.

Many people have accused Mr Jinnah and the Muslim League of intransigence at this juncture. They say he should have conceded the point to the Congress, for although the Muslims in the Congress ranks could have been counted on the fingers of one hand, they were all men of distinction—this carried no weight with the Muslim League. Even so, had it been Maulana Azad or Mr Asaf Ali, who were likely to be nominated by the Congress, the League might have given in. But it was known that the person who was to get this non-Muslim League Muslim seat was Khizar Hayat Tiwana, then Prime Minister of Punjab a man whose name was already anathema to the Muslim Leaguers. The British favoured his nomination because he came from a family with a long tradition of devotion to the British; his war efforts in the present war had been considerable and the British felt they could not overlook his claim.

It was a pity that this was so and that just as power was to fall into new hands, the British should still cling to this old outmoded point of view and fail to realize that those who were to hold power in the new India and in the yet unborn Pakistan would be men chosen by the people and not those put on the *gaddi* by the British. And so, after nearly three weeks of debate, of discussion lasting all day and late into the night, of meetings between people who could bring agreement between leaders, the Simla Conference came to an end. It had failed. Probably, the reason for its failure lies with all three parties; the British, the Congress and the Muslim League. Perhaps none of them had been as far-seeing and diplomatic as the occasion demanded of them.

As far as I remember, it was late in the evening that the official announcement came that the Simla Conference had ended in failure. Everyone more or less expected this, because the news for the last two or three days had been most disheartening. Yet I had gone on hoping for a last-minute compromise. The official announcement extinguished that last flicker of hope and I suddenly felt deflated and went about with that hollow feeling that comes after one has been living through a period of intense excitement.

But at that moment, Simla was seething with excitement, and though I was still young enough to be thrilled by it all, I was not quite oblivious of the growing tension between Hindus and Muslims which augured ill for the future. The *Hindustan Times* published a virulent article attacking me. Lady Chelmsford's Ladies' Club, the majority of whose members were Hindus but of which I had been a most active member for about twelve years, refused to invite me to a party they gave. My political activities had ceased to be merely something very exciting and wonderful for me personally. It had become a matter of public concern, which affected people's attitude towards me. It had begun to curtail my freedom of action, for while the Congress attacked me virulently for my active championship of the Muslim League, a whispering campaign had been started against me by recently joined members of the Muslim League for my continued friendship with such prominent Congress members as Mrs Naidu and Mr Asaf Ali. I began to realize that I had chosen to tread a very difficult and tortuous path and could not be sure where it would lead me.

CHAPTER 14

THE GATHERING STORM

Soon after this the Labour Party came to power in Britain. Many of its prominent members had been known to have sympathies with India and on coming to power were more or less pledged to give her independence. As a first step towards this end, general elections were to be held in India. The last elections had been held in 1937, nearly ten years ago, and during this period great political changes had taken place in the country. The most remarkable of these was the growth of the Muslim League, which now claimed to have the allegiance of 90 per cent of Muslims in India. The Muslim League was handicapped by the fact that its representation in the Legislature did not reflect this. Therefore the news of general elections was very welcome and both Congress and the Muslim League plunged into preparations in order to justify their previous claims to represent their country.

It was essential that the Muslim League should be able to substantiate its claims to represent the majority of Muslims in India. As opposed to Congress, it had had a very short time, a bare seven years, in which to educate public opinion in its favour and so it was with a certain amount of apprehension that the candidates for the Muslim league decided to contest the elections.

During these elections much work was done by students and by women. It was almost the first time that Muslim women *en masse* had taken part in political activity. For me it was an interesting and exhilarating experience. The election campaign was opened on 27 January 1946.

I happened to be in Calcutta then and attended the mammoth meeting in the famous Calcutta 'Maidan', addressed by my cousin, Huseyn Shaheed Suhrawardy. I also accompanied him and my father in their first election tour, which was rather like a triumphal march. We went to Kharagpur, the big railway junction near our own village of Midnapur. We left by train from Calcutta and at every little station the train stopped, we met hundreds of people who crowned us with garlands, shouting League slogans. There was such a surge of enthusiasm among these people! They could not have understood many political details, but a new hope had been kindled in their hearts, a hope for a better world. It is a tremendous responsibility to have raised such a hope and not yet to have been able to fulfil it.

In Kharagpur, my cousin and father were taken out in procession throughout the town, and I went in another car to the house of one of the chief Muslim League workers. We were overwhelmed with hospitality. In my country, specially in small towns and villages, till this day visitors are really given a royal welcome. For whatever purpose they may come, or how many they may be and however long they may stay, the host never slackens his efforts to entertain them. This was no exception.

From the moment of our arrival to the moment of our departure, we met with nothing but kindness. There was a tremendous banquet prepared for that night, after which we all went to attend the meeting. It was the biggest political meeting that I had as yet attended. People for miles around had gathered there. There was the usual unfurling of the flag and singing, after which my father and my cousin both made very moving speeches in which they explained the significance of this election for the Muslims of India.

I was extremely surprised when I too was suddenly requested to speak. As yet, I had not addressed a mixed gathering, and this was not even mixed but almost exclusively male. There were just twenty or so women behind the purdah among whom I also was sitting. When the request was made by the local Secretary, my father sent a message to me that I had better speak, otherwise they would feel hurt. I don't remember much of what I said. But I remember that I was feeling extremely moved at the sight of so much enthusiasm. The people seemed to be ready to make every sacrifice, and I felt that with such enthusiasm it was impossible for us not to succeed, and I was not wrong. We did succeed in achieving our objective. The people did not let us down. We asked them to unite to vote for the League and they did. It is we, the so-called leaders, who have not been able to redeem our pledge, the pledge that we gave them that if they did what we asked them to do, we on our part would be able to mitigate their sufferings.

One thing, however, this political struggle did achieve for us: it brought women into the forefront of public life. I have just mentioned the fact that the Secretary of the Muslim League himself requested me to speak at a political meeting. He was not a modern Westernized man, but the political struggle had somehow generated such enthusiasm that all old prejudices and taboos seemed to have been swept away. And so it was that, during this electioneering campaign, women worked in towns and in villages among every stratum of society, trying to get votes for the Muslim League. And men were grateful for their help and forgot their centuries-old prejudice, as they worked side by side to usher in a new era.

Soon after the Kharagpur meeting I came back to Delhi, and for the rest of the election campaign I remained there, working with other members of the Delhi branch of the All India Muslim League sub-committee.

But the Delhi election itself was not of great consequence to us. The most important election, the one on which all our interests were concentrated was the election of Liaquat Ali Khan, the General Secretary of the Muslim League. His constituency was in the United Provinces, the most politically conscious province of India and the stronghold at once, of both the Congress and the Muslim League. Liaquat's election was symbolic. The Congress felt that his defeat would mean the defeat of the League and so they put all their strength to achieving that end. We fought with equal zeal, and as the day of the results drew near, excitement mounted to fever pitch. The whole of the day on which the news was to come through, we kept telephoning the League office in Delhi. At last the news came through that he had won.

The most spectacular victory of the League, however, was in Bengal, the largest Muslim province in India, but one in which, though the Muslims were in a majority numerically, economically and educationally they were more backward. The Hindus of the province were not only head and shoulders above the Muslims in literacy and in wealth, but also in almost every other sphere, so the fight there was a very unequal one. In spite of this, we won because of the superior discipline and unity shown by the people, who were ably organized by Shaheed Suhrawardy. In this province, the Muslim League did not lose a single seat, thus securing an absolute majority in the Legislature.

As soon as the results of the elections were announced, Quaid called all the newly elected Muslim League members of the Legislature to meet in Delhi. This was called the Convention of the Muslim League and its purpose was to formulate the League's policy for the future. It differed from the Muslim League meetings of the past in this, that its members were elected by the people on Muslim League ticket and their claim to speak for the people could not be questioned by anybody.

The arrival of the members was awaited with great eagerness by the Muslim Leaguers in Delhi, who looked upon the Convention as a sort of celebration of our victory, for this election was no ordinary election. On its results depended the future of a hundred million Muslims in India.

It is for this reason that it was conducted with a crusading zeal, and its success was hailed with such delight.

The last to arrive and the most eagerly awaited were the contingent from Bengal. There were more than two hundred members from there, so a whole train had been engaged to bring them. It steamed into Delhi station, bedecked with flags and with League slogans chalked all over it. Even the engine had 'Muslim League Zindabad' chalked in big letters right round it. The platform was packed to capacity, and as the train was sighted the sky was rent with shouts of 'Allah-o-Akbar' and 'Muslim League Zindabad'. It was a proud moment for me as my cousin stepped out of the train and came up to where my father and I were standing and embraced my father, bending his head down as is the custom to receive his blessing. My father had come out of a nursing home to meet Shaheed; his fatal illness had begun, though as yet we did not know it.

The crowd pressed on us and was so dense that I felt I was going to suffocate. The meeting was to be held almost immediately, and therefore it was important to get to our car. How we ever reached it, I don't know, for it was impossible to walk. I was somehow propelled by the moving crowd, clutching desperately at my father's arm. After what seemed like ages we found ourselves at the exit of the station and in front of our car. We somehow got my cousin detached from the crowd and bundled him into the car to proceed to the meeting.

Having reached the place where the meeting was being held, I went over to the women's enclosure. As it adjoined the platform, we could see and hear everything very clearly. This time, a very large area had been partitioned off for us, for political consciousness had grown to such an extent that it was expected that a large number would attend. That evening there was only to be the opening ceremony, always very moving with its unfurling of the flag and reading of the Koran and today even more so. The important day, however, was tomorrow when the official resolution of the

League, solemnly reiterating their demand for the establishment of Pakistan, was to be put forward by Shaheed Suhrawardy.

As soon as the meeting was over, I rushed home, as all the Party workers who had come with my cousin were staying in my house and I was anxious to see how they were faring. I had as usual a tent put in the grounds for them, for whenever my cousin stayed with me he brought at least half a dozen people with him. But this time the number seemed to be much more than that. In fact, about fifty people had arrived, tired, hungry, demanding refreshments and expecting to be looked after.

My servants had risen to the occasion manfully. Another tent had been rigged up to accommodate those who said it was necessary for them to stay at the same place as my cousin. Others were put in touch with the Muslim League Reception Committee office which arranged for their accommodation, but before they left all of them, fifty or more, were given tea and refreshment by my servants. I asked my bearer how on earth he had done it, for there was strict rationing still in force and I hardly had enough tea and sugar in the house for half a dozen extra people, let alone for a whole army. He replied he had borrowed from every house in the road, and added quite unconcernedly: 'I told them you would let them have it all back again.' I could not reproach him or point out how difficult, if not impossible, it would be for me to do that. I realized that he could not possibly have done anything else, for not to entertain guests is unheard of by our standards. Those who come to your house, no matter how large a number or what hour of the day, must be fed. Changing conditions of life are making the keeping of this tradition very difficult, but every effort is still made to try and keep this tradition of hospitality.

CHAPTER 15

UNDER THE DARKENING SKY

My life in Delhi had now fallen into a familiar pattern. We lived in one of the Government-built houses which, if not distinctive, was very comfortable and had a nice large garden. I do not know of any part of the world where the climate is more healthy and invigorating than it is in Delhi in winter. The air is like a tonic, the rays of the sun like a caress and each part of the day has its special charm.

I remember the early mornings, when mist hung like a veil and dew lay sparkling like frosted glass. We would sit on our verandah, muffled in warm clothes, drinking steaming cups of tea, after which my husband would work in our garden and I would follow him round, trying to sound knowledgeable about vegetables. I love gardens, in fact I spent a large part of my time in them, but my knowledge of gardening, particularly vegetable gardening which was my husband's speciality, is very scanty, and however hard I try I find it difficult to distinguish between cabbage and turnip leaves.

Every day I spent the whole afternoon in the garden. The children rested on their brightly coloured *durees* and later played about in the shade. I lay under a tree, just my head in the shade and the rest of me soaking in the sun, with my books and writing material and knitting spread around me. I used to stay there till the afternoon light took on a mellow hue, and then I would get up and go inside and, after tidying myself a bit, go for a walk. The short winter's day would be drawing in and the air would be unutterably calm and full of wood smoke. I used to come back in the gathering dusk, and after a hot bath, sit beside the crackling fire. The children, also fresh and sweet-smelling from their bath, would sit round me, warming their little hands and feet, and I would tell them stories. In a little while, my husband would come in and we would have the first hour in the day together with the children, for he was in the War Supply department and could never get away earlier than seven o'clock or seven-thirty in the evening.

There was much less official entertaining now that there was a war on, but a good deal more was done unofficially because there were many more people in Delhi than before. Delhi had become much more cosmopolitan. It was not only the headquarters of the Government of India's War Effort, but it had also become the stage of the most important political conferences that were taking place. Because of this, both English and Indian journalists were always present in large numbers, and most of the first rank official leaders, both of the Congress and Muslim League, were in Delhi as well. Efforts were being made to ascertain the political situation in India, and for this purpose both official and non-official politicians and writers from England were constantly visiting Delhi. They were all interesting people and interested in what was happening, and so I saw a great deal of them at parties.

Large buffet parties became popular about that time. They made service easier and one could have many more people. They were not as elegant as the sit-down dinners had been, but being more informal they were greater fun. There would generally be some music or singing or poetry recitations afterwards, and always a good deal of laughter and talk. We gave such parties regularly, but the part I enjoyed best was when most of the formal guests had left, and we would collect all the chocolates, fruit and sweets and bring them from the dining-room to the drawing-room, make up the dying fire and sprawl round it, nibbling at the nuts and sipping at left-over drinks, discussing the party.

We called this the 'Post-Mortem' and never held a party without one. Very often the conversation would turn on serious matters. Then the discussion would get heated and would continue until late into the night.

Lunches followed the same pattern as the dinners, except that they were nearly always in the garden, but best of all were the breakfast parties. I liked these very much and gave them often myself. They would, of course, always be on a Sunday morning and naturally consist of people one knew very well. Nobody dressed up for them, in fact some of our friends who lived near enough came in their dressing gowns. We would all sit on the verandah leading from the dining-room, so as to be near the kitchen and be sure everything was piping hot.

At these breakfast parties, one ate enormously. We had sizzling *parathas* with a sort of Indian scrambled eggs called *khagina*, or we had delicious *halwa, puri* or *jalebi*, straight out of the frying pan, wrapped in dried leaves to retain their heat and moisture, and of course we ate *nehari*, the traditional breakfast dish of Delhi. It always had lots and lots of chillies and everyone's eyes would be streaming before they finished, but nobody ever stopped till the plate was empty. Then we ate thick clotted cream and carrot *halwa* to take away the effect of the chillies. By the time we had finished it all, there would hardly be room for tea, but of course we would drink it and, after that, sit chewing *paan* and talking in a desultory fashion for hours.

When there was not a breakfast party on a Sunday morning, there would always be a picnic in the afternoon. Delhi provided such ideal sites for picnics; each of the old historic buildings had beautiful rambling gardens and terraces, which commanded a magnificent view. Their gardens were so large that though there would be dozens of people, it would never appear crowded and one could always find a secluded spot.

At this stage, I feel I must say something about how wonderful servants were in our country. They formed an important part of our background and it is they who made possible that life of leisured grace that we led. They were exceedingly well-mannered, efficient, reliable and absolutely devoted to the members of the house they served, making the interests of their masters their own and accepting whatever they did unquestioningly, as the only right thing to do. If they worked with Europeans, they gave them the same unquestioning loyalty. They were not concerned with politics, their devotion was to their immediate masters and to nothing else.

This type of servant was becoming rare by the time I set up my house, but I was fortunate enough to have found a set that had many of these old-fashioned virtues, and I was consequently envied by my friends. There is no doubt that had I not been so fortunate I could not have given my time to political and social work as I did, for I am not one of those social workers who is indifferent to her home. I could go about canvassing votes for the Muslim League only if I was sure that my house was well-run and that my children would be getting their meals on time.

But as it happened I could be sure of it, and not only this, any number of people could drop in at a very short notice and I need have no qualms about it. I would walk into my kitchen, looking apologetic and saying that those three people who had come to see my father at ten-thirty were still there and looked as if they would be staying to lunch. The cook would serenely assure me that it would be all right and that he had realized this and had already added to the menu. After a while I was so sure of this that I would issue the invitation without even dashing to the kitchen to make sure that it would be all right.

It is not possible to have this type of servant or get this type of service any more, but in 1940–7 in Delhi one could still keep a large staff, and though it had already become very expensive, food was still the cheapest item of expenditure. I am not thrifty by nature; I would rather do without half a dozen sarees, than waste my time doling out sugar and tea, or go marketing to check prices and so forth.

All my neighbouring housewives disapproved of me, and this made me feel guilty, but try as I would, I could not come up to their standards of efficiency. 'How much do you pay for chicken nowadays', I would be asked by one lady with that unmistakable aura of efficiency that surrounds good housewives. 'Oh, twelve annas', I would reply meekly, knowing full well that she would reply in a shocked voice: 'What! twelve annas! I get mine for ten', and then I would be treated to a minute description of the superior merits of her chicken.

Another would come with keys jingling at her waist, proclaiming her vigilance in household matters and no sooner would she be seated than one of my servants would come up asking for my keys and of course I would not be able to find them. I would make a frantic hunt for them, getting more and more nervous as I sensed the unspoken criticism of my guest, and finally one of the servants would find them in some unlikely place, such as behind the cushion on the garden chair. At this, my neighbour would not be able to restrain herself any longer and would say: 'If you are so careless with your keys, your servants could take them and help themselves to whatever they like.' 'Of course they could,' I felt like saying 'and for that matter they could murder us all in our beds, but somehow or other they never do it.' But I never had the courage to say this.

In fact, it was years before I even had enough self-confidence to ignore these criticisms. Even now I can't help feeling guilty when one of these efficient women fixes me with a steely eye and demands to know what I pay for my coal or butter or meat or whatever it is. For the life of me I can't remember it, and even if I do it always seems to be too much! Once I tried to get over this difficulty by telling a lie. I quoted an absurdly low figure, but I got into more trouble this way, for then the woman wanted to know the address of the shop from where I got my stuff. So I never dared try that again.

In the third year of the war, we did not go to Simla in the summer as usual. We discovered, however, that summer in Delhi—though very hot—had its compensations, such as sleeping out of doors under a clear, star-studded sky. The afternoons were long and very hot, but made bearable by closing all the doors and windows and fitting them with *khas* screens. *Khas* can best be described as sweet-smelling hay. It is plaited and made into screens which are then fitted in the windows and doors. They not only keep the rays of the sun out but, when moistened, give out a wonderfully refreshing fragrance. This can be said to be our way of air-conditioning, and I must say that it was very pleasant.

At six o'clock the doors and windows were thrown open, chairs, tables, beds and electric fans were all taken out into the garden. We forgot the heat of the day, as after a cold shower we sat and sipped ice-cool sherbet. It was during this time that moonlight picnics came into their own, and once again the wonderful historic buildings of Delhi proved an ideal setting for them. The dim outline of the old buildings made one feel pleasantly melancholy. So we sang sad love songs, or passionately nationalistic ones, recited poetry or played a game called *baitbazi*, which is very popular with both old and young in our society. One needs to have a good memory for verse to be able to play it, for one has to cap the verse recited by the opposite party with another which should begin with the letter the last verse ended with. It is the sort of game which even the most literary people in the West would find difficult, but in our society, quotation is so much a part of our life that nearly everyone can play it with ease. To us, poetry is the substitute for opera, ballet and theatre. It is the very woof and warp of our life. We can truly be said to lisp in numbers.

We read poetry all the time, we recite it and quote it without any feeling of self-consciousness. We talk of the new verse that has come to our notice, as in the West one talks about the latest novel one has read, and one of the most popular social-cum-literary functions amongst us is the *mushaira*. That is a gathering in which poets read their latest compositions. It is done with a great deal of ceremony, for poets are very protocol-conscious. The recitation begins with the younger poets present, and goes in a very strict order of seniority. If a poet is called even one or two places out of turn, he would refuse to recite and may even be offended enough to leave the gathering. All the poems recited in a *mushaira* have to follow the same metre and pattern, and the poets are informed of the pattern chosen beforehand. These days, however, this rule need not be strictly adhered to and poets are at liberty to read poems in verse and metre of their choice.

Living in Delhi, I had plenty of opportunity of going to *mushairas,* for there was always one on. Two or three times a year, there would be a grand *mushaira* arranged by some literary society, or under the auspices of one of the colleges, but besides these there would be small gatherings in the houses of friends throughout the year, in which just two or three poets would be present. These were the most enjoyable ones.

The *mushaira* I went to most regularly and which to my mind had the full flavour of the old days, was held in the house of Khawaja Shafi. Khawaja Shafi, like Asaf Ali, was essentially a product of Delhi culture. Though a young man, he had the same courtly manners of the old world, and spoke the same chaste and fluent Urdu. His manner of giving praise to the poet was, in itself, so poetical that it was worth attending the *mushaira* only to listen to that. Syed Reza Ali was also one of those people who enhanced the interest of a *mushaira* by presiding over it, for as I have said before, there was a great deal of ceremony involved. There were unwritten rules about how one presided and what one said and how one said it, and yet within the formal framework there should be spontaneity, and therefore not everyone was able to achieve it. Those who could, were as much in demand as good poets.

The most well-known poets of this time were Josh, Jigar, Majaz, Mahirul-Qadri, Danish and of course, Hafeez, and I had the opportunity of listening to them all. The most elusive amongst them was Josh. Nearly everyone who was arranging a *mushaira* would announce that Josh would be reciting, and people would flock to it. I myself spent much rationed petrol in this quest before I had the good fortune of listening to him. This was at a delightful informal gathering presided over by Mrs Naidu in her own inimitable manner.

Delhi also provided opportunities for listening to some excellent *qawwalis*. This was the nearest we came to a concert, that is to say music played and sung in chorus, for mostly our music is performed in solo. Shrines are the most appropriate settings for *qawwalis* and as Delhi abounded in them, there was ample opportunity for listening to *qawwalis*. The best known was held at Dargah Nizamuddin. It was famous all over India and people came each year from all parts of the country to listen to it. It lasted a week and at the end of it, one's head reeled with music.

During those years in Delhi, my life was full of varied interests and activities, which provided amusement as well as intellectual stimulation. And though there was a war on and we ourselves were in the grip of a national struggle, it did not seem to disturb the even tenor of my life in Delhi. That I would ever have to leave this city which I loved in its every mood, as one does a person, I never even dreamt. The frontiers of Pakistan had not been defined and it never entered our heads that Delhi would not be included within it. How sure we were that Delhi was ours and would come to us can best be illustrated by this incident. We were having a picnic on the terrace at Humayun's Tomb one afternoon, when my sister-in-law remarked: 'Do you think we will get Delhi if Pakistan is established?' My husband replied pointing to the domed and turreted skyline of Delhi:

'Look at it—whom do you think it seems to belong to?' and Dina could not deny that the essentially Muslim character of its architecture seemed to proclaim that Delhi belonged to the Muslims. And so it did, in every way, except population. No, that is not true, even by counting the heads it would have been ours, had the dividing line come below and not above Delhi. But by dividing Punjab, our overall majority was lost, so we lost Delhi. And today its mosques and minarets join the mosques and minarets of Cordoba and Granada in saying:

> The descendants of Arabs, they were, those who created me.
> I stand here, a memorial to their vanished glory.

Chapter 16

THE STORM BREAKS

The failure of the Simla Conference in the summer of 1945 caused tension and bitterness. Elections, following in 1946, further intensified this—one could feel it everywhere. Social relations between Hindus and Muslims which, up till now, had been free and easy, became increasingly strained. Things one had once done without thinking, now seemed to have political implications. For instance, Hindus had used *adaab* and *khuda-hafiz* which are forms of greeting of Persian origin, but in common use among both Hindus and Muslims in polite society, particularly in Uttar Pradesh. Now their use was considered to be an indication of a pro-Muslim attitude.

Similarly the use of *teeka* (a red spot on the forehead, originally a caste-mark among Hindus but now used more or less for its decorative effect) by Muslim girls was frowned upon by the equally communal and narrow-minded Muslims. The atmosphere was becoming so charged with suspicion and hatred that one felt one could hardly breathe. Thinking men of every party were beginning to get alarmed. And everyone began to realize the urgency of coming to an agreement soon. Now that the election results had clearly and unmistakably shown the Congress and the Muslim League to be the two political parties, claiming the allegiance respectively of the Hindus and the Muslims, Britain had to come to terms with them and somehow to reconcile their claims, so that a transfer of power might be possible.

For this purpose a Parliamentary Delegation composed of such eminent persons as Lord Pethick-Lawrence and Sir

Stafford Cripps came out, bringing with them what came to be known as the Cabinet Mission Plan. The subsequent division of the Indian subcontinent was based more or less on the proposals contained in this plan, though, at this stage, it was still hoped that it would not be necessary to follow it. But by conceding the maximum amount of autonomy to the provinces, within a united framework, the claims both of Congress and the Muslim League would be met. And for a brief period that hope looked like being realized.

The members of the Cabinet Mission arrived in New Delhi in March 1946, when the hot weather was at its height, a time when the British Government normally used to retire to the mountains to escape the dust and heat of the plains. The arrival of the Cabinet Mission almost at a time when normally work tapered off, was itself significant of the fact that the British had realized the importance and urgency of solving the Indian problem. Sir Stafford Cripps and his colleagues, though they bravely tried to carry on during the gruelling heat of Delhi, soon found it impossible to continue and so had to retire to the heights of Simla, hoping that its cooler climate would be more conducive to cool and calm judgement.

Both Mr Jinnah and Pandit Nehru went up to Simla as guests of the British Government and we followed the reports of their daily talks with the members of the Cabinet Mission with interest and anxiety. After what seemed like an interminably long period, though it could not have been actually more than a fortnight, it was announced that an agreement had been reached. It was such a relief after the last six months, during which time agreement had seemed to recede farther and farther. One hardly dared to believe that the miracle had happened and all the three contending parties had finally come to an agreement. But it seemed that this was so, for Mr Jinnah was coming down to Delhi and had called a meeting of the All India Muslim League in order to announce to them his acceptance and to ask for their support.

THE STORM BREAKS

It was on 9 June 1946, in the spacious hall of the Hotel Imperial that this momentous session of the All India Muslim League was held. I remember Mr Jinnah looking pleased and confident as he sat on the platform, overlooking the packed hall. I remember his speech almost word for word. He explained clearly and lucidly, as he was wont to do, the reasons that had led him to the acceptance of the Cabinet Mission Plan. I remember the end of his speech, when he said with a smile; 'They say that at last reason has dawned upon me. Well, that is a very good thing. I only hope that reason will also dawn on the leaders of the Congress.' And that is what all of us, hearing that speech, fervently and ardently hoped for, a dawn of reason, for all concerned in solving the problem on which the well-being of millions rested.

But this fervent hope was very short-lived. On 9 June, I attended the League Council meeting. The next morning I left for Calcutta, for my father was very ill, and from now on, for the next year, while the dramatic struggle of the people of India was reaching its climax, I went through a period of great personal anguish and suffering. Because of this I ceased to be an active participant in the events that took place during this period, while the heightened sensitivity which comes with personal sorrow made me react to the suffering and tragedy around me more acutely. For this year in the history of India and Pakistan can truly be called a black year. The short-lived agreement between the Congress and the Muslim League had come to nought and thus resulted in the long pent-up tension and hatred breaking out into terrible communal riots all over the country. Calcutta, my home town, where my father lay ill, was the scene of the first of the terrible riots that were to break out in India with increasing ferocity during the next few months. My cousin, Shaheed Suhrawardy, was the Prime Minister of Bengal at this fatal hour and this made us, the members of his family, somehow feel more responsible for what was happening than we would perhaps have felt otherwise.

A really objective view of the horror that began on 16 August 1946 cannot be taken as many of the members of my generation were too personally concerned with it all; it lasted for four whole days, but the effects lasted for months and, in fact, can even be said to have lasted until today.

This briefly is what had happened since 9 June 1946. Congress repudiated the agreement reached. It began by Pandit Nehru's statement in the Press on 12 July that he had accepted nothing but the convening of a Constituent Assembly, to which the British would transfer power and then get out, after which all questions would be decided by the majority vote, which meant by the Hindus, as they were in absolute majority. It meant that none of the provisions regarding the division of power between the provinces and the Central Government could be taken as binding. That meant that Muslim majority provinces of Punjab, Bengal, Sindh, NWFP and Balochistan could not expect to be virtually autonomous, as proposed by the Cabinet Mission Plan, but could be subject to the Central Government in every detail. This statement of Pandit Nehru was preceded and followed by statements by other Congress leaders. It created a wave of distrust among the Muslims, who reiterated the demand for Pakistan, saying that they could never hope to have a fair deal within a united framework. Another fateful meeting of the Muslim League Council was held, this time in Bombay, and many momentous decisions were taken at this session. The dramatic return of the British titles took place there. One by one, the prominent members of the Muslim League came up to the platform and pronounced the returning of their coveted titles and honours, bestowed by the British Government. Holders of the smallest to the highest of the British titles, from MBE to the Knight Commander of the British Empire, one and all were glad to be able to give this proof of their adherence to the League command.

So far the Muslim League had studiously refrained from getting involved in the virulent anti-British activities of the Congress. Mr Jinnah's greatest achievement was that he had kept Muslims from losing sight of their main objective, which was to secure a fair deal in free India. But it was now felt that the British, because of the Labour Government's well-known partiality for the Congress, were deliberately bypassing the Muslim League. This was amply proved by their refusal to implement the Cabinet Mission Plan, because the Congress did not accept it, even though the Muslim League had accepted and stood by its commitments. It seemed after all we would not get our rights through negotiation and would have to be ready for action. This was the gist of most of the speeches delivered in the Bombay session, and it was decided to hold a Direct Action Day when the future plan of action for the League was to be explained to Muslims all over the country.

It was on the Direct Action Day that the Calcutta riots broke out, and the Congress has always tried to fasten the blame for this on the Muslim League, but as far as I can judge the matter dispassionately I feel that this is not true. In fact, nothing was planned for Direct Action Day except large-scale meetings all over the country, and it was while the Muslims of Calcutta were attending such a meeting that the riot broke out, *not in* the area of the meeting, but in the areas of the unprotected homes of these people. And the carnage that took place during these first few hours, where women and children fell as completely helpless and defenceless victims, was greater than the subsequent retaliatory attacks by the Muslims on the predominantly Hindu areas. Those returning from the meeting were also attacked unaware and so could not retaliate. I personally, however, do not think this sort of argument is a justifiable one. The riots in Calcutta were terrible, no matter who was to blame. The suffering that it caused to thousands of people shocked and horrified us all, and even though, since then there have been still more terrible riots (I have seen the victims of the East Punjab riot after Partition which made the Calcutta riots seem insignificant), I somehow have never been able to get over the shocked impact the Calcutta riots had on me.

It made me realize what a terrible responsibility we take on ourselves when we champion a cause and ask people to be ready to sacrifice and die for it. How few of us realize, as these words glibly pass our lips, what it actually costs people in blood and tears. I know that I at least have never again, after the Calcutta riots, been able to make a speech exhorting people to sacrifice. It seems too great a price to ask for so lightly from a public platform. I feel only those who themselves are ready and willing to pay, or rather who have already paid, are entitled to demand this supreme sacrifice; for only then can we be sure that they have done, and can do, what they are asking others to do.

It was during this period, when the rioting was at its worst in Calcutta, that my father's illness also took a serious turn. It was very difficult in a riot-torn city to get proper medical attention for him. We lived in Park Circus, a predominantly Muslim residential area. The doctors, who were Europeans and Hindus, lived in other parts of the city. The hospital, where one had to go constantly for various checkups, was in a predominantly Hindu area, and nurses lived in still another part of the town. My father's condition was already so serious that a few days' neglect could have fatal consequences and therefore, somehow or the other, medical attention and nursing had to be secured. For two nights and a day, neither doctor nor nurse could come, for all communications were at a standstill.

I was also faced with the problem of feeding all the people who were staying in our house. We had a large number of servants. My two young cousins and their small child were also staying in our house at that time, and now we had the two nurses and another child added to the household. All the shops were closed and we were more or less cut off from the rest of the town; so getting food presented a real difficulty. All of us who were well managed to live on boiled rice and *dal*, but in the case of my father it was necessary that he should have nourishing food. It was here that the poor people in the village tenements near us came to my aid.

These village tenements are a special feature of the city of Calcutta. Right in the middle of the most industrial part of the city, or in the heart of its residential district, one sees these village tenements which are known as *bastis*. They are, for all intents and purposes complete self-contained units and the people living in them have the same characteristics as our villagers. These *bastis* had started to disappear under the new town-planning schemes, and ours would have gone too, but because of the war, many of these plans had been shelved. And at this moment I was certainly very glad of the proximity of these *bastis,* though in the past at times I had deplored it. The people in their kindness, kept me provided with new-laid eggs, vegetables from their meagre little plots and even once let me have a whole chicken, and in this way I could tide over the worst period of food shortage.

We tried to keep the news of what was happening as much as we could from my father, but of course it was impossible to do so. Though he was very ill, his mind was perfectly clear and he insisted on listening to the radio, and so he knew exactly what was happening. It distressed me greatly to see his anguish, for my father was a man who really loved humanity and suffered for it. The fact that he was helpless and could do nothing to alleviate the misery of his people made him suffer all the more.

My father, throughout his political career, had never been virulently anti-British. He was by temperament a kindly person and vehemence was alien to his nature. He had throughout his life tried to serve his country in a constructive and not in a destructive manner. His contribution towards its struggle for liberation had not been of a spectacular kind, but consisted of solid work in the fields of health and education. But when he heard the Muslim League resolution about returning the British titles, he immediately decided to act on it.

I remember that evening so well. I had gone downstairs to see my uncle, who came every day to inquire about my father's health, but as he was old and had heart trouble, he could not come up the stairs. When I came upstairs, father told me that he had just listened to the radio, and in obedience to the Muslim League resolution, wanted to return his titles. He asked me if I would take down a letter to that effect. I hesitated to do so and said: 'Why, you never believed in such gestures. Why do you now want to do this?' 'It is all I can do', he said, and my heart seemed to break as I realized his utter misery at his helplessness. I tried to forestall his taking such a drastic step, but I should have realized that my father was not a man who, after having decided on a course of action, changed his mind. Next morning, when a young cousin of mine came to visit him, he got him to take down the letter renouncing his titles. This gesture, as a friend of ours so aptly said, was 'his last salute to the Muslim nation'.

Because my father could do nothing himself to help and serve the party, which at the moment was going through its most critical period, he insisted that I did whatever I could. At a short distance from our house was Lady Braebourne's College for Girls, which had now become one of the refugee centres. Truckloads of men, women and children were brought there daily from other parts of the town. Their homes had been burnt and looted. Many of their men killed, many more wounded, all of them were suffering from shock, none of them possessed anything but the clothes they stood up in and sometimes even those were torn to shreds. I was later to see many more such people, to get used to them almost, but at this moment it was still unfamiliar enough to be an appalling shock. Those that were seriously wounded were taken to hospital, but

1. Nawab Syud Muhammad

2. Hasan Masud Suhrawardy

3. Hasan Masud (aged 18)

4. Begum Ikramullah (aged 12) with her father, Sir Hassan Suhrawardy

5. Receiving Ph.D. from the University of London

6. Muslim Women's Students' Federation, 1941

7. With the Quaid-i-Azam at Simla, 1945

A family portrait

9. Mohammad Ikramullah, Sarvath, Salma, Begum Ikramullah, Naz, and Inam at their Clifton home, December 1947

10. Mohammad Ikramullah

11. With her Mamoo, Syud Hussain, the first Indian Ambassador to Egypt, 1949

12. Begum Ikramullah, Fatima Jinnah, Naz, Salma, and Inam at Flagstaff House, September 1949

13. With her husband and Mr and Mrs Alva Warren, US Ambassador

14. Inter-Parliamentary Conference, Dublin, 1951

15. With Begum Raana Liaquat Ali Khan and wives of diplomats at a lunch at PM House

16. Huseyn Shaheed Suhrawardy, Hasan Shahid Suhrawardy (Pakistan's Ambassador to Spain), Mohammad Ikramullah (Pakistan's Ambassador to France), and Begum Ikramullah, 1953

17. With Queen Elizabeth II at the Pakistan Stall, British Trade Fair, 1956

18. With Vijaya Lakshmi Pandit (sister of Jawaharlal Nehru) at the UN, 1956

19. With Prince Wan (left) at the UN, 1956

20. Deputy Chairman of the Pakistan Delegation, UN 1956–57

21. Security Council meeting, 1956, Front: Feroze Khan Noon
Second Row: Begum Ikramullah and Mohammad Ali Bogra
Third Row: Aftab Ahmed Khan and Rahat Said Chhatari

22. With President Ayub Khan and Zulfikar Ali Bhutto

23. Presenting her credentials to King Hassan Thani of Morocco, 1964

24. Leaving the royal palace with Siddi Mameri (left) and the Protocol Officer (right)

25. With her daughters and staff at her house in Morocco

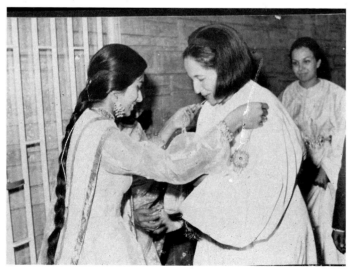

26. Sarvath greeting Lalla Aisha, the first Moroccan woman to be appointed Ambassador to England

27. With Lalla Aisha

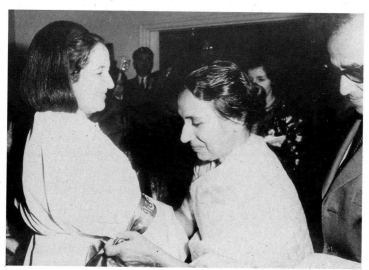

28. Tying the imam zamin on Lalla Aisha's arm

29. Begum Shaista Suhrawardy Ikramullah

there were many amongst them who had very bad cuts and who also had to be attended to.

Dozens of women among them had seen their menfolk dragged from their homes and killed before their eyes. Some of them were so numbed with shock that we could not even get them to move or eat or lie down. They sat looking into space with fixed vacant stares. It was terrible to see them. There were some who could give vent to their feelings by crying. Their wails were like Rachel's mourning for her children and they would not be comforted. Some of them had been separated from their husbands or children, who had been taken to another refugee centre. They were distraught and begged us to somehow try to trace their families. It was extremely difficult to do this, as everything was in such a state of chaos, but we tried to do what we could.

My young cousin, Mrs Ahmad Sulaiman, daughter of Shaheed Suhrawardy, and her husband were working day and night at this centre, and thought nothing of going through the most riot-ridden areas to rescue those who were trapped. And it was Mrs Sulaiman who went to the various police stations to try and trace the members of families who had got separated and bring them together. I will never forget the expression on the face of one of the refugee women when she got her three children back again. The oldest among them must have been about ten and the youngest was a few months old. The eldest child had looked after this baby, begging a little milk at the other refugee centre and feeding it by soaking cotton wool with milk and squeezing it into its mouth. The little baby did not look any worse for this method of feeding, and the joy of this family at being reunited was a sight to bring tears to the eyes. This woman had been stunned by a blow on her head, and that is how her children had got separated from her. Her husband had been badly wounded and was in hospital, but later got better and was able to rejoin them.

But there were women whose entire families had been

wiped out; husbands, brothers, sons, just leaving five or six defenceless women. What were we to do about these was the question that was to come later. At the moment, it took all our time and energy to feed and clothe these people somehow. Food was cooked in huge quantities by the men volunteers of the Muslim League Party, who also served the men refugees. But we, women volunteers, undertook to serve the women. It meant two or three hours of back-breaking work, and as soon as we had finished this, it seemed to be time for the evening meal and in between there were a hundred and one things to do.

Fearing an outbreak of cholera or smallpox, we tried to inoculate these people. Not having enough nurses or doctors to do this, those of us who had some sort of a first-aid training undertook to do this ourselves. All the work was organized and directed by Mrs Sulaiman, together with the group of ladies, most of them society women, who for the first time in their lives had come to do work of this kind. Later on, our women were to do much more than this and it explains how more or less overnight, they became social workers. The need was great; there was almost no choice. Whenever a challenge as tremendous as this faces a nation, it must rise up to meet the challenge or perish. Thank God, we were able to meet the challenge.

Our house itself had become a sort of refugee centre, because people from the village tenements would all flock to take shelter whenever there was a scare that rioters were coming. My father was very concerned that all those taking shelter in our house should be properly cared for. The first night that they came in, my father told me that they should be given something to eat. 'But how can I,' I said aghast, 'we have hardly any food in the house.' My father paused for a minute to think, and then told me that in one of the storerooms there were some large canisters of tea that he had brought from Darjeeling some time ago. Would I go and take these canisters out and at least give these people some tea?

I did as he told me, and in the same room found a samovar which, I remembered, was used in election days for making tea for the voters. So I had this samovar taken downstairs and handed over the making and distributing of tea to one of the village headmen who did the job very efficiently. This was the month of Ramadan and most of these people had been fasting the whole day and had had nothing to eat, even after breaking the fast. So the hot cup of tea was very welcome.

This became a daily occurrence while the scare continued, and even after this, when they no longer came to the house in the evening, I would get constant requests for help. A woman would come to say that her husband, who had gone out working in the morning, had not yet returned, and she feared that he might have been wounded or killed; would I try and find out what had happened. And either my cousin Mrs Sulaiman or I would telephone the police station and hospitals and try to trace the whereabouts of the person, and more often than not, he would turn up safe and sound later in the evening, at best having been delayed by a rowdy crowd.

I used to try and keep things from my father as much as I could, but as I tried to spend as much of my time with him as possible, he always found out when any such request had come to me, and he often told us what was the best way to help. One day, feeling rather irritated by these constant demands on my time, when I felt I had more than enough on my hands, I said: 'Why can't these people go to so and so for help', mentioning the names of our neighbours. 'They are also influential people and should be able to help.' My father was deeply shocked by this remark of mine. For a minute he looked up at my face and I could clearly see the surprise in his eyes, that I should have said something so contrary to the creed he had tried to bring me up in. He said, 'My dear, it has always been the tradition of your house to help other people', and then sighed gently, closed his eyes and turned over.

Many a time during the last few years, when I have felt the same sort of mounting irritation and have thought: 'Why can't such and such a person do something, or why should I always be bothered', I have remembered that scene in the sickroom of my father and heard his voice saying those words to me in the gathering twilight.

The actual rioting, the killing, the looting and the burning stopped after five days or so, but the dislocation that it had caused continued for days, indeed for months. Not only this, almost every other day there would be a scare, a false alarm or an actual instance of stabbing or arson, which would result in shops closing or traffic coming to a standstill for several hours at a time. My father's condition was deteriorating so rapidly now that the doctors felt that it was too much of a risk for him to continue staying in the house, because there was no certainty of medical aid reaching him when it was critically necessary. Colonel Pasrischa, the Director of the School of Tropical Medicine, where father's check-up was being carried out, said to me, 'I am prepared to turn your house into a hospital, give you oxygen cylinders, blood transfusion equipment, everything that is necessary, but what I cannot guarantee is my doctors and nurses getting to your house in time of necessity, if there is a sudden outbreak of violence, and therefore I beg you to bring your father over to my hospital.'

In my country, people who have got homes and dear ones to look after them do not go to hospitals. It is considered *infra dig*. We have still a conservative society's prejudice against institutions, and when one is seriously ill and chances of getting well are remote, one never goes to hospital, because together with the ordinary distrust of going to hospital there is a sort of religious prejudice against it as one would be surrounded in one's last moments by doctors and nurses who were of another faith, and one would not perhaps have an opportunity of receiving religious consolations.

It was therefore very difficult for me to decide to take my

father to the hospital. My aunts, that is my father's sister and sister-in-law and my mother's aunt looked aghast at me. 'What! Take him to the hospital in this condition!' and I could read what was in their minds. I was torn with conflict and did not know what to do, but my cousin Shahid, who throughout my father's illness had been a source of spiritual and physical strength to me, helped me to make up my mind on this issue also. 'You must not pay heed to meaningless convention, my dear. You must try and do everything that you can to prolong your father's life', and so it was that I decided to take my father to the School of Tropical Medicine. We were there only for a week. It was a week of great loneliness and trial for me, but during it I met with the greatest of kindness, consideration and sympathy from the entire hospital staff, nearly all of whom were Hindus. I mention this specifically because I am truly and deeply grateful to them for having been good to me. I am particularly grateful to them, not only because their kindness made my ordeal bearable, but because of it I can look upon these days without any feeling of bitterness, and I am glad that it can be so, for bitterness had no part in my father's philosophy of life.

CHAPTER 17

THE YEAR BETWEEN

My father died in September 1946 and Pakistan was established as a sovereign independent State on 14 August 1947. The year between was one full of momentous events, and for me a year of much personal worry and anxiety.

A central interim government, consisting of representatives of the Congress and Muslim League, had been formed soon after the Calcutta riots, but it was not a coalition government, because the two parties had not agreed on a common policy. They had come together only for the purpose of seeing that their separate points of view should get translated into action. It was hoped that working together might bring about a better understanding and result in a compromise. This hope, however, was not fulfilled, and though the representatives of the two major parties continued to sit round the same table, trying to tackle the various problems that confronted the nation, the bitterness amongst their people continued to grow. The Calcutta riots were followed by still more terrible riots, lasting for a much longer period, covering a much greater area and taking the toll of many more lives.

The first of these was the Bihar riot. Bihar is a province between Bengal and the UP. It was a predominantly Hindu province with a Muslim minority of 8 per cent. It was a province that had retained much of the old-world charm and its people, particularly its villagers, were noted for the gentleness of their manner. It therefore shocked everyone profoundly when the people of this province suddenly ran amuck and indulged in an orgy of killing and burning. The population of Calcutta consisted of Hindus and Muslims in almost equal proportion. The Muslims were in fact in a minority. They were about 48 per cent, but as there was a Muslim League government in power, the Hindus insisted that the riot had been instigated by the government and therefore were determined to take revenge for it. As a result the Bihar riots were planned. And the Hindu population being in absolute majority, the Muslims, particularly in the villages, were more or less wiped out. It was estimated that after the riots the total Muslim population of Bihar was reduced by half. The area covered also was enormous. The whole of the province was affected, and the riot continued unabated for nearly a month. Pandit Nehru, who had already become Prime Minister, rushed to the scene, as also did Gandhi, and there is no doubt that they tried to stop the carnage, but their efforts did not meet with much success.

The riots in Bihar were followed by equally terrible riots at Gurmakteshar, on the occasion of a Hindu festival. This festival took place annually on the bank of the river Jumna. How terrible the riot was can be gauged from the fact that it is said that the water of the river seemed to have been turned into blood. On this occasion also the victims were Muslims, and the riot was a planned one, calculated to strike terror in our hearts. But unfortunately it did not have that effect. A wave of indignation passed through the entire Muslim population of India and caused riots to break out in Noakhali, a district in Bengal with a predominantly Muslim population. Here the victims were the hapless Hindu minority.

These successive riots alarmed the British, who feared a complete breakdown of the government machinery, and decided to transfer power before that could happen. Lord Wavell was then the Viceroy of India, a man of high moral principles, great integrity of character and honesty. He refused to undertake such a task in a hurry, he was therefore recalled and Lord Mountbatten, who had a reputation for getting things done, was sent out as the last Viceroy of India, for the express purpose of liquidating the Empire.

There is no doubt that the increasing lawlessness in India alarmed the British, but it was not this that made them decide to quit India. There had been rioting and civil disturbances in India before, and they had managed to quell them and remain there. But something else had happened as the war came to its close which made the British realize that the time had come for them to leave. This was the INA trials and the reaction they had in the length and breadth of India.

The INA, or the Indian National Army, consisted of the Indian prisoners of war in Japan, who had been released by the Japanese Government on their having given up their allegiance to the British. These had been formed into a National Army of Liberation under the leadership of Subhas Chandra Bose, Congress Leader, who had escaped to Japan. Some of these men may have actually fought against the British troops but most of them had been kept in reserve for such time as the Japanese hoped to invade India, when these men would have been most useful to them. After the Allied victory these men were naturally brought to trial as deserters, this made them heroes overnight in India. So many things have happened during these last years that many people have forgotten the importance and significance of the INA trials, but there is no doubt that it was one of the deciding factors which made the British leave India.

I was fortunate enough to manage to be present at the trial of three of the INA officers. It seemed as if I was watching a dramatic play. The atmosphere was charged with emotion, the fact that the trials were being held in the Red Fort of Delhi added irony to the situation. And among the lawyers who had been elected to defend the accused, were not only the most famous names in the Indian legal profession, but the most prominent in the political field as well. Pandit Jawaharlal Nehru himself was among them, and I am almost certain that if this was not his first appearance, it was certainly the first in thirty years in the role of a barrister. Asaf Ali, Katju and Bhulabhai Desai were the other bright stars in the galaxy. They looked most impressive as they walked in and took their place opposite the prosecutors.

I cannot remember what the prosecution case was. I know that it was a brief one, after which Bhulabhai Desai got up and opened the case for the defence. Desai, who was known as the silver tongued orator, spoke for two whole days and he brought the full battery of his eloquence to bear upon the case. I could not judge its legal merits, but as a piece of oratory it was superb. As he ended his speech with the words:

> If it be treason to try and break the shackles of foreign rule, then these men are traitors; if it be treason to adopt whatever means presents itself to free one's country from hated foreign rule, then these men are traitors; if it be treason to work to free one's country from bondage, then these men are traitors, and not only these men, all of us are traitors. All of us, every man, woman and child in India, are today working for the same end.

There was such tension in the atmosphere that one could almost feel it. Desai had expressed what, rightly or wrongly, was felt about the INA by everybody in India. I say rightly or wrongly, because in this matter issues were not clear cut. There is no doubt that according to ordinary normal criteria of conduct, the action of the INA could not be considered anything else but treason. There was not an exactly comparable case with the ordinary civilian. They had chosen to wear the King's uniform. They had taken up arms to fight for one cause and then decided to change sides. But such was the atmosphere in India at that time that it was impossible for anyone to see or think clearly. The British in realizing this showed great perspicacity, because when people get to the stage when they cease to differentiate between right and wrong in their struggle, they have reached a dangerous point, and to try and hold them down further could only mean disaster. The British Government were wise not to have tried to do the impossible.

We heard on the radio in February 1947, that the British Government had decided to transfer power, and that Lord Mountbatten was coming over to put the decision into effect. The work of transferring power was expected to be completed by June 1948. We heard this announcement sitting in our drawing-room in New Delhi, and after it was over the room seemed suddenly very quiet. The régime, under which we had been born, and to which we had grown accustomed, was to be changed; and even though we may have wished for it, and I, in a small way had worked for it, it was a bit frightening now that it was actually going to take place.

I went to see the procession of the Mountbattens arriving in New Delhi, because I knew that it would be the last viceregal procession that I would witness. Soon after their arrival, I left New Delhi and so I missed getting to know the Mountbattens, whose extraordinary conduct in the last year of the British rule in India has made them the most controversial figures amongst the long list of royal representatives that have graced the Viceregal Lodge. I also missed the exciting and the momentous events attendant on the last phase of transfer of power to our hands.

I went to Nagpur to attend the wedding of my husband's nephew. A period of great personal worry and anxiety followed. My eldest daughter, Salma became very ill and her condition gave me cause for anxiety for months. Her illness coming so soon after my father's death worried me much more than it would otherwise have done. The strain of it affected my health. My youngest child, Sarvath was born prematurely and was so weak that it further added to my anxiety, and so it happened that while a revolution was more or less taking place around me I was so engrossed in my personal worries that I was hardly aware of it. My husband had become a member of the Partition Committee, which had been set up to carry out the onerous task of dividing the country, and except for making frantic telephone calls from Delhi was unable to help me in any way. On 11 August he left Delhi, accompanied by our son Inam, to set up the Foreign Office in Pakistan.

On 14 August 1947 Pakistan was established. Sarvath was barely three weeks old, and it was impossible for me to travel. I longed to be in Karachi and to take part in the joyful celebration that were taking place there, but I could not do so.

My daughters, Salma and Naz, however, made little green flags themselves and went up and down the long verandah, singing Pakistani songs and shouting, 'Pakistan Zindabad'. This was all the celebration we could manage on this long-awaited day.

The next day was 15 August the day of Indian Independence. Since the Calcutta riots, things had never been normal in Calcutta, and for the last few weeks as the day of the Independence drew near, tension had reached fever pitch. It was rumoured that Hindus meant to wreak their vengeance on the Muslims on the day. This was no idle rumour, there was concrete proof that a large-sale disturbance was being planned. That it did not take place is almost a miracle, and this miracle was brought about by the superhuman efforts of Gandhi and my cousin Shaheed Suhrawardy.

Gandhi was proceeding to Noakhali, to be there in case fresh rioting should break out. He had to pass through Calcutta to go to Noakhali. My cousin met him at the station and said to him that it was Calcutta and not Noakhali he was needed at. My cousin, who was still the Prime Minister of the whole of Bengal, said he knew exactly what the condition was in the various parts of the province, and it was not in Noakhali but in Calcutta that trouble was brewing, and by staying here Gandhi could stop a flare-up. Gandhi said he would agree to stay on and do what he could, provided my cousin agreed to work with him.

Agreeing to work with Gandhi meant, of course, agreeing to work in his way. In this case, it meant going and staying in a mud hut in the poorest and the most badly affected part of the town, eating vegetarian food and following the routine that he followed. This must have entailed a lot of discomfort for a person like my cousin who was used to a very different sort of life, but so great was his desire to prevent another holocaust that he agreed to these conditions and carried them out meticulously for over a fortnight. It also meant facing much physical danger; several attacks were made on his life, and his car was blown up by a hand-grenade, but he persisted in the task he had undertaken.

Mahatma Gandhi and Shaheed Suhrawardy started their crusade for peace together on 11 August. They went to different parts of the town and held meetings in which they exhorted people to be worthy of the new independence that was coming to them, and asked Hindus to treat Muslims as their brothers and asked Muslims to think of Hindus in the same way. They sent volunteers in lorries shouting peace slogans all over the city, and somehow managed in three or four days to ease the tension and bring out an upsurge of goodwill. For on 15 August, the day that was dreaded, Hindus and Muslims instead of killing each other fraternized together and celebrated the coming of independence joyfully. It was a wonderful achievement and I am proud of the part my cousin played in it. I think that in his long record of public service, there is nothing else that matches this. On this occasion he showed courage, boldness and most of all, a real concern for the people's welfare.

This act of my cousin was misconstrued by his enemies and eventually cost him his career in Pakistan, though in actual fact this was not only an act of service to Muslims in

Calcutta, whose elected representative he had been for twenty-seven years, but also a great service to the newly established State of Pakistan. For if he had not acted in the way he did, riots would have broken out in Calcutta also, in which case Pakistan would have had to cope with an influx of refugees on both its fronts.

It took all Pakistan's resourcefulness to deal with the five million refugees that poured into West Pakistan within the first three months of its establishment. That it could stand up to this terrific strain is incredible, a proof of the courage and determination of its people. But it is doubtful if even their superhuman courage and determination could have withstood a double attack. Even if it could have done so, the strain would have been terrible, and Shaheed deserved gratitude, not censure, for having prevented the catastrophe. But such is the way of politics that this, his greatest act of service, was misconstrued as an act of disloyalty.

As conditions in Calcutta improved, disturbing news began to come through from Punjab. The very day after the Partition, Sikhs and Hindus together had started a systematic massacre of Mussulmans in East Punjab. All the villages were destroyed and men, women and children in thousands, killed. This started such a panic and terror in the hearts of people that within a few days millions were trekking their way from East Punjab into West Punjab.

The riots had now spread to Delhi and terrible things were happening there. Gandhi, on hearing this, left for Delhi, to try and do there the same wonderful work he had done in Calcutta.

CHAPTER 18

ARRIVING IN PAKISTAN—THE PROMISED LAND

I arrived in Karachi on 17 September 1947. I travelled from Calcutta to Bombay, and then to Karachi by the steamboat named Bamora. The deck class was full of Muslims emigrating from various parts of India. They were travelling in great discomfort, were overcrowded and, on strict rations. I went down more than once to see them and found their morale very high, they were full of hope and courage. There was not a single word of complaint. They were counting the hours till they could arrive in Pakistan.

As we neared Karachi, we saw a small boat (I believe it is called a sloop) flying the flag of Pakistan. My cousin, Shahid Suhrawardy, my daughters, Salma and Naz, my nephew Rashid, and I leaned over the rails to get a closer look at this boat. It was the first symbol we saw of our independence, and even Shahid Bhai, who was by no means an emotional person, was deeply moved. I heard him saying, 'It is very small, but it is ours'.

It was already dark when the Bamora entered the harbour of Karachi. The passengers had all assembled on the deck, straining their eyes to catch a glimpse of the shore, and as soon as it was sighted the cries of 'Allah-o-Akbar' rent the air, and became more and more vociferous as the ship drew nearer to Karachi. I found the next day that I was completely hoarse!

There was a big crowd waiting at the shore. These were the refugees who had arrived from India and were more or less stranded here, again this had not dampened their enthusiasm for Pakistan. They welcomed us with resounding slogans of 'Allah-o-Akbar' and 'Pakistan Zindabad' and for about fifteen minutes one could hear nothing but these cries of exultation, triumph, and hope—mingling with those of the ones on board. In the midst of it, the ship docked and we arrived in Pakistan—the promised land.

My husband and son, Inam, had come to meet as. They found us with some difficulty because of the disembarking crowd. The atmosphere was charged with emotion, and almost everyone was in tears. I myself was deeply moved. As it had already grown dark, I couldn't see much of Karachi on my drive home to Clifton. Next morning, I got up feeling strange and unfamiliar. Then a flood of realization swept over me that I was in Pakistan. Actually in Pakistan—the land of promise, the land of hope, the land for which millions had sacrificed their lives so that the Indian Muslims could have a homeland of their own.

We had been given a house in Clifton, a suburb of Karachi. In 1947 there were very few houses in that area and we felt cut off from the town and its activities. So, as soon as I could I went into Karachi to look at the city which was going to be my home. I saw the flag fluttering from the Government House and realized that it was now inhabited by Quaid-i-Azam. I, who for years had avoided calling at Government House, immediately went in and signed my name in the visitor's book with a flourish! I beamed at the policeman and the ADCs, for all these appurtenances to the British Raj had now become symbols of our own sovereignty. We were now a nation and a state, the realization went to my head like wine. It made me feel as if I was walking on air.

But there was no time for joyful celebrations, for the price paid for Pakistan was very great indeed: no less than five million people had been uprooted, many thousands of whom had been killed, their houses looted and their womenfolk raped. Now they were trekking their way to the newly established State. This had begun twenty-four hours after Pakistan came into existence, and before the State was more than a few days old it had to face the alarming task of absorbing five million refugees. That it could do so was a miracle, a miracle made possible by the grace of God and the determination and endurance of its people in the face of unparalleled misery, and the grim determination of those at the helm of affairs to surmount the unprecedented difficulties that faced them, are equally praiseworthy, and have evoked the admiration and wonder of people in all parts of the world.

I have often heard people say : 'Isn't it remarkable that in the brief period of seven years, Jinnah put forward the idea of Pakistan, had it accepted by the people and sanctioned by the British?', but that is not so. It is true, the demand for Pakistan was made only seven years before it was established, but this demand only gave concrete expression to the dream of the Indian Muslims to have a 'local habitation and a name'. This dream they had cherished since 1857 when the last vestige of their rule in India came to an end. But I must go back farther than that in order to explain it all.

Muslims had come to India as conquerors and for 800 years had ruled the country. During this period, they had settled down, married and accepted many of the customs of the land of their adoption, but had never become absolutely one with the people of the country. The reason for this continued detachment lay in the religion these people followed. It baffles Westerners that it should be so, but the fact remains that religion did make different people of them, influencing their way of life and their pattern of thought. Hinduism had hitherto absorbed most conquerors, but the clear-cut tenets of Islam defied amalgamation with any other creed. The rigid caste system of the Hindus was a barrier that prevented free social intercourse; there was also the gulf separating the rulers from the ruled. And though in the case of the Muslims and Hindus, this difference was not as great as between the British and the Indians, it still existed.

When Muslim rule in India was succeeded by the British, the basic differences between the two peoples did not disappear, if anything, they grew stronger. The Muslims felt themselves threatened both by the supremacy of the British as rulers and by the numerical superiority of the Hindus, and in order to preserve their separate entity they held more tenaciously to their own way of life, and to every little thing that made their culture different from that of the Hindus. These differences may seem trivial to an outsider, but to the Muslims they were like sentinels guarding their separate existence in a sea of aliens.

After some years of British rule, a new nationalism was born which was the result of Western education and the product of Western thought. Influenced by it, the Hindus and Muslims—for the first time—came together for the attainment of a common objective—independence of India through constitutional methods. But this type of nationalism had no mass appeal because the very language of parliamentary democracy that it used, was unfamiliar to the common people. No doubt in time it would have succeeded, but the process would have been a slow one. It would also have been a peaceful one and in the long run would have saved a great deal of pain and suffering, but this did not come about. Many things stopped the evolution of nationalism of this Western pattern, and it would take too long to recount them here.

Gandhi changed the whole character of the national movement. He gave it mass appeal by introducing a quasi-mystic element into it. At the same time, it took on a more definite Hindu colour. Gandhi's national movement also advocated non-violent non-cooperation as the method and kept the achievement of parliamentary democracy in the Western pattern as its object. But neither the end nor the means used to attain it appealed to Muslims as a whole. *Satyagraha*, *Ahimsa*, separate electorates, reservation of seats, minorities and weightage—none of these succeeded in creating any enthusiasm among the Muslim masses. But they could understand, visualize and thrill to the idea of a separate state of their own, and that is why the idea of Pakistan, from the minute it was put forward, caught their imagination.

So great was the enthusiasm for this idea that all the difficulties that lay in its way were ignored, all the sacrifices that would have to be made to bring it about were unheeded and all the contradictory factors of the case were lost sight of. We did not realize that it would mean sacrificing the very centres of our culture, the very monuments of our glory, the area that had been the cradle of our civilization. But although no one realized what price would have to be paid for the realization of this dream, when the time came for its payment, it was paid—almost without regret.

The people of Pakistan made superhuman efforts in the first weeks of its existence for survival. They were fired by the desire to make this State of theirs succeed against all odds. For it was something for which they had waited subconsciously for nearly a century. For this end, a handful of officials worked twenty-four hours a day in offices that lacked tables and chairs, typewriters and stationery, that had neither pen nor paper, that in fact were bare of all office equipment. Officers sat on packing cases and wrote orders on backs of used envelopes. No one grumbled, no one minded the discomfort, no one grudged the long hours that they were required to put in, for they realized that they were making history.

Post offices were short of stamps, railways were short of fuel and yet somehow they continued to function, because of the initiative and resourcefulness of the men in charge, who were mostly young men with very little experience but a tremendous faith and belief in themselves and in the cause that they had elected to serve. Business and commerce were completely disrupted. These had always been the preserves of the Hindus, and no one in Pakistan knew much about these matters, but somehow courage and enterprise took the place of experience and knowledge, and the gap was bridged.

On returning home I phoned Miss Jinnah. She expressed her pleasure on my arrival and asked me to see her straight away as there was much to be done. She also invited me to a meeting of the newly formed Women's Relief Committee. Later that afternoon Begum Raana Liaquat Ali Khan came over. She came right into my bedroom. I had not even unpacked yet and offered to take her to the drawing-room. She refused and sat there on a bedding roll and recounted harrowing stories of the refugee camps. On hearing about the horrible sufferings of the refugees I felt guilty that I had not been able to come earlier and could hardly wait to begin work.

The Pakistan Government had been formed barely a month back, and was doing whatever it could. It was in this task that the women were of great help, refugees in their millions were looked after, fed, clothed, nursed, and a large proportion of them rehabilitated, in record time. Society women, who until now had done very little work of any sort, spent hours at refugee centres. They worked in groups, and individually and did all they possibly could. They dressed wounds by tearing their *dupattas* to make bandages, collected soap, iodine and bandages, took them round to those in need, and tried to keep the refugee centres clean. Cold weather added further hardships to the lot of the refugees. We went from door to door collecting blankets and warm clothes for them. I can say without exaggeration that there was not a house left in Karachi that winter, where anybody, however rich, had more woollen clothes than they absolutely needed. Everything that could be spared was given.

There was no rest, no relaxation in our efforts for the first few months, but gradually things began to improve. The influx of refugees slowed down, the government machinery began to work more smoothly and surely, and we felt that we had weathered the storm. So far there had been no functions, for no one had the time or the inclination for them. But by now we had ambassadors from most of the important countries, so parties had to begin, the first of them was given for the Diplomatic Corps by the Foreign Office.

Christmas Day was drawing near, which also happened to be Quaid's birthday. For the last few years, the Muslim League had celebrated it with much ceremony, and now that Pakistan was established, we thought that we should celebrate it with all the more éclat. The idea was ours, that is, the women's. The officials at first smiled at it, but later when they agreed to our suggestion, their arrangements for it left nothing to be desired.

In the morning, there was a parade. We have had much bigger ones since, for at that time we had very little to show, but I have never felt so proud as when those small contingents of our Army, Navy and Air Force smartly marched past, while Quaid stood proudly taking the salute, with the Services Chiefs by his side. It underlined the fact that we had truly become a Nation. I remember leaning over and saying to Chaudhry Muhammad Ali, 'What do you think the Indian ambassador is thinking,

یہ کیسی قوم ہے کہ اسے ایک سیٹ نہ دو تو ایک ملک لے لیتی ہے۔

(What kind of a nation is this, that if we don't give it one seat it takes a country instead).

In the evening there was a reception at the Prime Minister's and a State Banquet at the Governor-General's House, but the function that was the grand finale of it all was the banquet held at Sir Ghulam Hussain, the Governor of Sindh's house the next evening. Sir Ghulam Hussain and Lady Hidayatullah were known for their wonderful parties and lavish hospitality and on this occasion they had excelled themselves. The whole of the Governor's house was ablaze with light, the table groaned under the plates of food, men looked smart in their uniforms and women resplendent in gorgeous dresses and beautiful jewellery. Everybody felt gay and happy and in a festive mood.

Towards the end of the evening, we all gathered in the spacious hall to drink to Quaid's health. I can see the scene so clearly in my mind: Quaid sitting in the middle of the room on a sofa, relaxed and happy. By his side was Lady Hidayatullah. All of us gathered round in a semi circle, holding glasses of ruby-red pomegranate juice in our hands, and a group of lovely girls, led by Pasha Haroon, standing opposite Quaid and singing a song, which had as its refrain: 'May you live long, O Quaid-i-Azam.' And though Quaid did not live for very long after this, I do not think that our prayers went unanswered...for he lives as long as Pakistan lives.

Chapter 19

INSIDE PARLIAMENT

In February 1948, I took my seat in the Constituent Assembly of Pakistan. I had been elected to the Constituent Assembly of India in 1946 during the brief period of agreement between Congress and the Muslim League, but as the agreement had broken down almost immediately, Quaid-i-Azam had asked the Muslim League members not to take their seats in the Constituent Assembly of India and consequently I had not done so. When the Partition was agreed upon, I was again elected to the Constituent Assembly of Pakistan. This was a period of great personal anguish for me. My father had died in September 1946. Calcutta riots were raging during his illness and its aftermath continued to disrupt life. Therefore, though I had been elected at that time I had hardly realized its significance. Sitting in the Assembly Chambers that morning, however, the full realization came over me and I was awed to think that I should be amongst those who had been chosen for the proud and onerous task of framing the Constitution of my country.

> To take the sorry scheme of things entire
> And to remould it nearer the heart's desire.

Yes what an honour it was and what a chance—a chance that comes but once in the life of a nation, to mould the destiny of its people, and lay the foundation on which the generations to come will build. The future was ours to shape—it was a momentous occasion.

A hush fell over the room as the Secretary of the Assembly announced the entrance of the President. The *chaprasi* lifted the curtain behind the presidential chair and Mr Jinnah stepped on to the platform. We all rose to our feet, Mr Jinnah bowed ceremoniously, we returned the bow, and then resumed our seats. One by one, the members were called to come up to the platform and take their oath. When my turn came I went up, my heart beating and my knees trembling, I somehow climbed the three steps of the platform. The Secretary handed me the card on which the text was written for me to read. After I had finished taking the oath, Mr Jinnah smiled at me encouragingly, rose, shook hands and said a few words, after which I walked across to the other side of the dais, and climbed down. For the next half hour, this continued, member after member went up, took his oath, shook hands with the Quaid and returned to his seat. There was a great solemnity about the occasion, and though later many of them were to forget it, at the moment, under the eagle eye of the Quaid, all of us were aware of the greatness and importance of our task.

One prepares for one's maiden speech in the Legislature with great care—it is a great occasion, the initiation of one's political career. I had also looked forward to doing likewise but as it happened I could not do so. My first speech in the Legislature was more in the nature of an intervention (*see* Appendix 1). It happened like this. After the oath had been taken, a member from Bengal got up and moved a resolution, suggesting that the Constituent Assembly should meet once in Karachi and once in Dhaka. Discussion followed. The members from East Pakistan felt that being the majority it was their right that the constitution-making body should also meet in Dhaka. The members from West Pakistan objected that Dhaka was a provincial capital, and if this demand was acceded to, other provinces could also claim that the Assembly move from capital to capital of each province. It was not feasible for the Constituent Assembly to go on a circuit. During this heated discussion I, forgetting my nervousness, joined in. I supported the idea whole-heartedly, pointing out the great benefits that would come of it. The Prime Minister, Liaquat Ali Khan got up to reply, and looking at me said in mock horror: 'Women never understand practical difficulties', to which I retorted: 'If we had considered the difficulties in our way we would never have supported the demand for Pakistan.' There was an applause at that. So I began my parliamentary career with a dissent, and continued in this manner for as long as I was in the Assembly, and outside it.

In my speeches I not only always disagreed with government policy, but being quite young (I was about thirty-two years old), I had the audacity of youth, bordering on rudeness. The Prime Minister Liaquat Ali Khan always took it in good humour. While his rejoinders had a sting in them, they were always well within the parliamentary norm. What a contrast to the prevalent conditions in the august House of our Representatives today! How lucky I was to have been a member of the First Constituent Assembly of Pakistan when its Prime Minister and other members were gentlemen.

I was to remain a member of Parliament for nearly seven years, and these years were full of interest and activity. Our Parliament had a dual function—framing the Constitution and carrying out the day-to-day legislature. I was very ignorant and it took some time to understand the Parliamentary procedure, but once I had done this, it was like taking part in a large-scale debating society. With this difference only—on the result of the debate depended the fate and welfare of millions. It was a tremendous responsibility and in all my years as a member, I felt overwhelmed by it. For by either supporting or opposing a motion, or by putting forward a resolution and getting it carried through, one could do such great good or countenance a great evil.

The tradition of respect for women had been set by the Quaid-i-Azam in the public meetings of the Muslim League where Miss Fatima Jinnah always sat on the dais alongside the Quaid. She sat in full public view and so the rank and file of the Muslim League's women workers could also sit in like manner on the benches facing the dais. There was a separate enclosure for women and many sat there behind the purdah. But for those of us who preferred not to do so there were no cat-calls, no rude remarks. We were treated with respect and deference, and this tradition once established continued in the House. We were two women in a house of seventy-nine members. Begum Jahanara Shahnawaz, a veteran political worker from Punjab who had attended the Round Table Conference in London as early as 1923 was one, and I from Bengal, was the other. We each had a small desk to ourselves and though there was room for two to sit no one else shared our desk. It was a small thing but it was a gesture of deference which we appreciated.

The Assembly met two or three times a year and its total sitting time was not much more than three months, but being a member of the Assembly meant that one's time was always at the disposal of the people. Everyone with any sort of grievance or any idea on any subject, had a right to come and see one, and as I was particularly concerned with the refugees and with education, there was a great deal that could be done and said about these matters. I soon found that I did not have a moment to spare. Besides this, there were endless requests to me to make speeches, preside over societies and take part in charitable organizations. Before I realized it I had become a member of no less than a dozen societies, besides being a member of semi-governmental organizations such as the Red Cross, the Anti-Tuberculosis Society and the UNICEF.

During this period I was sent as a delegate to several International Conferences as well, including the third session of the UN in Paris in 1948. In 1951 I was invited, by the

State Department of the United States, to study educational institutions and was given opportunities to speak about Pakistan. It was all very interesting and, at the same time, a great strain; for besides all this I had my home to run and my children to look after. I was not prepared to neglect these, not only because I considered it to be my first duty but because I really enjoy being at home and seeing that it is well-run, comfortable, and a place where my family and friends like to be.

I also love being with my children. They were now at a most interesting stage, and I did not propose to miss watching the fascinating process of their growing up. I also felt that I was somehow on trial, that all eyes were on me, waiting to see if it were possible to combine a home and a career, and if I failed it would have an adverse effect on other women's chances of doing the same. I tried very hard not to fail.

In order to get through my day's work I learnt not to take more than five minutes to dress, to give up the pleasure of shopping or even of window shopping, to never curl up on a sofa with a book whenever I wanted to, or visit a friend in mid-morning for a cup of coffee and gossip. In the dust and strife of life in Parliament I often longed for the peace and leisure of the days in purdah. But there could be no turning back, no return to the secluded and sheltered existence of the past. I had to continue on this new road on which the women of my country had set out, in which one could taste the joys of achievement as well as the bitterness of failure, to know both hope and fear, disillusionment and attainment. And who can deny that this is a richer, fuller and a more rewarding way of life?

During the period when I was a member of the Assembly, the greater part of my time was given over to speaking on matters pertaining to education—its availability or rather the lack of it, and its quality.

Educational backwardness has been the cause of all our ills. After the Mutiny of 1857 we did not cooperate with the British and did not accept Western education. This left us behind in the vanguard of progress and the Hindus having taken advantage of the opportunity got in the forefront. They had no hang-ups as they merely had to begin learning English instead of Persian which they had to do during the Muslim rule. Sir Syed Ahmed Khan realized that this was the cause of Muslim backwardness and he tried to remedy this by starting the MAO College, which later became the Muslim University of Aligarh in the subcontinent. The Hindus were a generation ahead of us in educational achievement which gave them financial advantage, too. This disparity was the root cause of the many ills that the Muslim in the subcontinent suffered and which eventually led to Partition. This is a well-known fact. I will, therefore, not go into detail about it. I passionately believed in education, it could be said that I had inherited this passion, for I came from a family of educationists. My grandfather, aunt, uncle, and my father had all in turn made this their chief subject of interest, and therefore it was only natural that I followed in their footsteps.

I was pleased when on 27 November 1947 the newly established government of Pakistan called an All Pakistan Educational Conference in Karachi to discuss and debate on the future programme of education in Pakistan. I felt that this was the right attitude and showed that the newly formed government realized the vital importance of education and was keen to remedy the woeful deficiencies in it without any loss of time. The calling of the Educational Conference so early after its inception was a happy augury.

The persons who attended the conference were prominent intellectuals, and educationists of Pakistan. There was Professor A.S. Bokhari from Punjab, Professor Shahid Suhrawardy (not to be confused with his brother the politician, Huseyn Shaheed Suhrawardy) from Bengal and Dr Daudpota from Sindh. Besides them there were men and women whose academic qualifications, liberal outlook and service in the cause of education made them eminently suitable for the task of laying the educational policy of the newly formed State of Pakistan. This euphoria of mine did not last long because in this conference alongside the eminent and liberal minded educationists, were persons of rigid, narrow and reactionary views, and my six years membership in the Assembly was a struggle against the domination of these retrograde elements.

I had thought that those who had a say in forming the policy of Pakistan were people who realized the paramount importance of education. I had come to this conclusion because of the convening of the education conference at an early stage of Pakistan but the successive action of the government belied this. The Minister chosen for education in the first cabinet of Pakistan was Mr Fazlur Rehman, a God's good man no doubt, but far from my idea of an educationist or I should qualify it by saying a liberal educationist. Mr Fazlur Rehman was narrow, rigid and doctrinaire, totally unable to even comprehend the tenets of a liberal education. For the few days in the conference I had had the support of Professor Bokhari and Shahid Bhai and other intellectuals who were attending it. They were opposed by the traditionalists—there was difference of opinion on almost every point. Religious education, whether it should be compulsory? If so of which denomination? or should it be non-denominational? or should it consist of the fundamentals only?

The Education Minister wanted that not only religious education but party policies should also be included in the curriculum. The party history should be taught not in the broad spectrum of the struggle for independence but in a narrow one-sided manner. To think, to evaluate and assess were to my mind the essence of education. But the Education Minister could not understand what I was talking about. Looking back upon it after nearly fifty years I think that I was probably being as doctrinaire as the Education Minister. I was certainly being unconventional. Education has been considered the inculcating of certain moral principles and of learning by rote, the objectives being to qualify or rather train one to be good civil servants in the lower grade of government service. Now the horizon had widened but the objectives remained exactly the same. This difference of perception became apparent in the few days of the conference.

I felt this was a desperate situation. I had grown up in a liberal atmosphere and this attitude had gathered strength because of the Second World War which was supposed to have been fought for individual freedom and for freedom of thought and expression. I went to the Prime Minister, it was the second time that I did so. I had gone to him once before, that had been in connection with the ejection of the refugees. I have mentioned that in context of their plight.

The Prime Minister was as usual kind and reassuring, 'That is why you are on the Educational Board,' he said. 'This is what it is for, try and discuss this with the Education Minister.'

'I can't discuss it with the Education Minister,' I replied. 'I have tried to do so but he does not understand what I am talking about. I cannot undertake the education of the Education Minister,' I added. The Prime Minister was much amused, he used this phrase of mine later on, in the Assembly.

The aims and objectives of education was not the only matter I disagreed about. There were other subjects such as teacher's salary, conveyance allowance, and other practical matters. I was at loggerheads with the Education Minister over all of them. I considered the salaries to be inadequate (I still do so). I think reducing the status and salary of teachers and by bringing their emoluments down to the lowest level has made the teaching profession so unattractive that only those who can find no other means of earning their living go into it.

I do not have to elaborate its disastrous effect on the quality of education. Conveyance allowance was a related subject, and here also I think I was right though I realize now that I could have chosen a better way of expressing myself. But then I was young, impetuous, and impatient with the red-tape and modalities of the government.

Together with Mian Iftikharuddin I got the reputation of being a maverick. Mian Iftikharuddin and Sardar Shaukat Hayat resigned from the Muslim League Party after two and a half years. I however continued to be a Muslim League member till November 1953 when I resigned, as a protest against the continued delay in framing of the Constitution.

Chapter 20

THE PLIGHT OF THE REFUGEES

My first experience of work in a refugee camp had been after the Calcutta riots of 16 August 1946. The riots had been deliberately provoked by the Hindus but the responsibility for it had been unfairly put on the Muslims because the Muslim League was heading the government. So powerful was the Hindu propaganda machinery that even now when these riots are mentioned, the opprobrium for it is put on the Muslim League government and its Chief Minister, Huseyn Shaheed Suhrawardy, while the carnage of the Bihar riots and the slaughter of Muslims at Gurmakteshar have been forgotten.

The number of people in Haji Camp in Ranchore Lines and other refugee camps in Karachi were much greater than the victims of the Calcutta riots, who had been sheltered in the Lady Braebourne College for Girls. Yet these were not the ones who had faced the real brunt of the disaster, it was Lahore that had the brunt of the influx.

Haji Camp, one of the buildings built for the Hajis in transit, was now taken over to provide shelter for the refugees, so were schools and colleges and any vacant buildings that could be found. The trickling in of the refugees had begun even before Pakistan had been established but now it became an avalanche. We were able to face it and survive for at that time there was no feeling of provincialism or regionalism. The word 'ethnic' was unheard of—we were all Muslims, no matter what part of India we had come from, we had taken shelter in Pakistan.

We must not forget the warmth and hospitality with which the people of Sindh received us. What happened to make that feeling of unity disappear and be replaced by discord and hatred of today, is another story.

Words fail to describe the plight of the refugees—the sufferings, the harassments that they had endured. Their homes had been burnt, their children killed before their very eyes, all their worldly goods looted, they had walked wearily towards the promised land—Pakistan. On crossing the border they had knelt down and kissed the ground of Pakistan in *sajdah-e-shukar.*

People I talked to in the refugee camps never complained, never asked for anything but were grateful for the help they were given. In Karachi, the number of refugees was so great that the Army personnel took over the entire work of looking after them. We women tried to help in small ways, and worked from morning to noon. Our backs ached from bending over to feed hundreds of people. Most of them were incapacitated by illness. We tried to dress their wounds, both mentally and physically. There were just not enough doctors, nurses or medicines. In hospitals, every bed was occupied and verandahs were full of seriously ill and dying patients. It was not only a time of great trial and tribulation, but of great courage and a feeling of great exultation also. A great price had been paid but Pakistan had been achieved.

Today after fifty years and many heartbreaking events and much disillusionment I still remember the feeling of that time and hope and pray that their sacrifices were not in vain, and that we have not lost sight of our vision, and will achieve our goal.

These men and women who had been uprooted from their homes and had trekked for miles to Pakistan *en route* had been attacked by Sikh and Hindu fanatics, and being unarmed had been literally butchered. Women had seen their husbands and sons killed before their very eyes. Even children and infants had not been spared, old men had been beaten and women molested. But the caravans trudged along carrying their pitiable bundles, joined by refugees from other villages. Some times a bus or truck gave them a lift.

The trains that were running, were attacked and passengers killed. The ghastly massacre on the Peshawar Express with 6,000 passengers, all were killed, can never be forgotten. When the train reached Lahore it had only dead bodies, on board and the compartments were flowing with blood. It was a horrible scene. The incident of the Peshawar Express and similar killings of that period makes one think that human beings seem to have completely forgotten the meaning of compassion and decency.

Amidst it there were such heartbreaking cases of love and sacrifice. Amidst the loot and carnage I remember a woman who had lost all her children; a widow whose twelve year-old son had been her only support since her husband died. 'He was a such a good boy', she kept saying. The day of the trouble he had gone out to get some food and never returned. We listened to her and promised to look out for the boy, knowing as we made the promise that it was a hopeless task.

There was another widow with three daughters, she had stitched and sewed for years to feed and clothe them. She had made the *jahez* of the two elder ones, sewing every thing with her own hands—they were to get married in the coming month of *Eid*. When she had to leave everything was also left behind, even the *jahez* got together with such labour of love. The groom who was of another *mohalla* had disappeared without a trace. She begged us to look for him. 'Yes we will,' we promised, knowing as she also knew that it was an empty promise.

And so the story goes on—of loss, of suffering, of man's cruelty to man.

* * *

The first weeks of Pakistan were given over to dealing with the day-to-day task of looking after the refugees, feeding, clothing and dressing their wounds and finding shelters for them. I have briefly recounted how we coped with this great and unprecedented challenge. But the really onerous task still remained—the task of resettling them permanently and finding means of livelihood for them. This was by far the most difficult work.

The refugees from East Punjab were mostly farmers, owners and cultivators of land. The Hindus who left West Punjab were of like occupations therefore, the settling of the East Punjab refugees was comparatively a simple matter. Simple but by no means an easy one. Those Pakistani Government servants who under unheard of difficulties and most unusual circumstances accomplished the task of resettling five million refugees in Pakistan deserve great praise—their work has not yet been given the recognition they deserved.

The refugees in Karachi were from urban and not rural background like those of East Punjab. Their resettlement posed greater difficulties. Small shopkeepers, factory hands, and domestic servants found employment similar to what they had been engaged in, in India. But I find that it was the highly skilled artisans and craftsmen amongst them that were completely stranded. They could not be settled on land and the guild system under which they worked had completely broken down. I felt that if we did not do something about rehabilitating them we would lose our proud heritage of craftsmanship. I therefore suggested in the Assembly that something specific should be done about these people (*see* Appendix 2). I was fortunate that Mr Ghulam Muhammad, the Finance Minister, was an imaginative person, he immediately responded to my request and formed The Artisans and Craftsmen's Committee.

At first it met with opposition even derision. 'Begum Sahiba this is not the time to talk about *gota thappa*,' said some members with heavy sarcasm. 'But the present crisis would not last forever,' I replied that Insha-Allah things will get normalized and then there will be demand for these luxury items and if we do not rehabilitate our artisans and craftsmen we will have to import them from abroad, i.e., from India, and this skill of our craftsmen would have been lost forever. And we will want these artisans not only for domestic competition but these will be the most attractive items for import.

The Committee's object was to rehabilitate what is known as Cottage Industries, i.e., handicrafts. But as I have said my colleagues looked upon this idea with tolerant amusement, as a folly to be expected from fashionable ladies. Some other members of the Committee however saw in it an opportunity to further their own interest. Suggestions were made and grants were asked for establishing other industries. No doubt this was also very necessary. But my objective was to save our precious heritage of craftsmanship from disappearing.

I was sure that this would happen because the upheavals had completely disrupted the guild system under which these people worked. Now they were completely uprooted and were forced to accept any work which provided them with a livelihood. The financial gain in rehabilitating artisans may not be so great but the publicity value will be tremendous. It will create an image of Pakistanis as a gifted people—no image of them existed at the moment. But my voice was a cry in the wilderness. But I carried on with my effort. I went to the various refugee camps trying to locate the jewellers, the makers of brass and copper utensils, goldsmiths and silversmiths, all those whose skills had contributed to the making of our way of life picturesque and colourful. This was about a year after Partition, when I asked at the camps the whereabouts of the artisans and craftsmen, I remember the exact words of the reply given to me by one of the persons there: 'Begum Sahiba you have come now looking for the *karigars* whose one hand was gold and the other silver, they have all either gone back to India or have become *thelaywallas* selling *chaat* at Clifton Beach'. And this was true. It is exactly what had happened. Vallabhbhai Patel—realizing that Muslim artisans' presence in India was vital for preserving its arts and crafts, which gave India the image of a civilized nation—had gone to Benares offering security and protection to the weavers of Benares silk and *kamkhab*. He had also sent emissaries to Pakistan to ask artisans to go back to India offering them security and every inducement to do so, and quite a number had gone back.

I felt that if we did not do something about rehabilitating our artisans and craftsmen we would soon be completely denuded of our heritage and we who had lost the monuments of our culture would also be bereft of our craftsmanship which can add some beauty in our daily lives.

* * *

It was August 1948. A year had passed since Pakistan had been established but there had been no mitigation in the suffering of the refugees in Karachi. It is human nature to become indifferent to suffering if it goes on for long. When the barefoot, lacerated, destitute refugees had begun pouring into Pakistan from India, there had been a tremendous surge of sympathy for them. Not only the government and the government institutions, but every man, woman and even children had reacted with horror and sympathy and did whatever they could to alleviate their misery. The task however seemed unending and the fonts of sympathy were drying up. People turned to their everyday tasks. The government had other things of importance on hand. The task of having to run a state, without any experience, buildings and equipment was not an easy one.

Government personnel were housed wherever they could find space—colleges, schools in erstwhile Army barracks—

and still there was not enough accommodation. The government was hastily building clerical grade quarters. They were nearing completion but as yet there was no water, electricity or any other amenity installed in them. When the rains came, the refugees took shelter in them, this caused a furore and was looked upon as illegal encroachment. The suffering and sacrifices of the refugees for the cause of Pakistan were already forgotten.

The government ordered their eviction. The refugees in their desperation sent their spokesman to the government officials. I do not have any personal knowledge of how the spokesman was received, but I do know that they also sent telegrams to the members of the Constituent Assembly imploring them to come and see their plight and help them. I also received one such telegram and went to Lalukhet. I found the position of those sheltering there desperate. They told me that they had been ordered to vacate these buildings within forty-eight hours, and no alternative accommodation had been provided for them. They were to be given five rupees and four *chattaies* per head. This was their compensation, they who had lost their hearth and homes for Pakistan!

I was distressed beyond words and said that I would see the Prime Minister and apprise him of their plight.

Next day I went to the Constituent Assembly before the start of the session. I asked the Prime Minister's personal secretary if he would kindly get me an appointment. The Prime Minister very kindly gave me one the very same day.

'What is the matter? You look very upset,' he said solicitously.

'I am very upset,' I replied and proceeded to tell him in detail of the events. He was visibly moved.

'You mean to say that these people are being turned out without any sort of alternative accommodation?' he asked incredulously.

'Yes!' I replied. 'That is just what the government orders seem to be. They are being given five rupees and four mats per head which seems like adding insult to injury.'

'I will immediately look into this matter,' said the Prime Minister, and he did so.

I think he spoke to the minister-in-charge of the refugees and then to Mr Hashim Raza, Collector of Karachi. On verifying the above matter, he sent for me immediately.

'What do these occupants want done? What is their demand?' he asked.

I was ready with my answer, because they had told me what they wanted. It was a Stay Order issued by the government so that they could remain in these partially built houses till alternative accommodation could be provided to them.

The Prime Minister countered, 'But I understand these buildings are for lower grade government servants who are also staying in great discomfort. What is more, the quarters are not yet completed and I am told they cannot be completed if they are already occupied.'

'I am sure what you have been told is correct. No doubt these lower grade government servants are staying in great discomfort in crowded rooms or as unwelcome guests with relatives. They are scattered all over the city, which makes office attendance in time difficult. I know all this,' I replied. 'But at least they have some sort of roof over their heads, they are earning, however small the amount and can get themselves food and other basic necessities of life. Their discomfort is nothing compared to the plight of the refugees, who have nothing. They are truly in a desperate position.'

'What do they want me to do for them?' asked the Prime Minister. I reiterated that the Stay Order would ensure that they are not thrown out in the streets again in the rains.

'All right,' said the Prime Minister. He made no further comments. I felt that the interview had ended so I took my leave.

THE PLIGHT OF THE REFUGEES

Next morning the Stay Order was issued by the Prime Minister. He said that the homeless occupants would not be ejected from the government buildings but would continue to live there till alternative accommodation could be arranged.

No alternative accommodation was arranged for them (not for this particular group of people of this area) but they were allowed to stay on, and the buildings were modified. These quarters offered one room, a kitchen and a bathroom (in each quarter) with enough space for the occupants to build at least two more rooms if they wanted to do so, later. They were to pay the government a nominal sum till the cost of the house was paid up. This became the pattern for the refugee quarters in Malir, Korangi and other parts of Karachi.

The refugees were relieved beyond measure—they could not find words to express their gratitude. They wanted to name the area after Mr Hashim Raza and myself. Both of us begged them not to do any such thing as it would be said that we had done this to get publicity. So, the area was named Liaquatabad, and quite rightly, too, for neither Mr Hashim Raza nor I could have done anything concrete, no matter how great our sympathy. It was the Prime Minister's concern for them, and his immediate decision that solved their problem. So that is how Lalukhet became Liaquatabad.

CHAPTER 21

THIRD SESSION OF THE UN (1948)

I was first asked to go as a delegate to the United Nations in 1947, I was surprised and pleased that such a prestigious offer should come to me so early in my career. But I had to turn it down because Sarvath was only a few weeks old. It was sometime in July 1948 that the Prime Minister Nawabzada Liaquat Ali Khan informed me of my appointment as a delegate to the Third Session of the UN which was being held in Paris. I then remembered what Quaid-i-Azam had said when he had asked me not to go to the Pacific Relations Conference. The whole episode came back to me as I sat on the terrace of the Prime Minister's House on Victoria Road.

In 1945, the Indian Government had asked me to go to the Pacific Relations Conference. I was naturally very pleased but thought to apprise Nawabzada Liaquat Ali Khan, Secretary General of the Muslim League. I asked for an appointment and informed him of the offer. I asked him whether I should accept it or not. He thought for a moment and then replied, 'I do not see why you should not go, after all you are not an office bearer in the Muslim League.'

I think that he might have been motivated by kindness to stretch a point in my favour, as going to international conferences was not such an everyday occurrence as it has now become. I then informed Sir Sultan Ahmed, Advisor of the Viceroy's Council, who had very kindly made this offer to me. When the list of the delegates came out in the papers, my name was in it.

The same evening I was walking in my garden when I heard the telephone ring. I went inside and picked up the phone and said nonchalantly:

'Hello, who is speaking?'

'Jinnah speaking,' came the reply.

It is difficult to convey to people today the awe in which we, the followers of the Quaid-i-Azam held him. For a minute I was speechless and then I found my voice and muttered something in reply. Quaid-i-Azam then said, 'I want to see you.'

'Yes Sir,' I said.

'Can you come tomorrow morning at 9.30?'

'Yes, certainly,' I replied.

'Then I will see you tomorrow. Good-bye.'

I remember the occasion very clearly, I was alone in the house. My family and guests had gone out shopping. It seemed ages before they came back but in actual fact it could not have been so long.

'What is the matter ?' asked my husband and sister-in-law, Dina, when they saw my face. I told them about the telephone conversation.

'I don't see it as any reason to get so worked up about,' said my husband. 'Probably Mr Jinnah wants to talk to you about your going to the Pacific Conference.'

'I suppose so,' I replied but without much conviction.

The evening seemed very long, we somehow got through dinner, the others seemed to have also been affected by my nervousness, and after some desultory conversation we all went to bed. Next morning after breakfast I got ready to leave.

'I'll come with you,' said Dina and she did so.

Quaid-i-Azam met us in the spacious hall of his house. He greeted Dina courteously and then turned to me and asked me to follow him. Dina also got up, wanting to accompany me.

'No!' said Quaid-i-Azam politely but firmly. 'I want to talk to her alone.' We went to his study. Quaid-i-Azam sat down in one of the chairs and motioned me to sit down on the other. He said, 'I saw your name among the delegates to the Pacific Relations Conference. I am afraid as a Muslim Leaguer you cannot go to it.'

'I asked Nawabzada Liaquat Ali Khan if I could go,' I managed to stammer out. 'He had said that I may.'

'No, you cannot go because the Muslim League is not cooperating with the Government of India in any of their projects,' said the Quaid.

I was disappointed for, as I have mentioned before, going to an international conference was a rare honour in those days.

'Can't I go and not speak on behalf of the Muslim League,' I asked.

'What are you going to speak about—the man on the moon?' said the Quaid with slight irritation. Then he added gently, 'Don't you realize you have been asked because you are a member of the Muslim League.'

I could and did realize it. In fact I had always known subconsciously that I could not go. The interview finished, the Quaid got up and so did I. He walked with me to the door, and before holding it open he turned towards me and said: 'One day you will go as the League's representative with honour.' It was an implied promise, he kept it.

I came back to the present as I heard the Prime Minister saying, 'So, you will prepare yourself to leave.'

'But I cannot go for so long,' I said.

'Send me instead to the International Parliamentary Conference in Dublin. I can manage that because it requires being away from home for a shorter period.'

'But Quaid-i-Azam wants you to go to the UN,' said the Prime Minister.

'Can't you suggest someone else's name,' I replied. I mentioned a name.

THIRD SESSION OF THE UN (1948)

'Give me credit for knowing Quaid-i-Azam's mind after knowing him for thirteen years,' said the Prime Minister.

'Only thirteen years,' said I mischievously quoting a verse of Ghalib:

شبِ حال ہجر کو بھی رکھوں گر حساب میں تو سکتنے ہوتے ؟

As usual the Prime Minister took my impertinence in good humour. So, I accepted to go to the Third Session of the UN. It was to meet in Paris in the third week of September (for till then the original decision to hold the yearly session of the UN in different capitals of Europe was still being adhered to). The Third Session of the UN was being held in Palais de Chaillot, Paris. It was later that the UN sessions began to be held every year in New York, thereby contributing to it coming completely under the influence of the United States of America—leading to many of the ills of post-war politics, but that is another story.

I arrived in England a little ahead of time, the Session was to meet in Paris. I was in Manchester staying with a friend, when I saw the news of the greatest tragedy yet to befall our nation and people. In the morning paper of 11 September 1948 I read that Quaid-i-Azam had passed away.

It is difficult to convey our feelings about Quaid-i-Azam, the mixture of affection, the respect and the regard—it is just not possible to give any idea of how bereft, how shattered, how completely lost we felt at the news that Quaid-i-Azam was no more. Our ship had weathered many storms but with the Quaid at the helm, but now what? I was still staring at the paper trying to take in the dreadful news, when the phone rang—it was from the High Commissioner of Pakistan in London, informing me officially of the disaster, also telling me that a meeting would be held at the Caxton Hall that afternoon to mourn the passing away of the greatest statesman of our time and asking me to come. I left immediately—my friend Gillian whom I was visiting, was most sympathetic, 'We felt just as devastated when Roosevelt died during the war, but great nations survive great leaders—you will also do so,' she said. I went straight to the residence of the High Commissioner. A number of Pakistanis had gathered there, each and everyone of us looked shattered, as if we had lost our dearest and nearest, and so we had. The High Commissioner's house was a house of mourning. I think it was about four o'clock when we proceeded to Caxton Hall.

There was a large gathering there. The meeting was being presided over by the Secretary of State for the Commonwealth, Mr Pethick-Lawrence. There were many speakers; they all paid glowing tributes to the man whom many of them considered difficult and non-compromising but whose integrity and single-mindedness of purpose they had never doubted. Among the many speakers was Miss Agatha Harrison, the well-known Quaker leader. She said she had known Quaid-i-Azam for a long time—she had met him when he was a student in England. She said that he used to come to their women's suffragette meetings and used to speak in their support. 'Even then he was not afraid of championing an unpopular cause,' she added. I still remember for it was a very significant remark.

The next few days are a blur in my mind. I read the English papers, and came to know that Khawaja Nazimuddin had been chosen as Governor-General. There was no other change. We proceeded to Paris in this dazed state of mind.

In 1948 it was only three years since the Second World War had ended. The devastation wrought by it was still fresh in people's mind—never, never again should such a thing be allowed to happen, vowed the people. It was on the lips of everybody. We must do something that will prevent the repetition of such horrors. It was with this objective in view, that two momentous resolutions, the Convention against Genocide and the Universal Declaration of Human Rights was deliberated upon and passed. It was a privilege to have been associated with the drafting of these documents.

The Convention against Genocide spelt out what must not be done to impair the dignity of the individual. Professor Raphael Lemkin was the author of the Convention of Genocide, he was a Polish Jew and a jurist whose entire family, twenty-four individuals in all, were killed by the fascist forces of Hitler.

Professor Lemkin had made it his life's work to see that this horror was not repeated. Clause by clause in the Convention against Genocide, he tried to safeguard the rights of the individuals against brute forces. Though he was not a member of the Committee dealing with the drawing up of the Convention, yet he was the inspiration behind it. For me also this subject was a very emotive one. Thousands of Muslims had been killed, their homes and hearths destroyed, their culture and identity shattered as a consequence of the Partition of India and the price for establishment of the Muslim majority state of Pakistan. I had worked for a year—before coming to the UN session— in the refugee camps and seen with my own eyes the devastation, I therefore shared Professor Lemkin's feelings. I also wanted to do something which would make such a disaster impossible again. But I had thought that Genocide was a moral and emotional matter, I had not realized that it was a highly controversial and legal issue. The countries of the world that have a large number of minorities within their jurisdiction were against the passing of such a Convention, because they feared it might be used against them, unjustifiably, as a political weapon. I had thought that all I had to do was to get up and make a moral and emotional speech—which I did. I was extremely surprised when I found Sir Hartley Shawcross, an eminent jurist speaking opposite me in very complicated legal terms.

I was completely out of my depth and I would have floundered if Agha Shahi had not come to my rescue. He explained to me the meaning and implication of words like 'sanctions', and he gave me Mullah's book on Muslim Law. I found it very informative and read it with great interest, asking Shahi to explain the points which I could not understand. When my turn came to reply I had made myself familiar with enough legal terms to give a speech, which did not reveal my complete ignorance.

I was extremely pleased when one of the members of the Fifth Committee congratulated me on my speech, and asked where I had studied Law! My entire knowledge of it was confined to Mullah's book together with Agha Shahi's explanations! This was the sum total of my legal knowledge, but I got away with it.

However the Fifth Committee was not my committee. I was accredited to the Third Committee which was dealing with Human Rights. I had asked to work in the Fifth Committee as the subject of Genocide was one with which I was emotionally involved, because of what had happened to the Muslims in India. I had however got much Press coverage at home for the work I had done, for the question of Genocide was a very relevant one, and its consequences could be seen all round us. The delegate who was officially accredited to the Fifth Committee thought that I was getting an unfair amount of kudos, and that the Fifth Committee's work and its attendant publicity were really his due! As I did not want to be the cause of any misunderstanding and seeking publicity was not my objective, I went back to the Third Committee where the work on Human Rights was also very interesting and absorbing.

It was December, the Session was drawing to a close. The questions that had been debated and discussed in the Committees (there were six of them) were to be formalized and presented at the General Assembly to be voted upon. I was therefore very surprised when I was asked by the secretary of my delegation, Mr Agha Shahi, to speak on the Convention of Genocide at the time of its introduction in the General Assembly, because the accredited delegate had left for Pakistan to take on the post of minister in the Cabinet!

At first I refused as I had not followed the Committee's discussions on Genocide and did not know the developments that had taken place.

'O you don't have to bother about writing a speech yourself; I have a complete speech written here', Agha Shahi said, pointing to some papers before him. 'All you have to do is read it.'

'But I don't read speeches written by somebody else, I write my own speeches,' I said. Agha Shahi appeared to take umbrage thinking that I did not consider his speech good enough. I assured him that I thought his speech excellent, but I had a casual style and it was very different from his and therefore I could not do justice to a speech written for him. After a long discussion I agreed to speak at the General Assembly provided that all the daily reports of the proceedings dealing with the Fifth Committee for the last three months were to be sent to my room immediately. I also asked that Clara Khan, the secretary who used to type out my speeches be asked to please come up to my room at 5.00 a.m. Both my requests were accepted.

I had an early supper, and began reading the reports of the Fifth Committee. By 3.00 a.m. I had finished them. Thereafter I managed to get about two hours sleep. Clara came to my room punctually at 5.00 a.m. We ordered hot coffee for ourselves, and sat down to work—I to dictate and she to take down. Clara was a quick and efficient typist and therefore within two hours she typed out a rough copy of the speech for me to see. I made some minor corrections. By 7.30 a.m. Clara went back to her room to make a clear copy of the speech and to give it for duplication. I had a bath and breakfast, and was at my seat in the General Assembly by 9.00 a.m., the pile of the typed copies of my speech before me. Punctually, at 9.30 a.m. the General Assembly began. There were the usual introductory speeches, and then the Committees were called upon to present their resolutions for acceptance by the General Assembly. It was quite a while before my turn came.

I went up to the dais with fear and trepidation. I felt my speech did not do justice to the subject but that was not my fault. I went ahead and read it, there was quite a bit of applause which was very heartening—perhaps because the subject was emotive and the events which had led to the demand for the Convention were recent enough for people to remember them in their horror. Even so the countries that had objected to the drawing of the Convention remained adamant in their objections, and refused to vote for its acceptance. The countries that had suffered Genocide voted in its favour. There were fifty-eight delegates and fifty-five voted in its favour.

Professor Lemkin had been watching the proceedings from the side, and as I came down from the dais, he stepped forward and congratulated me. I felt I couldn't have done so badly after all! When the Session was over and I met him again, he again thanked me for my work on the cause that was so dear to his heart. I told him it was dear to mine also as my people had also been victims of Genocide. We were both sad that the so-called great countries had not voted to declare Genocide a culpable crime! But at least the question had been brought to the forum of the world, and we would go on trying, and a time will come when the world will declare Genocide a crime. Not only that, we hoped there would be no Genocide in the world of tomorrow and our children would grow up without knowing the horrors of Genocide. Convention on the Prevention and Punishment of the Crime of Genocide was unanimously adopted on 9 December 1949.

Alas! that bright hope has not been fulfilled, and unfortunately there have been terrible cases of Genocide in the world. Even the nations that were signatories to the Convention have failed to abide by it, but still there is a touchstone that we can refer to in cases of violations, and continue to hope that a day will come when mass extermination of people on basis of race and religion will be a legal and punishable crime.

The Universal Declaration of Human Rights tried to preserve the dignity of the individual. It was discussed, drawn up, and passed by the Third Committee of the UN. The Chairman of the Third Committee was Dr Charles Malik, a seasoned politician from Lebanon. Mrs Eleanor Roosevelt was the person, entrusted with the day-to-day work of drawing up the Declaration. She worked tirelessly, and showed exemplary patience. The Cold War had just begun. She was harassed at every step of her work by the representative of Russia in the Third Committee, who was an extremely adroit and vocal person, who objected to almost every clause in the Declaration and tried to trip Mrs Roosevelt if he possibly could. As I have said she showed exemplary patience in dealing with him, she replied to every objection he made very politely, and let him have his say at length without interruptions. The question of human dignity, personal freedom, sanctity of the family life and rights of dissent were the most significant items, and on each and every one there were long discussions. Representing Pakistan, I also spoke at one such discussion:

> It is because we believe in the fundamental... Rights and dignity and worth of the human person that this organization has been formed... But while there are codes and conventions by which international conduct can be judged, so far there has been no universally accepted Charter of Human Rights... The discoveries of science have brought and are bringing the world very close, and, therefore, it is imperative that there must be an accepted code of civilized behaviour... We cannot today sit in the comity of nations and behave in the accepted international manner and yet in our domestic matters (if it suits us) revert to barbaric practices and refuse to give an explanation of our conduct on the score of it being an internal matter... I realize that neither the draft declaration nor the convention is a law nor are they backed by a sanction although I hope that the nations will incorporate it in the laws and make it the corner stone of their constituencies... I hope that this declaration will mark a turning point in history as did Thomas Paine's Rights of Man and the American Declaration of Independence.

There were other items on the agenda of the Third Committee as well, but most of its time was taken up in discussion of the Declaration of Human Rights. It was scheduled to finish by the end of the Session. The Committee worked very hard to make this possible; despite the delaying tactics of the Russian delegate, it achieved this goal. The Universal Declaration of Human Rights was passed at midnight on 10 December 1948 by forty-eight votes to nil, with eight abstentions.

This Declaration was made with the hope that the people of the world had now reached a state of civilization and maturity to be able to honour it. This hope has not been fulfilled. There has been continued violence and abuse of Human Rights in every part of the world. Those who get into power by objectionable and undemocratic means, try to remain in power by crushing dissent in flagrant disregard of human rights. But still there is a Declaration of Human Rights, a Charter of human freedom, and the oppressed and their champions can at least refer to it when those who having seized the reins of power try to trample on the people. The struggle between right and wrong continues. The ideas emphasized in the Declaration of Human Rights are far from being realized, but there is a goal, to which those who believe in the freedom of the human spirit can try to reach.

Chapter 22

PROPHETIC WORDS

Basic Principles Committee's first draft was presented for discussion in the Constituent Assembly in March 1949. There was a vociferous criticism of it in the press. Influenced by it, the Prime Minister decided to refer it to public opinion, even though it had not been fully debated in the Constituent Assembly. I thought that that was a mistake and said so very emphatically to the Prime Minister of Pakistan, Nawabzada Liaquat Ali Khan. I am still of the same opinion, that had this not been done and had the first report of the Basic Principles Committee been passed by the Constituent Assembly during Nawabzada Liaquat Ali Khan's life time many of the ills that Pakistan has been suffering, in fact, could have been avoided.

Though the first report was not fully debated in the Constituent Assembly, there were still murmurs of dissent and these were pointers of what was to follow.

The debatable point was the division of the seats in the Legislative Assembly between East Pakistan and the provinces of West Pakistan. The Constituent Assembly in the beginning consisted of only seventy-nine members. The total number of seats allocated to East Pakistan was forty-four. The total number of seats in West Pakistan including each of the four provinces were: Punjab twenty-two seats, Sindh five seats, NWFP three seats, Balochistan one seat, and one member each to represent the Balochistan states union, the states that had opted for Pakistan such as Bahawalpur and Khairpur, and the NWFP princely states. Amongst the seventy-nine seats were included two seats for women. The women members were Begum Jahanara Shahnawaz from West Pakistan and myself representing East Pakistan. It was quite obvious that if there was any point of disagreement then East Pakistan had a clear majority and could overrule West Pakistan. This was the question that was to bedevil all the subsequent attempts at drawing up the Constitution.

In the brief tenure of Shaheed Bhai's Prime Ministership this Gordian knot was cut. His getting East Pakistan to accept parity was made possible by his powerful personality and the influence he had over the people there because it was an unheard of concession where the majority had voluntarily conceded in spite of its numerical superiority. It was only Shaheed Bhai's popularity in East Pakistan that could achieve this, even so it was a tough fight, and there are still people in Bangladesh who have not forgiven him for it. This was a supreme act of statesmanship, in which he staked his own political future but did not get any appreciation from West Pakistan either. I think that Nawabzada Liaquat Ali Khan's referring the Basic Principles Committee Report to elicit public opinion may have been motivated by the fact that he wanted to postpone dealing with the thorny question of East Pakistan majority which was resented and feared by West Pakistan.

How small was the flicker of dissent in 1948–49, and how easy it would have been at that stage to deal with it, for the feeling of unity that had led to the establishment of Pakistan was still not dead. But this was not done. The provincial elections in the Punjab were to take place and it was very important that the Muslim League should win. So a policy of procrastination was adopted instead of statesmanship. It was time to remind people that three years ago they had been united in their demand for Pakistan, and that they were Pakistanis first and Punjabi, Bengali, Sindhi and whatever else second, and it did not matter which province had more and which had less seats—if there was trust and unity between them, each and every province would work for prosperity, development and a place of honour for the other. In short, the reasons for which Pakistan had been created had not been lost sight of yet. But these ideals were being blurred, and the ugly head of provincialism was trying to raise its head. It could have been and should have been squashed at this stage, but it was allowed to grow like a monster, which eventually lost us half the country and is still aiming at destroying what is left of Pakistan.

* * *

Pakistan's first Prime Minister, Nawabzada Liaquat Ali Khan, was assassinated on 16 October, 1951. It was the second great loss that befell Pakistan after the passing away of Quaid-i-Azam Mohammad Ali Jinnah. Liaquat Ali Khan had been Prime Minister for four and a half years. There had been ample time for the Constitution to have been completed and passed, but it had not been done. This was the single unfortunate fact in Pakistan's history which led to all the misfortunes that have befallen our country. Had the Constitution been passed, it would have been as if the rails had been laid, and the train of our nation's destiny would have followed on the tracks; but this was not done and one blunder followed another.

After the Quaid's passing away, Khawaja Nazimuddin was chosen to be the Governor-General of Pakistan. He was a veteran Muslim Leaguer, a seasoned politician and a truly religious man. He was eminently suited to be the head of an Islamic state. He did his duty with dignity and impartiality during the four years he held office. He never stooped to any intrigue or interfered in the day to day running of the government. In fact the only time we had a Head of State that conformed to the requirements of a parliamentary form of government was during the time of Khawaja Nazimuddin.

After the assassination of Prime Minister Liaquat Ali Khan, Khawaja Nazimuddin was persuaded to relinquish his high office and take on the onerous task of becoming the Prime Minister of Pakistan. It was one of the biggest mistakes that his advisors made. Mr Ghulam Muhammad, the former Finance Minister in Liaquat Ali Khan's cabinet was chosen as the next Governor-General.

The Head of State in a system of parliamentary democracy is supposed to carry himself with grace and dignity and on occasions such as visits of foreign heads of state and other representatives to welcome and entertain them as befits their position according to Pakistan's tradition. Khawaja Nazimuddin filled this role admirably. Therefore we should have looked for and found the person suited to be the Prime Minister; it was a formidable task but not an impossible one. Even if Shaheed Suhrawardy—the most obvious choice—was to be disregarded for reasons not relevant to be mentioned here, yet there still remained amongst the first rank of Muslim League, men, who had worked with the Quaid and could have filled the role admirably. Sardar Abdur Rab Nishtar was actually considered and he would have been an excellent choice. But this did not suit the king-makers.

Mr Ghulam Muhammad had had a massive stroke a few weeks before the assassination of Liaquat Ali Khan. He had barely recovered and had gone to Rawalpindi to rest and recoup when the Prime Minister was assassinated.

He was a bureaucrat and in choosing him the contenders for power thought that he would agree to leaving the decisions in the hands of the politicians. This was their big mistake. Ailing and inarticulate though he was, Mr Ghulam Muhammad was determined to play a hand in the power game and as it turned out the game was entirely played according to his manipulation. How he did it is a wonder, and a mystery but he did do it, and for three years Pakistan's destiny was in the hands of a sick man.

The riots against the Qadianis erupted for the first time during this period. This was the beginning of the sectarian violence which was to increasingly grow in Pakistan in later years. Disturbances were put down firmly, Martial Law was declared for the first time. Khawaja Nazimuddin, let it be said to his credit, tried his best not to give way to the narrow and sectarian demand but unfortunately the Chief Minister of the Punjab was not above the temptation of giving in to the fanatics. Soon after his return from Lahore, Khawaja Nazimuddin was dismissed by the Governor-General. This was the first fatal blow to the democratic system. Khawaja Nazimuddin was too weak to put up a fight, on behalf of his democratic rights—short of declaring that he had the budget passed just before the dismissal of his Government so he could not be said to have lost the confidence of the House, which is the only valid reason for the dismissal of a government.

Khawaja Nazimuddin left the Prime Minister's house with the quiet dignity which was characteristic of him. Though having held high offices for the best part of his life, being of exemplary honesty, he did not possess a house of his own; and was dependent on the courtesy and kindness of the Adamjees who put one of their spacious flats at his disposal.

* * *

After the dismissal of Khawaja Nazimuddin in April 1953, Mr Muhammad Ali Bogra, Pakistan's Ambassador to the United States of America, was recalled and sworn in as Prime Minister. The first session of the Constituent Assembly, under his aegis was called and it was emphatically declared that the long delayed Constitution would be drawn up and this task expedited as quickly as possible. In fact, if I remember rightly, it was said that the Assembly would not adjourn till it had completed this task.

In October 1953, my husband was posted as Ambassador of Pakistan to France, and had just taken charge. As an

Ambassador's wife, I had numerous tasks connected with settling in a new assignment. But I left all this and came back to Pakistan to attend the session of the Constituent Assembly because I firmly believed that this time the Constitution would finally be passed but I was to be bitterly disappointed!

The completion of the Constitution was being held up because the delicate issue of division of seats between East and West Pakistan was still unresolved. This was a crucial matter, but instead of dealing with it, a resolution was passed, which said 'the Legislature will not enact any law which is repugnant to the Holy Koran and the Sunnah'. This resolution was passed with much fanfare. I was rather puzzled and wanted to know who would pass a law against the tenets of Islam when the elected members of the Constituent Assembly were overwhelmingly Muslim and if by some inexplicable reason, Muslims—who formed 85 per cent of the population and had gone through untold suffering to establish Pakistan so that they should have a state in which their culture would flourish—were to pass such a resolution, what could prevent them from doing so? I added that if Muslims could have passed this resolution in the Indian Constituent Assembly it would indeed have been an achievement.

Nobody paid heed to my doubts and questions. Another resolution was introduced, purporting to safeguard the security of Pakistan. I considered some of its clauses to be against the tenets of democracy such as the right to dissent. This to my mind was the essence of the freedom of speech. I objected to this as I felt very strongly about it. My action caused great indignation amongst party stalwarts. Mr A.K. Brohi, the law minister, who was considered an intellectual and a person of liberal views, tried to persuade me to vote in favour of the resolution. He assured me that later he would introduce an amendment modifying the part of the resolution that I objected to. So I agreed and voted in favour of the resolution. The amendment was never considered much less adapted and passed!

I felt that the resolutions that were being tabled were narrow and reactionary, so I decided to see the Prime Minister, Mr Muhammad Ali Bogra (during the time of some of the discussions, he had been indisposed). He was kind enough to give me an appointment and I went to see him. He heard me in detail, patiently, and agreed to do everything I suggested. It had been so easy to persuade him that I felt doubtful whether he had taken my suggestion seriously or understood the implications of the objections I was making. If he was really going to accept it, it would take him a long time to persuade the House to do so. 'I do not think he means to do anything,' I thought to myself as I walked along the corridor of the Prime Minister's House to the lift which took me down. My apprehensions proved to be correct because when I went to attend the session at eleven o'clock next morning I was told that it was postponed. I was completely taken aback and went to the meeting room of the party to find out more details. I was told that there would be a party meeting at six o'clock that evening. There I strongly objected to the suggestion that the Assembly be prorogued. I reminded members that they had promised not to do this before completing the Constitution, and why were they going back on their word? Mr Nurul Amin, Chief Minister from East Pakistan, stood up and said that he had had the resolution passed regarding the Koran and Sunnah and that was enough for his election purposes! I was extremely upset and said, 'In that case I will resign from the Muslim League!' This caused a real commotion as it was an unheard of thing to do. Nawab Mushtaq Ahmed Gurmani came up to me and tried to dissuade me from taking such a drastic step. I thanked him but said that I could not be a party to such hypocrisy.

As the session of the Assembly was about to start, we all walked towards the Hall of the Assembly. The proceedings started and I objected. The matter was put to vote. There was a division with my solitary voice saying 'no' three times. My small voice, amplified by the microphone resounded in the large Hall of the Assembly. I was alone in my dissent. Mian Iftikharuddin and Sardar Shaukat Hayat Khan were the ones who used to ask for and get a division and who used to voice their dissent were absent so I was alone—it was my finest hour. After voting I gave a brief speech and announced my resignation from the Muslim League (see Appendix 4). Mr Nurul Amin sarcastically criticized my decision and suggested that if I disagreed with the policy of the Muslim League, why did I confine myself to resigning from the Party, why did I not resign from the seat. But I was not going to do that. I intended to be a thorn in their side, to be a lone voice of dissent among the 'yes men'. But I was not to get that satisfaction for long.

In one of my speeches made in the Assembly—which unfortunately turned out to be prophetic—I had said that by delaying the framing of the Constitution in this manner we were betraying a trust, and if we continued to do so we would ignominiously be turned out (see Appendix 3). This is exactly what happened. I resigned on 14 November 1953 and the Governor-General, Mr Ghulam Muhammad dismissed the Assembly on 24 October 1955.

Maulvi Tamizuddin Khan, the President of the Constituent Assembly, presented a writ petition in the Sindh High Court against this action of the Governor-General. Sir George Constantine upheld the objection and gave a decision against the Governor-General's action. Mr Ghulam Muhammad appealed against this decision to the Supreme Court. Justice Munir, Chief Justice of the Supreme Court, upheld Mr Ghulam Muhammad's decision, justifying it under 'doctrine of necessity'. Justice Cornelius, who was one of the judges of the Supreme Court, disagreed with this decision. He did not confine himself merely to a verbal disagreement but had the courage to write a note of dissent of several pages explaining his reasons. These pages will remain in the history of the judiciary as a testimony to the courage of one man to save the reputation of the Pakistan's Judiciary and democratic practice.

I feel sad, in fact ashamed that the honour of the Judiciary was upheld in both the cases by non-Muslims, in the Sindh High Court in the first case by an Englishman, Sir George Constantine and in the second in the Supreme Court by Justice Cornelius, a Pakistani Christian who showed extraordinary courage in taking this action. Justice Munir though upholding the decision of the Governor-General however ordered that the Constituent Assembly should be re-elected. This was a lame effort to save the judiciary from the impression of complete subservience.

After nine years of independence, in 1955 we went back to square one. We not only did not have a constitution but we had to re-elect the Constituent Assembly afresh. The Electoral Colleges once again acted as the provincial legislature. But their composition was now different to that in 1947, both numerically and otherwise. The members of the Constituent Assembly were now numbered eighty instead of the original seventy-nine, the task of drawing up the Constitution began all over again.

CHAPTER 23

ELEVENTH SESSION OF THE UN (1956)

After my resignation I returned to Paris where my husband had been posted. After a stay of a little more than a year in France we were transferred to London. It was while we were in London that I was once again sent as a delegate to the UN. Its sessions were now being held regularly in New York.

My cousin Shaheed Suhrawardy had become the Prime Minister (he was to remain in this office for barely thirteen months). He had decided to take the question of Kashmir to the UN which had become moribund, and had been in cold storage for four and a half years. Therefore it would take not only some time but a great deal of political manoeuvring to revive it and get the support and attention from the members of the UN. The time was particularly inauspicious as the interest of the world was wholly and totally focused on the important questions of Suez and Hungary.

How fate favoured us, and how by sheer chance the question of Kashmir was able to hit the headlines I shall recount later. Sir Feroze Khan Noon the Foreign Minister was the leader of the delegation. I was appointed Deputy leader and was told that I would have to take over as the leader after the departure of the Foreign Minister. I felt awed but also thrilled to have the opportunity to deal with this most momentous question for my country. It made me overcome my initial reluctance to again enter the arena of politics, and I accepted the offer.

There were about nineteen members in the Pakistan delegation and they seemed rather a mixed lot. I did not realize how intractable and uncooperative most of them would prove to be. I had great difficulty in keeping discipline, and getting them to accept my authority. I expect that is what every woman faces when she finds herself in a position of authority over men.

In the months immediately preceding the 1956 session of the UN there had been two international crises. The crisis now referred to as the Suez Crisis, and the invasion of Hungary by Russia. These two questions dominated the entire session and was the subject of discussions, debates and acrimonous exchanges between the two great powers, the USA and Russia—it was full-fledged Cold War.

The Suez Crisis can be considered as Great Britain's last effort at gun-boat diplomacy. It ended in a fiasco for a number of reasons. The chief of these being the fact that the United States, Britain's greatest ally, did not support her in this venture. Not only did it not support Britain, but actively opposed it by moving a resolution in the Security Council asking that Britain and France withdraw their forces from the area. The Security Council was convened at the instance of Britain and France who were allies in this venture. The United States moved a resolution condemning the action of its allies and asked for the withdrawal of the British and French forces that had landed, and were landing in the Suez Canal area. Though this was a terrific blow to the *amour propre* of the British they complied and withdrew their forces from the Canal-Zone in Egypt. This, described as a great victory of the United Nations, can also be called the death knell of British Imperialism.

The atmosphere in the United Nations was electric, the tension in it was further heightened by the invasion of Hungary by Russia. Hungary, like other countries which came to be known as eastern Europe, had been under Russian domination after the Second World War. This was the beginning of what came to be known as the Cold War.

Hungary had made an effort to break the shackles of Russian control and rid itself of communism. Their feeble but heroic effort failed by a massive invasion of Russia and the rising was crushed with great ruthlessness. This having taken place immediately after Suez became a touchstone for the UN as to how it dealt with aggression.

The Security Council meetings were called, and the usual procedure of framing a resolution condemning aggression and asking for the withdrawal of invading forces was tabled. It could not be passed because Russia as a permanent member of the Security Council had the right of veto which it exercised, much to the chagrin of the United States. There was one other method to stop aggression or rather to condemn it and that was known as 'Uniting for Peace'. This was when all the member nations of the UN joined together to condemn an act of unprovoked or unjustified aggression, but this option could not be exercised either, for it to be mandatory, it had to have two-third majority and this was not possible, particularly after the Swiss Crisis which had ruffled the feathers of most of the non-European countries and they were not likely to join hands with the UN and the West in condemning Russia, no matter how flagrantly it may have defied the UN.

Delegates of country after country came to the forum and made a speech. Though the purpose was to present a résumé of their country's achievement during the year under review, their speeches, inevitably, slanted in favour of one or the other of the great powers—United States or Russia. Each side made out that they were the great champions of justice and wanted to condemn the other side for their aggression. Much heat was generated and the speeches on both sides were fiery and eloquent.

Each delegation sat together in the seats reserved for its members, we were in the front row. I sat next to the Foreign Minister, Sir Feroze Khan Noon and listened to the outpouring of nations on both sides of the divide. Each of them expressing the righteous indignation and horror at the tampering of the rights of smaller countries in defiance of the ruling of the United Nations. But nobody mentioned Kashmir! These exponents of human rights, the defenders of freedom and the right of self-determination etc. did not remember that there was a small country called Kashmir where each of the values, these men championed had been trampled upon. I listened with mounting anger. I knew that this was only the preliminary session where the member nations were supposed to present a résumé of their country's achievement during the past year. But they were using this occasion to voice their sentiments regarding the crisis of Suez and Hungary. Could we not also intervene and bring Kashmir to the notice of the assembled nations? I could not bear to remain silent any longer. I asked Sir Feroze Khan Noon to permit me to say something about the Kashmir issue, he very graciously agreed. I will always be profoundly grateful to him for the generosity in giving me this chance for had he not done so I would not have been able to make the impact that I did. Having got the permission I went over to the rostrum and said:

> ...We are opposed to the last ditch stand of the waning imperialism of Europe and are equally determined to oppose the nascent rise of imperialism in Asia....

I expressed shock at Britain being one of the aggressors since it was one of the foremost countries working for,

> a new morality in international affairs and which had so gracefully accepted the liquidation of an empire and welcomed, instead, a free cooperative of like-minded nations which is the Commonwealth.

It was, therefore, in Britain's own interest

> ...that their unfortunate reversion to imperialist tactics be rectified immediately and they together with France and Israel withdraw their troops forthwith from Egypt.

The UN would lose its new found strength if its resolutions were not complied with... Time has come when it must make it clear that Security Council resolutions are not mere pious declarations, but must be obeyed and applied without fear or favour...

Pakistan sponsored the resolutions because it was against foreign troops or troops of occupation anywhere under any pretext by anybody.

I ended my brief speech by saying,

We condemn aggression and oppression equally in Egypt and in Hungary, in Algeria and in Kashmir.

I walked back to my seat amidst a thunderous applause.

After this I sat glued to my seat expecting a retort, from India's delegation. I had been long enough in the United Nations to have heard that V.K. Krishna Menon made mincemeat of anyone daring to contradict or even disagree with him, but nothing happened! I sat day after day in my seat in the Assembly Chambers not daring to go even for a cup of coffee in case Menon may say something in reply to my provocative remarks. What I did not know was that he always made the valedictory speech, in which he settled all outstanding scores. Several days passed. Sir Feroze Khan Noon went back to Pakistan and I took over the leadership of the delegation. This meant that I had to keep myself apprised of what was happening in other Committees and could not be in the General Assembly all the time.

I was asked by the Fifth Committee to settle a point, having done that I went to the Delegates' Lounge to dictate a note. The stenographer Mr Razaullah began preparing to take down the dictation, he said *en passent*—'It is a pity, you were not in the General Assembly for Menon has been speaking and has just attacked Pakistan'.

'What!' said I. 'Menon has been speaking! What did he say?'

ELEVENTH SESSION OF THE UN (1956)

'Oh he has been speaking for some time and said the usual things against Pakistan,' Mr Razaullah replied.

'I must go immediately', I said and got up to leave.

'Oh he has been speaking for some time and must have finished by now,' said Mr Razaullah. But ignoring this I continued with as much speed as I could muster with dignity, reached one of the side-doors, and opening it I saw that Menon was still speaking! I went straight to the table of the Secretary who takes the names of the speakers, to give my name.

'There is no more time,' said the girl at the table. 'It is lunch break now, and the President has already declared a closure.' I made my way back to my seat feeling very angry and dejected. I sat down and listened to the venomous outpouring of Menon against Pakistan. I could bear it no longer, 'I must do something,' I told myself. 'There must be some way of replying to these vilifications.'

I got up and went to the Secretary and said, 'I absolutely insist that you send my name to the Chairman'.

'All right! All right!' said the girl, 'Don't get so excited, Portugal is also insisting on his right of reply, so the closure has been withdrawn, you will also get a chance.' I came back to my seat much relieved. By this time most of the members of my delegation were back, and Mr Chhatari who was my adviser, bent over my chair and tried giving me some points which might be of use.

'Please Mr Chhatari' said I, 'I cannot at this time take any briefing. Please let me handle it the best I can.' He kindly agreed and sat back. It seemed that Menon would never finish; after him came the Portuguese. If not as long winded as Menon, he seemed to me long enough. At last my turn came and I went up to the dais with trembling feet and with my heart in my mouth. I am never very long in my replies. This was a plus point for me and was a welcome change after Menon but he being master of procedure, asked under some rule or other, 'the right of reply,' the President agreed reluctantly. 'Please be brief, I am hungry.'

Menon went up to the dais, of course he was constitutionally unable to be brief, but he was comparatively short. He repeated further blatantly untrue charges against Pakistan.

I sent a note to the President requesting him to give me just three minutes, and I assured him that I would not exceed my time! The Prince Wan graciously gave me the time I required. I went up, made my point in just two and a half minutes as I had said and came back to my seat, amidst loud applause.

The President then declared the session closed. Menon made another dash to get to the rostrum but Prince Wan said, 'The lady has the last word', and struck the gavel three times.

The house got up amidst laughter. Menon said to the President, 'You were hungry when I wanted to speak but it seems a lady's voice can assuage hunger and thirst.' (*See* Appendix 5)

Chapter 24

THE YEARS IN MOROCCO

The years in Morocco seem like a golden dream to me. I went there during a very sad period of my life but the charm of Morocco, the kindness and friendliness of its people, and the fact that there was a job to be done prevented me from sinking into apathy. Yes, I have to be grateful for the years in Morocco.

I had come back from England after dealing with a myriad of problems that seemed to have cropped up in the wake of my husband's death. I had also been quite ill and had to undergo a serious operation for a thyroid condition. On my return home there were still more problems to face: income tax arrears, death duties, etc. So far I had been lucky as my husband kept me completely sheltered from the mechanics of day to day living. With him gone, I now found them overwhelming. On coming back home after dealing with one such problem, I was told that there had been a call from the Foreign Secretary and would I call him back. 'I wonder what he wants,' I thought to myself as I dialled the number. I got his PA who asked me to visit his office the next morning at 10.00 which I did.

Establishing the Foreign Office from scratch was not an easy job as my husband Mohammad Ikramullah, the first Foreign Secretary of Pakistan, found out. There were literally not even any typewriters or stationery, and the first thing he did was to send one of the clerks to purchase these. The first telegrams to Heads of States—thanking them for their felicitous messages—were sent sitting on packing cases as there were no chairs or tables. The making of Pakistan's

Foreign Service was my husband's contribution towards the building of Pakistan and he was very proud of it.

Mr Aziz Ahmed, the Foreign Secretary, greeted me formally. He told me that the Government had decided to offer me the ambassadorship of Ceylon, and asked me how soon I would be ready to take it up. The question whether I would want it or not had not occurred to him. I told him that I had a great number of things to deal with after my husband's death and, therefore, could not think of leaving the country for sometime. Mr Ahmed seemed to be taken aback and repeated the Government's decision and suggested that I should accept the offer. I said that I would think it over.

The next morning I went to see him and informed him that I was not prepared to leave the country just yet, and also that I was not very keen on the post offered. However, if later there was a chance of going to a Muslim country I would be interested. I mentioned Jordan and Morocco as the two Muslim countries I would like to go to. Both were monarchies and I am a monarchist.

Mr Aziz Ahmed replied, rather brusquely, that somebody had already been appointed to Morocco and the Foreign Office was not thinking of opening an embassy in Jordan, yet. I said rather nonchalantly, 'I myself am not prepared to leave the country at the moment but if and when one of these countries becomes available I would be prepared to consider it'. After this I left and thought to myself, 'This is the end of that'.

A few days later I was called to the President's House. President Ayub Khan met me with great courtesy. He spoke for sometime reminiscing about my husband, his devotion to duty and his working tirelessly even when his health was visibly failing.

'I told him not to come on that last trip for it was a very strenuous one but he insisted on coming,' he said.

'That was typical of him,' I said.

We talked for a little while in this strain, and then he asked me: 'Why did you refuse to go to Ceylon as an ambassador?' 'You should try to use your talents to serve your country,' he added.

'I did not refuse completely,' I replied. 'I did tell Mr Aziz Ahmed that I was prepared to consider the offer for a Muslim country'. I repeated what I had said to Mr Ahmed and his reply. I was amazed when the President said, 'You can have Morocco if that's what you want'.

'But Mr Ahmed said it has been promised to someone else,' I said.

'He has promised it. I have not,' was the reply.

'Who is it?' I had the temerity to ask. The President told me it was someone from East Pakistan, I knew him, a very decent person.

'But he will cut no ice in Morocco,' I said.

'No, he will not and you will,' he said as he rose from his seat signifying that the meeting was over.

On returning home, I found a message a waiting for me: I was supposed to go and see the Foreign Secretary. I did. Mr Aziz Ahmed was standing near the fireplace. He said with suppressed irritation, 'The President wants you to go to Morocco, when can you leave?'

'But I told you I cannot leave for sometime,' I replied.

'But we have to have an ambassador in Morocco immediately as Morocco is one of the non-official countries that have been selected for the membership of the Security Council this year, and we want their support for Kashmir.'

I could see the importance of the point. Also, that I could have a country of my choice and have it when I wanted it. But going immediately was impossible and I said so to Mr Ahmed.

'I cannot leave before my husband's *barsi*'.

'When can you leave then?' he asked. I thought very quickly, a year would be completed on 12 September, I said, '12th of October'.

'Right!' said Mr Ahmed, but not a day later, he almost seemed to imply by the manner of his acceptance.

I could understand his chagrin. It was not every day that someone is offered an ambassadorship, which is turned down because the country does not interest her particularly! and because she is not prepared to leave immediately. Then she gets the country of her choice and she is still reluctant about leaving! I realized a compromise had to be made, and I did so in the matter of timing but it was a great strain having to do so.

* * *

I arrived in Morocco on 15 or 16 of October after having stopped for a day in Paris. There was no direct flight at that time from Karachi to Rabat. I stayed in Paris with our Ambassador Mr J.A. Rahim who was a cousin of mine. I was pleased to see how well his wife had done up the ramshackle embassy that we had inherited.

Within a week of my arrival I was informed that His Majesty the King of Morocco was pleased to allow me to present my credentials immediately. This was a great privilege, but how much of a privilege it was I only realized after I had been in Morocco for sometime. I saw that ambassadors had to wait for weeks, sometimes for a month or more before being received by His Majesty. It was a privilege to be allowed to present one's credentials as soon as possible, because till this was done one could not participate in any diplomatic activity.

The presenting of credentials was a very formal affair, for Morocco was not only a monarchy but a monarchy that went back to several hundred years, and which had maintained all its picturesque traditions. Earlier, the ambassadors used to go in a coach of four to present their credentials to the King. I was sorry that practice had been discontinued just before my arrival. I went in a large and impressive saloon car accompanied by the Protocol Officer.

A motorcade followed us which comprised of my First Secretary with a protocol officer, my daughters Naz and Sarvath, and various other functionaries.

The motorcade arrived at the Palace Gate; there I was presented with an Honour Guard, who were very impressive in their colourful uniforms. Music was being played as I inspected them. At the conclusion of the inspection I proceeded towards the entrance to the Palace.

I entered a vast hall, at the end of which there was a dais, on which there was an ornate chair on which the King sat. I slowly proceeded towards the dais, stopping whenever indicated by the Protocol Officer for bowing low in salutation—I think I repeated this three times before I reached the foot of the dais. I then climbed the steps and stood facing the King, who very graciously got up to receive me.

I presented my credentials, and His Majesty very kindly directed me to sit down on the vacant chair next to him. He talked to me through an interpreter and said how pleased he was to welcome me and hoped that during my term of office the ties of friendship between our two countries would be further strengthened. He was also kind enough to say that I could approach him freely at any time. After a few minutes I got up, bowed and took his leave. Protocol demanded that I do not turn my back to the King, therefore, I had to negotiate the steps of the dais walking backwards and had to do this for the whole length of the hall stopping in between to do my salutations!

The hall was divided in a split-level right in the middle and I was stopped from falling by the presence of mind of the Protocol Officer who took my arm. I finally got to the end of the hall, made a final salutation, stepped out, and the door closed behind me. Now I could turn my back and proceed to where my car was standing.

I got into the car and it drove back to my house. My daughters, who did not come by the longer route, were at the gate to greet us. As tea was ready I asked the Protocol

Officer and the other attendants to join me in having some refreshments. After some polite conversation they left.

I was now the accredited Ambassador of Pakistan to the Court of His Majesty Hassan Thani of Morocco.

* * *

After a week or so of presenting my credentials, I received an invitation to attend the wedding reception of the King's third sister Lalla Nezha. I had met her in London where she was staying with her aunt, Lalla Fatimah Zahra, the wife of the Ambassador of Morocco. I was therefore very pleased to be present on the occasion of her wedding.

It was an afternoon reception but even so the glitter and glamour was dazzling and it looked like a fairyland. I arrived at the entrance to the Palace and from there was conducted to the ladies section of the Palace. Here I was greeted by His Majesty's mother, Lalla Abla. She was a real personality and had had much influence during the reign of her husband Sultan Mohammed V, and continued to do so during the reign of her son. I had met her once before the wedding when I had come to the Palace to give presents to the Queen and the Princesses. The Queen Mother was gracious and though the language barrier prevented a proper conversation, I could still appreciate her kindness and sense the quality of her intelligence from the questions she asked through the interpreter. Lalla Latifa, the King's wife was young and pretty, she was very fair as she was a Berber. The King had married into the Berber clan for political reasons. She had a daughter and a son, and her two other daughters were born whilst I was in Morocco. I had the unique honour and pleasure of attending the *Tasmiyah* of her third daughter.

It was a royal custom that on the occasion of the wedding of a prince or princess half a dozen or more young girls from good families in straitened circumstances were also married at the royal expense. So Princess Nezah sat at the centre of the long gallery, flanked by half a dozen other brides. The guests sat facing them.

The Moroccan ladies unlike the Arab ladies in the Middle East, and those of Iran and Turkey had not given up their national costumes. They wore a long dress which was called a caftan which had wide sleeves falling well over the wrists. The folds of the dress was gathered together at the waist by a fabulous jewelled belt. This piece of jewellery was really dazzling. When worn by aristocratic ladies it would be of gold, studded with precious stones of various shapes. Those who could not afford gold and jewelled belts still had beautiful ones embroidered in gold and silver threads. It was the *piece-de-resistance* of their ensemble. Besides this they wore beautiful necklaces, bracelets, and jewelled head pieces. The effect was dazzling, eyes could not take it all in.

I was taken to Princess Nezah who recognized me and expressed her pleasure to see me again. We were served tea in the Moroccan manner. Yes, making and serving tea was a ceremony itself but I shall speak of it later. After tea, we were asked to come and help ourselves to the refreshments. We went into another large room where the tables were laden with sweets and pastries in silver dishes. Besides Corn-de-Gazelle there were other Moroccan and French pastries. We helped ourselves to a few and sipped some more tea. Ladies were chattering like birds in a gilded cage. Alas, I could not understand or join in the conversation but I smiled and they smiled back expressing what I could guess as friendly greetings. They admired my saree and I returned the compliment. There was an atmosphere of goodwill and enjoyment. Goodwill can get across even without the aid of words. His Excellency Mr Balafrej was later to call it *Lughat-e-Qaloob*, 'The Language of the Heart'. This was to take me through my three years in Morocco.

After the ladies had their fill of chattering and admiring each other, brides began leaving for their new homes with the blessings of the King and a dowry fit for a princess. This was my first introduction to a palatial function. I was lucky enough to attend several more such functions during my stay in Morocco. I found everything fascinating and colourful. This was a sortie into another world, a glimpse into a fairy tale land. It never ceased to fascinate me. I loved reading about our past, the grandeur of Akbar, the splendour of Shahjehan, the glamour of Noorjehan and the beauty of Mumtaz Mahal. I read about them and felt a great sadness that it was all over in my country. I was fortunate to have had a glimpse of it in this wondrous world of Morocco.

* * *

Serving of tea on all occasions is a Moroccan custom and it is made with much ceremony. Though it is also made by official tea-makers it is to be seen at its best advantage when made by the lady of the house.

She sits herself comfortably on a low seat, the utensils and the ingredients necessary for making tea are brought one by one by the maids. The first to be brought is a small samovar which is placed near the lady. Then one or two silver trays with stands are brought and placed before her. On these trays are small, jewel-coloured crystal glasses, the tea-pot, several silver bowls, and boxes containing tea, sugar and fresh mint.

Now the process of making the tea begins: the lady tests the water by delicately putting her fingers on the samovar, having ascertained that it's right, she opens the samovar tap into the tea-pot to which tea has already been added. When the tea-pot is full, she removes it to the tray and lets it brew for sometime. A spray of mint is added for flavour. Before serving it to the guests she tastes it herself. She does this by pouring tea into a tall funnel-shaped glass, which she sips delicately; satisfied that the strength and aroma are right, she then serves the tea to the various guests one by one, who take a few sips and then return their glasses for a re-fill. The tea is made afresh, and the process is repeated at least three times. It is considered impolite to refuse after the first glass. The whole process is carried out in a leisurely manner with much grace.

Much has been written about the Japanese tea ceremony but I feel that the Moroccan tea ceremony is even more colourful, but since it takes place behind the veil it is not known to the West. Otherwise I am sure it would have caught their imagination and would have been written about.

* * *

I was fortunate that when I went as Ambassador to Morocco the men who had been prominent in the struggle to free her from the French Protectorate were still at the helm of affairs. They had suffered imprisonment and exile and therefore were looked up to as heroes by the nation. The most venerable and distinguished amongst this galaxy was Siddi Mameri.

Siddi Mameri had been King Mohammad V's tutor and was regarded with great respect and reverence by Hassan Thani himself and, of course, by all the people. He was designated as the Minister of the Household. It did not entail any specific duties except that he was present at important ceremonial occasions as when ambassadors presented their credentials.

I had the honour of his presence on the occasion of presenting my credentials. Siddi Mameri always wore a white cloak and hood over a white robe which is the traditional Moroccan dress. Though I met him on several occasions after the presentation, I did not have the courage to invite him to my house till he himself said so. It was when I was at the airport to receive the King who was returning from a foreign visit. There Siddi Mameri said to me, 'You invite my colleagues to your house but you have not invited me yet'. I did not know what to say. I murmured something like, 'It would be an honour to do so'.

On returning home I sent a formal invitation to Siddi Mameri suggesting that he choose a day when he should honour me by coming to my house. I received a prompt reply giving a day for lunch as he did not go out to dinner, he explained. After he had been to my house, the ice was broken and he often invited Sarvath and me for tea. These occasions will remain in my mind forever. Siddi Mameri was a walking history of Morocco and when he talked about events, it was like turning the pages of a history book. Realizing my ignorance of Arabic language, he spoke in French which I could understand but could not speak. Sarvath used to speak for both of us. He became very fond of her and when we were leaving for Pakistan, he presented her a beautiful hand-woven material with the beautiful words *May you wear it for many years and in great happiness.*

Mr Allal-Al-Fasi was the most prominent leader of the Istiqlal Party and was regarded with great respect and awe. He had not accepted any position in the government but his influence was greater than any one in it. He stood for complete independence from France. This had been achieved, but he felt there was still too much influence and deference towards the French. This opinion was shared both by the old as well as the younger generation. I remember an incident which showed the great respect Allal-Al-Fasi was held in. It was at a reception: there was suddenly a hush, then people stepped back, forming a passage, through it Allal-Al-Fasi came walking, with people standing on each side bowing their heads in reverence and greetings. I saw a similar scene in England on the occasion of one of the Queen's Garden Party. There also fell a similar hush and a passage formed through which Sir Winston Churchill came wallking. It is not given to many men to achieve such deference in their life time.

Ahmed Balafrej was honoured as much as Allal-Al-Fasi and had as distinguished a record of struggle for his country's cause and freedom. He had become Morocco's first Prime Minister and now his designation was The Personal Representative of His Majesty the King. He was an eminently civilized person and everything about him reflected his innate culture. He had a tastefully furnished home, his table serving the best of Moroccan and French food in European style which even Europeans might envy. Mr Balafrej's house was quite near to mine and I had the honour of coming to know his family quite well. Sarvath and his daughter, Mai, became great friends. On many occasions I went to his beautiful house, sat in his garden and talked to him. But my respect for him would not let me talk to him easily, that is informally. This has happened to me only with three people in my whole life—Quaid-i-Azam, Ahmed Balafrej, and Queen Zein El Sharaf of Jordan. I much regret this as I could have learnt so much from them.

Besides these national heroes the officials cadre was also a very distinguished one. The Minister for Religious Affairs was Mr Bargash about whom Rom Landau has rightly said, 'The office was honoured by him and not he by the office'. The Chief of Police, Mr Laghzaoui had a glamour which is not generally associated with someone holding this post. His daughter Aisha and his wife were two of the most elegant ladies of distinction in Moroccan society.

Such was the Morocco of my time but there were premonitions that all was not well. There had already been the incident connected with Ben-Barka and a little while after I left, I heard of a conspiracy involving an officer who was one of the most trusted persons in the King's Council. I however continue to remember my Moroccan period as golden.

The diplomatic corps in Rabat was very polished and urbane as was expected in a country that was a monarchy, and was as sophisticated as Morocco. I was treated with great courtesy by all my colleagues and became friends with most of them. I am still in touch with some of them. The first couple who met me at the airport and became close friends were Mr and Mrs Sulaiman Dhajani, First Secretary in the Jordan Embassy, who acted as Charge-de-Affaires after my stay. He was a born conversationalist. I enjoyed talking to him and learned a great deal of Arab history and politics from him. The other young couples who became close friends and remained so were William and Virginia Crawford. He was the political advisor to the American Embassy. His knowledge of current affairs and assessment of events was as good as Sulaiman's knowledge of Arabic politics and talking to both of them gave me a good understanding of events.

* * *

I feel I must say something about the administrative side of my job. I do not know of what use this would be to the readers, nor can I say that my experience is necessarily the same as of other women who have been in positions of authority over men. But I still want to tell about my own experience for whatever it is worth.

When I have to answer the question, 'What was it like in Morocco?' and I have to answer in one sentence, I say that the Government of Morocco gave me the courtesy due to a woman, and the seriousness due to a man. I have spoken at length about the courtesy and consideration shown to me. I will now say something about the work involved.

There are two instances which will illustrate this. One was in 1965 when we were at war with India. There was a conference of the Arab Muslim countries being held at exactly the same time in Casablanca, Morocco's largest commercial city. I thought this was a good opportunity to get the support not only of Morocco but of the other Muslim countries as well. I went and saw Mr Benjelloun, the Foreign Secretary, who had also been an Ambassador to Pakistan and was favourably inclined towards us, and was aware of the dispute over Kashmir. I asked him if the Government of Morocco would present a resolution at the Arab Conference condemning India's aggression in Kashmir. He was sympathetic and promised to try and do what he could.

The conference, as far as I remember, was held for a week and on the second or third day there was a resolution expressing regret at the war between India and Pakistan, and asking both the countries to desist from it. I read this in the papers and felt it was not good enough. I rang up Mr Benjelloun who explained that it was not possible to pass a more strongly worded resolution as some Arab countries, attending the conference, were friendly towards India. I then decided to go to Casablanca to try and make our case known to the delegates of the conference. I also tried to get the Moroccan Press' support.

In Casablanca I stayed in Hotel Memonia where most of the delegates were staying. I wrote a brief résumé on our case in Kashmir and asked the delegates of the conference to support us. In it I also mentioned the invasion of the Indian army in the past—supported by the British Governor-General—which had lost us Kashmir in the first place and now Lahore, the very heart of Pakistan, was being threatened. I added by saying that in our small way we had always helped and sided with the Muslim countries in their problems. Some of these Muslim countries were the participants of the conference. I reminded them the *ayat* of the Koran which said the only reward for *Ehsan* is *Ehsan* in return.

I talked to Mr Ghalab the editor of the *Alam* one of the most prestigious Arab papers not only in Morocco, but in the Arabic speaking world. Mr Ghalab was a member of the Istiqlal Party and in his youth an active worker in trying to free Morocco from the French shackles. I also knew the editor of the Moroccan English newspaper *The Nation* and sent my article to him also. Both the papers published my article, and what is more, through their editorials supported me. It said that Morocco should now support Pakistan in her hour of need.

The conference was coming to an end and I wanted a strong resolution to be passed. So I tried to contact Mr Ahmed Balafrej to whom the Government of Pakistan had given a Pakistani passport so that he could attend the United Nations' sessions, and sit with the Pakistani delegation to advocate the cause of his country. I succeeded in meeting him before the last day of the conference. I did not have to labour my point to him. Mr Balafrej agreed that this was the time to pay back the debt.

Next morning, before the concluding session of the conference, the resolution was passed unequivocally condemning India and asking it to withdraw from the territories of Pakistan that it had occupied. India's Ambassador was furious and called on the Moroccan Foreign Office to protest. Initially, his protest on the attitude of the Press had been given the bland reply: 'The Press is free in our country. We are Muslims and so is Pakistan. We cannot stop our Press from expressing its sympathies towards Pakistan'. Similarly about the resolution it was said that it was the united decision of the thirteen participant countries! But I knew and India knew that it was due to the personal support of only one person—Ahmed Balafrej—that this resolution had been passed. Needless to say it gave me great satisfaction and my prestige among my colleagues went up!

The other incident was the reverse of the coin. I to this day have not been able to understand why my government took the unnecessary decision to recognize Mauritania. It was a territory that Morocco claimed but France held on to. For the Government of Pakistan to recognize it, so soon after Moroccan support to us in our case of Kashmir, was not only unnecessary but an ungracious act. I was barely given any notice that this action was being contemplated but as soon as I got an intimation of it, I wrote with all the force at my command asking the government to desist from it. I suggested that even if Pakistan meant to recognize Mauritania we could wait till some other countries, who were also considering such an action, did so. But my suggestion was not taken any notice of. Pakistan's recognition of Mauritania was like a bombshell.

Mr Cherkaoui, the Foreign Minister, sent for me. After greeting me he asked me to sit down.

'We know your feelings towards Morocco, but your government without any notice or warning to us has recognized Mauritania', he said. Then he gave it to me straight from the shoulder and did not mince his words. He said that he was shocked by the fact that no prior warning had been given.

'I was having lunch with your Foreign Minister last week in New York and he did not do so much as hint at this'. He then went on to remind me of the close ties between our countries, and of the support Morocco gave in the case of Kashmir. He spoke to me as he would speak to a man and asked me to please convey his extreme chagrin and disappointment.

Shattered though I was at this encounter, I was still pleased that he did not take the attitude, 'Oh poor little woman she will not understand'. Instead he spoke to me as he would to a man. This incident cast a pall of gloom over me and for a while I went about in a daze. The courtesy and kindness of the Foreign Office and the attitude of my colleagues did not change. They were seasoned diplomats and knew that such things happen in diplomatic life.

Soon there was an interesting event. Lalla Aisha, the second sister of the King, was appointed Morocco's Ambassador to the Court of St. James. There was a ripple of surprise, a traditional country like Morocco had not only accepted a woman ambassador but was now sending one to England itself. I asked Lalla Aisha if she would do me the honour by having dinner at my house before taking up her appointment in London. She kindly agreed.

I made the occasion as colourful and traditional as I could. Lalla Aisha was received at the door by Sarvath with a beautiful gold-embroidered garland and presented with a bouquet of flowers. She was then taken to her seat where two girls presented her with *ittar* and anointed her fingers with it in the traditional manner. The dinner was Pakistani and as elaborate as I could make it, after which I made a brief speech to which she replied, thanking me. When I said good bye to her I tied an *imam zamin* on her arm. She found this gesture interesting, and appreciated it very much.

* * *

Happy days pass by very quickly. Soon it was time for me to return to Pakistan. Leave-taking was as formal as the presenting of credentials had been, except that there was an element of sadness in it for me. His Majesty was most gracious and through the interpreter expressed approval of my work. After a few minutes, I bowed and took my leave and had almost reached the door when the Protocol Officer came running. He said, 'His Majesty has inquired when exactly are you leaving?'

'In three days time,' I replied.

'If you can stay for a week His Majesty would like you to attend the *Tasmiyah* ceremony of his newly born daughter,' said the Protocol Officer.

'I will be honoured to do so,' I replied.

I got home and told Sarvath about it. We were both very pleased that we were to have another glimpse of the colourful ceremony of Morocco.

The next day I received a formal invitation to attend the *Tasmiyah* ceremony. The invitation was for the whole day beginning at 9 a.m. Sarvath and I presented ourselves at the Palace entrance at the required time. We were received as usual with great courtesy by Lalla Abla and taken through many corridors to a large room opening into a still larger courtyard. There were rooms on either side of the courtyard as well. The walls of the room, the arches, and the floor of the courtyard were inlaid with blue and white tiles; huge chandeliers suspended from the ceiling looked most effective, glistening as they caught the shaft of sunlight. There were dozens and dozens of beautiful ladies in gorgeous apparel. It was like a page out of the Arabian Nights. The older ladies had much grace and dignity as they sat on the banquettes while the younger ones frittered about. There was a large platform in the middle of the room covered with a gold-embroidered velvet carpet. A golden throne, obviously for the King, was placed on it. After we sat down at one of the banquettes, tea was served. Every now and then one of the ladies would come, smile, sit with us, and try to make polite conversation. I also would say a few words of thanks and appreciation but most of it was smiles and expressions of pleasure. After sometime we got up and explored our beautiful surroundings.

About midday lunch was served. A round table was placed before us around which were placed half a dozen cushions. As usual pastilla was brought and put right in the middle of the table. Pastilla is the typical Moroccan dish. It is made of several layers of pastry, each layer has sweet almond paste, pigeon, eggs and herbs between it. After we had finished, another dish was placed before us. It is impossible to say how many dishes there were on the occasion (even for ordinary dinners there used to be six to seven chicken and fish dishes) at the end of which, the typical Moroccan dish known as couscous was served. Food in Morocco was always eaten with one's fingers, as in Pakistan and India. The dish from which it is served is a communal dish, each person takes his share on his own plate or makes a portion in the main dish. It is done extremely neatly, keeping to one's own portion of the dish. Having the food in a communal dish is probably reminiscent of the Bedouin days when food was scarce, and whatever was available was put before everybody to help themselves accordingly.

After the meal was over our hands were washed in a beautiful inlaid ewer. After we had dried our hands rosewater was generously poured over them. We were so satiated that we could hardly move and sat around in a comatose condition.

The King then made his appearance. He mounted the dais and sat on the golden throne. Various members of the royal family sat round the dais. After about an hour, he got up and left. He must have gone for about five minutes or so when one of the fairy-like young ladies came and gestured to me to follow her which I did. She led me to a room where the King was waiting. I made my salutation and he said, 'I am very glad you could stay for the ceremony. I want you to know that you can always contact me for anything you want, or need'. I was deeply touched and expressed my gratitude. After which I finally took my leave of King Hassan Thani of Morocco—carrying with me memories of his great kindness and courtesy. I find it very difficult to believe when people talk about his arrogance. He certainly had not given me that impression.

* * *

The account of my time in Morocco would be incomplete without some mention of the help and support of my youngest daughter Sarvath. Salma was already married and settled in Dhaka. Inam and Naz had stayed back in Karachi. Sarvath (who was sixteen) had just finished her O levels and was the only one of my children who stayed with me in Morocco.

For the first year of my stay I kept her with me and arranged for her coaching—for A levels—through the kindness of the British Council. Though the teacher they provided was qualified enough and took great interest in her work, I felt she was not adequate for teaching A level subjects up to Cambridge standards which was Sarvath's goal. Therefore, I sent her back to England to stay with my friends Enid and Richard Davison who became her guardians and gave her much affection. She went to a proper tutorial—Bendixsons—as she had missed too much of the school to go back to Channing, her old school. During my second year in Morocco she stayed in London, coming back only for the holidays. During my third year she again stayed with me and prepared for her college entrance—more or less on her own—with the kind supervision of a retired English teacher.

The times Bitlum (Sarvath's pet name) was with me in Morocco she was of great help in running the house, managing the parties etc. In fact doing everything that falls to the lot of an ambassador's wife. Her most valuable contribution was that she made such an interesting circle of young friends. In this she was helped by my nephew Rashid who also spent his holidays with me. They made valuable contacts with the younger diplomats and with young members of distinguished Moroccan families. As it is in diplomatic life personal contact is of great value. Being singularly unequipped in my Embassy staff, Bitlum and Rashid's contribution was of inestimable value to me. How valuable was Bitlum's work can be judged by the fact that when I was leaving Morocco, not only was an additional toast drunk to her at my farewell parties but she also received almost as many farewell parties in her own right given by the young members of the Diplomatic Corps. The *épicerie* and flower shops paid their own tributes by giving her large bouquets of flowers. She received them graciously and expressed her thanks in an appropriate manner.

When she paid a visit to Rabat with her husband some six or seven years later, the flower shops still remembered the friendly girl who used to buy flowers from each of them, each time, so that no one should feel 'left out'. They were happy to see her again and it gave them much pleasure to see her in a new role as a Princess. They insisted on filling her car up with flowers, and were most offended when the accompanying Jordanian and Moroccan officials tried to pay them. That is the Morocco we remember with much warmth and affection.

APPENDIX 1

BEGUM IKRAMULLAH'S MAIDEN SPEECH AND NAWABZADA LIAQUAT ALI KHAN'S REPLY

24 February 1948

Begum Shaista Suhrawardy Ikramullah (East Bengal): Sir, I do not think that the practical difficulties of members travelling from Western Pakistan to Eastern Pakistan could be greater than that of the Eastern Pakistanis coming to the west, for their number is greater.

As regards administration and accommodation, I am not suggesting any remote village in Eastern Pakistan, but Dhaka which, I presume, has got sufficient arrangements to accommodate the House. Anyway, I think the psychological benefit far outweighs the practical difficulties. A feeling is growing among the Eastern Pakistanis that Eastern Pakistan is being neglected and treated merely as a 'colony' of Western Pakistan. We must do everything possible to eradicate this feeling. This narrow provincialism must be stopped. Justified or unjustified, we must not give any province a chance of feeling that it is neglected. I have lived many years with the Western Pakistanis and I feel that they are grossly ignorant of the people of Eastern Pakistan. I, therefore, think that at least once a year a meeting should be held in Eastern Pakistan. At the moment, we are faced with far too many difficulties. So let there be a meeting of this House only in Western Pakistan now; later on when it becomes a the Legislature only then let it meet at least once a year in Dhaka.

The Honourable Mr Liaquat Ali Khan (Prime Minister for Defence): I do not think there is any Honourable Member of this House who does not desire closer ties between the West and the East parts of Pakistan, but I am afraid this amendment, which has been moved, will not create those ties. As has been pointed out by Mr Tamizuddin Khan, there are, in fact, great practical difficulties. Begum Ikramullah has stated that it is easy to get over difficulties, I know that women never realize the difficulties, but I think those of my friends who have come from Eastern Bengal know fully well that the conditions in Dhaka at present are such that even the Eastern Bengal Government finds it difficult to function properly on account of the difficulties of accommodation and other problems of that kind. Apart from that, I think if my Honourable friends had read the rule carefully, those who had supported this amendment would have found that all that the rule says is that the business of the Assembly shall be conducted at Karachi, unless the President otherwise directs. So, therefore, it does not lay down that all the meetings of the Constituent Assembly and its Committees shall be held in Karachi and nowhere else. If it is considered necessary by the President, he can direct that such and such meeting will be held not in Karachi, but somewhere else; it may be Dhaka; it may be Peshawar; it may be Lahore; it may be any place. So, therefore, I would submit that we should not lay it down definitely that one meeting at least every year must necessarily be held in Dhaka.

Begum Ikramullah has stated that it is quite easy to move Government from one place to another. Sir, those who know what difficulties we had to experience in moving from Delhi to Karachi cannot support this contention of Begum Ikramullah that it is quite easy to move the Government from one centre to another. At least two months will be spent in this movement. The only safe and sure means of transport would be by sea. So, therefore, all your staff, all your files will be enjoying the sea air for two months—one month in going and one month in coming back—and during this period of two months the whole business of the Government will have to be suspended. It would not be expected that the business of Government would be carried on while on the high seas moving from one place to another. As I have stated, it is a wrong idea to have that because the meetings are held in a particular place, therefore the people of the State living in parts of the State are neglected. If the meetings of the parliament are held in one particular place, it does not mean that that particular place is given importance over other places in that State. It is only a matter of convenience. I submit, Sir, that it would be wrong to embody a rule to that effect that at least once a year a meeting of the Constituent Assembly must be held in Dhaka.

APPENDIX 2

BEGUM IKRAMULLAH'S SPEECHES REGARDING THE REHABILITATION OF THE ARTISANS AND CRAFTSMEN

2 March 1948

Mr Deputy President, Sir, Hitler made a psychological discovery when he said you tell a lie and keep telling it, people will believe it. We were told so often and by so many people that Pakistan cannot survive economically. American journalists told us, British Parliamentarians told us, Nationalist Muslims told us, till we began to almost believe it ourselves and this demon of doubt whispering in our ears has not been the least of many evils we have had to fight during these first six months after the birth of Pakistan. The most charitable of financial experts, the most optimistic of them gave us six months. By the Grace of God and the will of the people we have survived it and once a patient that has been given a bare six months survives, he usually lives to a ripe old age! The Honourable Finance Minister has been criticized by people for levying taxes on the common man. It has been suggested that he will resent these taxations? I humbly beg to differ. The common man is not likely to resent the taxations. He has made far greater and bigger sacrifices than these, when the History of Pakistan will come once to be written, this blood-red page of its History will be written in words of gold and the generations to come will value the freedom because it has been won by the greatest price a people can pay for it. But the common man does resent something and he resents it tremendously, resents it bitterly, it is not the taxes he might be asked to pay but the corruption that is prevailing in this State of Pakistan, which casts a slur on its otherwise brilliant record of endurance and sacrifices which is besmirching its fair name. Corruption came in during the war years, it is the legacy of the war years with its shortage of commodities, necessitating controls and permits. These have grown and taken on hideous proportions because during the last six months, the administrative machinery has been heavily burdened, because there has been chaos and unprecedented difficulty to cope with. Unfortunately some have seen in this the greatest tragedy that fell on their people, an opportunity to feather their nests. There is no word strong enough to condemn such despicable people, and I beg the Government to take action, strongest that they can take, the most comprehensive action that they can take, to root out this evil once and for all to do it speedily. We call our State 'Pakistan', it is an ambitious name and let us try to be worthy of it. Our public opinion is fully awake now, it was our public opinion that overthrew the British Imperialism, which refused to submit to Indian capitalism and I say to this House that it will not submit to exploitations of any kind. Public opinion is the strongest instrument; it is the strongest weapon people have and they know it and they shall use it against anyone or any person who tries to trample their lives.

It has been suggested also that the Defence Budget might be resented by the people. I do not think it will be resented by the people. It is the people who have suffered most by being defenceless and so far as I can judge the cry is, 'Never again, never again shall we be unprepared as we were on the 15th of August'. So they will not resent the Defence Budget, not while Tara Singh does his evil dance across the borders. People are prepared to pay for security so that they can build and plan a better future. But I am sorry to say that in this Budget there is not much evidence of such planning. The Honourable Member has not realized that Pakistan consists of those parts of India that are industrially undeveloped and educationally backward. I can call it the State of forgotten people. People who make the State of Pakistan, have always been forgotten by their former Governments for what reason I would not like to enlarge upon now. Perhaps they have always been far, too far, from the seat of Government; but they have made Pakistan, because they do not intend to remain forgotten. They want to take their place in this State and this is the reason why Member after Member from Eastern Pakistan and from NWFP have come and put their claims of recognition. These claims are not made in a provincial spirit. Their object is to bring to the notice of the Centre the claims of the far off people of Pakistan for whose sake Pakistan has been made. It has been made to give the common man, the neglected man, the forgotten man, full chance. The demand that there should be a development of the Port of Chittagong, that there should be Jute Mills and Textile Mills also, that there should be a Naval School in the Eastern Pakistan, is merely a means to an end, the end being giving the people of Pakistan a chance of being self-sufficient. They have been forgotten and neglected, they have been exploited for too long by everybody even by that clever twin sister, the West Bengal, for Calcutta became the second seat of the Empire because of the products of the golden fibre grown in the Eastern Bengal. We fully realize that our Government has much to do. We have full confidence in the Government of Pakistan. But we want it to realize that a nation on the morn of its freedom is anxious to remould its State nearer the heart's desire. Luckily we have in our Finance Minister a man who is not only a financial genius, but a man of vision and imagination, and he must realize this also. Pakistan grows food and goes hungry. Pakistan grows cotton and goes naked. Pakistan grows the golden fibre but no gold finds its way into the pocket of the grower. I agree with the Honourable Finance Minister that the refugees, who are mostly agriculturists, must be settled on the land and this work has been allotted to the Provinces. But I beg that the task of resettling the refugees who are artisans and craftsmen should be undertaken by the Centre. Some arts and crafts are particularly associated with the Muslim culture, such as, *Minakari, Zardozi, Kamdani, Sadakari* and so many other things. These arts are particularly associated with the Musulmans. Artisans are pouring in from Delhi, Lucknow, Moradabad and Jaipur. These artisans still work in guilds and they must be resettled accordingly. The glory that is the Taj Mahal and the grandeur that is Jama Masjid of Delhi will forever remain across the border, but may not we at least have a Billimaran, Dariba and Chandni Chowk here? They will make some people less homesick.

Sir, before I sit down I feel that I must compliment the Finance Minister for setting aside a lakh of rupees for the Iqbal Academy. It is fitting that Pakistan in its first Budget should pay this humble tribute to the man who gave the inarticulate dream of the Mussulmans a local habitation and a name and whose teachings brought forth self-respect, self-knowledge and self-confidence to Muslims again. So that his teachings should reach the whole of Pakistan. Sir, the first work that this Iqbal Academy should do is to translate his works in Bengali. It is necessary that this should be done so that his clarion call of unity should reach and resound in every corner of Pakistan and the Muslim nation may realize that we are a single nation, that they should realize that:

> *Munfaat ek hai is qom ka nuqsan bhi ek;*
> *Ek hi sab ka Nabi, din bhi iman bhi ek;*
> *Haram-i-pak bhi, Allah bhi Koran bhi ek;*
> *Kuchch bari bat thi hote jo musalman bhi ek;*
> *Firqa bandi hai kahin aur kahin zaten hain;*
> *Kya zamane men panapne ki yahi baten hain?*

(Common is the weal as well as woe of this Nation

Their Prophet (PBUH) is one, one religion and one faith
One Allah, one Koran and one holy Kaaba
Could not the Muslims be one
At one place is sectarianism and at other caste system
Are these the ways to flourish in the world?)

* * *

25 March 1950

Mr President, Sir, I notice with a feeling of satisfaction that our Government is trying to pay attention to the development of cottage industries. As has been said by the Honourable Minister for Industries in his speech at the Cottage Industries Advisory Committee's meeting the other day, the cottage industry in a country like ours, which is predominantly agricultural and is likely to remain so for a long time, can be of inestimable use to us. I want to draw the attention of the Honourable Minister towards the development and preservation of those particular cottage industries which have been a source of pride for us for many centuries. Though these industries cannot be said to be Pakistan's indigenous industries, but the craftsmen are all Mussalmans. I mean the industries such as Muradabadi utensils, Jaipur enamelled ware, Delhi *Sadakari* of *Bidar* Work, and other *Himrow* crafts for which Hyderabad Deccan, was noted. I drew the attention of this House towards the rehabilitation of those Muslim artisans who practised these crafts in the first budget session, and the Honourable Minister for Finance was kind enough to announce the formation of a Committee of Artisans and Craftsmen for this purpose. This Committee worked for six months and submitted its findings. I do not know if its findings were acted upon. Among its findings there was this point that although in Pakistan a large number of people depended for their livelihood on various types of embroidery work, like *zardozi, karchobi* and *kamdani,* the material for this embroidery work (that is gold thread), was done in India, particularly in Surat, and unless we had a factory in our country, the dependence of one of our great crafts would continue. The Committee also found that there were only two places in Pakistan where the climate was suitable for the establishment of a factory of this kind, namely Multan and Lyallpur. I know that when I am suggesting that these special crafts, the luxury crafts, be preserved, I am opening another venue of attack on myself. It will be said why in a country where people do not get sufficient to eat and dress, should these luxury crafts be preserved? I want to say that I do not deny for one minute that the primary duty of any Government is to supply food, clothes, medicines and education to its people. I do not deny it for a minute—no sane person can deny it. But Government has got other responsibilities also. We hope that a day will come when Pakistani cars will be able to compete with English and American cars. But it is not going to happen very soon. While these ancient crafts of ours are a source of great renown for Pakistan already I would like to point out to the Honourable Minister for Industries that in the industrial exhibition recently held in America the needlework of Balochistan secured the first prize. I believe that achievement is the best publicity and, therefore, development of these particular crafts will be the greatest source of publicity for Pakistan also. If they are properly organized and properly publicized, they will become a source of earning dollars and pounds. I would, at this stage, say that together with the development of these industries, we should try to encourage our people and draw their attention towards using Pakistani products, as it has been shown during the period of Khilafat Movement. We are not incapable of making great sacrifices if properly motivated.

APPENDIX 3

BEGUM IKRAMULLAH'S SPEECH DURING THE DISCUSSION ON THE REPORT OF THE BASIC PRINCIPLES COMMITTEE

26 October 1953

Mr. President! Sir, since the Objectives Resolution was passed in this House—I think it was in March 1949—we have heard innumerable speeches and seen writings in the Press on the Islamic Constitution, of the wonderful era that we were going to bring about and what wonderful people we were. As I heard these speeches, I thought of the line, I think it is of Roomi which says:

> *Zinhar az aan qaum na bashi kah faraaibannd.*
> *Haq ra ba-sajoodai wa Nabi ra ba darooday.*
>
> (Do not be amongst those people who try to deceive God by prayers and the Prophet by reciting blessings on his name)

and I think, Sir, that as long as we confine ourselves to mere talk, we will be open to the charge of deception.

Sir, as long as we remain what we are, no amount of speeches are going to convince them that Islam is a good thing, that Islam will give them fair play. You can only convince the minorities by living upto the precepts of Islam. What has been our record, I do not want to dilate upon it. I will not want to give instances for we are very thin-skinned and resent any criticisms, so I will quote the words of a poet, who next to Allama Iqbal is revered in society and regarded as a contributor to the building of Pakistan namely, Maulana Altaf Hussain Hali. This is what he said:

> Hamari har ek baat main sifla-pan hai
> Kameenon se bad-tar hamara chhaalaan hai
> Laga nam-e aaba ko ham see guhan hai
> Hamara qadam nang-e ahle-watan hai
> Buzurgon ki tauqeer khoi hai hamne
> Arab ki sharafat duboi hai hamne.
>
> Nahin koi zarra sharafat ka baqi.
> Agar ho kisi main to hai ittifaqi
>
> (We show our meanness in every word.
> Our actions are worse than those of the very base.
> We have besmirched the fair name of our ancestors.
> Our very existence is a standing slur on our countrymen.
> We have lowered the prestige of our forefathers.
> We have soiled the nobility of the Arabs.
>
> We have no trace of nobility left in us.
> But if anyone happens to have it, it is merely casual)

and it is as true of us now as when he wrote it, and do not pretend that it is not, or that you do not know it! And do not quote Koran in season and out of it, and do not quote from Allama Iqbal only such passages which are to encourage us to action, or where he wants to remind us of our glorious past! Our past was certainly glorious, our past was certainly wonderful, but our present is a sorry spectacle! Had Iqbal been listening to the cant that has been recited here for the last six years, his reply would probably have been in these words, it seems.

> Tumko islaf se kiya nisbat-e roohani hai?
> Tum Mussalman ho yeh andaz Mussalmani hai!
> Haidri faqr hai ne daulat-e Usmani-hai.
> Har koi mast ma-e zaque tan asani hai.
> Wuh zamanai main muazzaz they Mussalman hoker,

Aur tum khwar huai tarik-e Koran hokar.

(What spiritual affinity have you with your forbears?
You call yourselves Muslims but are these the ways of Muslims?
You have neither the resignation of Hyder nor the wealth of Usman.
Everyone of you is steeped in slothfulness.
They were respected and honoured as true Mussalmans.
Whereas you are disgraced for having forsaken the Koran)

Or he would have said:

Hath be-zor hain ilhad se dil khugar hain;
Ummati ba'is-e ruswai-ye Paighambar hain.
But-shakan uthgae baqi jo raha but-gar hain.
Tha Burahim pidar aur pisar azar hain.

(Your arms are weak, your hearts are inclined to atheism.
The followers bring disgrace to the Prophet
The idol-breakers are gone; the rest are idol-makers.
The father was no doubt Abraham but the sons are Azar)

Yes we were entrusted to lead the world, to frame a Constitution that was going to be a model, that was going to bring in a new order of things. Yes, that is what Iqbal had envisaged but he had asked us to fit ourselves for this task when he had said:

Sabaq phir parh sadaqat ka, adalat ka, shuja'at ka,
Liya ja'yega tujh se kam dunya ki imamat ka.

(Learn once again the lesson of Truthfulness, Justice and courage,
For thou art destined to be the Leader of Mankind)

Have you read that 'Sabaq' of 'Adalat' (Justice); 'Shujaat' (Courage) and 'Sadaqat' (Truthfulness)? I do not want to give unsavoury details but all of you know it, how we have lived up to this ideal and have qualified ourselves with the framing of a Constitution! You can say, as Mr Brohi has said, that there are Christians who do not live up to the precepts of Christ, there are Hindus who do not live up to the precepts of the Vedas, so what does it matter if we do not live up to the precepts of the Koran and Sunnah? The others, if they do not live up to their religion, do not go about proclaiming themselves to be champions of it. We do, and, mind you, to be champions something a little more than the mere acceptance of the creed is necessary. You say:

> Sufhai dahar se batil ko mitaya kisne;
> Noo'-e insan ko ghulami se churaya kisne.
> Meraay Ka'bay ko jabeenon se basaya kisne
> Meraay Koran ko seenay se lagaya kisne;
> Thay to aaba wuh tumharay hi magar tum kiya ho;
> Hath par hath dharay muntazir-e farda ho.

(Who has blotted out all trace of Falsehood from the World?
Who has delivered Man from his chains of slavery?
Who has rubbed his forehead in Thy Ka'aba.
Who has hugged Thy Koran to his bosom.
They were undoubtedly your own forefathers but what are you?
You just sit idle and hope for the best)

The answer is that. This is my reaction to all the speeches that I have heard, and I am not surprised that we did not carry conviction and I repeat, what I have said before, that no amount of haranguing of the minorities will convince them—no amount of quoting of unsavoury, indecent and obscene passages from the way of life of un-Islamic countries is going to prove—that we are going to do better.

Then what is the alternative; what are we to do? Pakistan was brought into being for two reasons: to satisfy the spiritual hunger of the Muslims of the Indian subcontinent and because of their economic necessity, but all we do is talk about religion—talk a great deal—we have done nothing but talk for the last six years without giving them a spiritual remedy and we do this because we do not want them to realize, to remember and to see that we are doing nothing—absolutely nothing—to mitigate their sufferings, or to provide the basic needs of food and clothing, a house and roof over their heads, of medical attention and education. We have done nothing; we propose to do nothing. We speak very little, if at all, about these things, but we think that as our people are religious—very deeply and sincerely religious—they will not clamour for it but keep quiet because of our talk of religion! It is true; every word of what these gentlemen have said about the sacrifice of these people in the cause of Pakistan is true. They did make sacrifices and they made those sacrifices because they wanted a country of their own, where the law of God will prevail, and that law of God meant that no man should go to bed hungry within forty houses of the house of a rich man. For that is what is ordained by the law of God. Talk a little more about this aspect of religion; think a little more about it, but do not try to deceive people by talking of religion, act on religion; that is what my advice is and when you begin to act, all the criticism will cease and the world will acclaim the birth of an Islamic State. Like the *Khulafa-i-Rashideen* you can usher in another period of golden age in the Islamic history, if you act on the true and real precepts of Islam. It is only by being sincere, by being true to the Islamic principles that you will be able to bring about a truly Islamic State in Pakistan. But not by mere talk!

Now I want to talk about the fears of my colleagues of the minority community. Unfortunately, I was not present when they made their speeches, but I have taken the trouble of reading all of the speeches of the prominent members of the Opposition and I find that they are in a state of panic and I honestly think I cannot understand why they should be! It seems to me that they have also got taken in by all this talk! Now I am not going to tell them that Islam is wonderful and that they have nothing to fear. I think they know that. I am merely going to tell them 'Please, just examine the provisions that have been made in this Constitution which are known as Islamic and examine them coolly and rationally—you are a very rational people, see how does it make your position any worse, see how it affects you at all?'

Now, take the provision that the country should be called as the Islamic democracy of Pakistan. Well, that is a fact—it is an Islamic democracy—and calling it so will not make it any less or any more of an Islamic democracy! Even in the Constitution of India it is said 'India, that is Bharat'. Every new nation likes to give an expression to their feeling of resurgent nationalism.

The second is that the Head of the State should be a Muslim. I expressed my view on this subject in a letter that I sent when this Constitution came up for discussion in December last, i.e., to my mind it was unnecessary to lay down this condition, but here I will only say that in a country of 85 per cent Muslims, it is inevitable that the Head of the State will be a Muslim; putting it down does not make it any more so.

I think the clause that caused a great deal of heart-burning and criticism is the one which lays down that no Legislature should enact any law which is repugnant to the Holy Koran and the Sunnah. Now here again, is this House likely to legislate a law or bring forward a provision that will be against the Koran and the Sunnah? 85 per cent of the people are Muslims, so it is not likely to happen, and I believe that some of our Members here have explained—I am not sure whether that explanation is coming or it has already been given—that it does not affect your personal law; if it affects anybody it affects the Muslims only. It is intended as a sort of brake on the more liberal elements in the Koran or Sunnah that prevents *Ijtihad*, for Islam is a living religion and its Commandments are capable of being adapted to every society. The fact is that Islamic law kept growing and changing for about 200 years or so but since then it has crystallized, because learning and research ceased amongst Mussalmans. I hope that with this new awakening there will be a revival of *Ijtihad*—a studying of the law will begin again and with that a further adaptation and changes will be brought about in the law to suit the modern conditions, but, till that happens—and it will take some time before that happens—many of the laws, which only a small section of the liberal elements in the country are likely to put forward will not be accepted, because of the narrow interpretation of the Islamic law, and I want to make my position absolutely clear by saying what sort of law I have in mind. For instance, polygamy is permissible in Islam but it is permissible under very strict conditions. Today, Mussalmans practise polygamy but do not conform to any of the conditions laid down. As a woman, I would like to bring forward a law restricting polygamy, because the way polygamy is practised by men today is not Islamic, but I know that I will not be allowed to do so.

Secondly, I come to the question of divorce. Divorce is easy in Islam, but it has been declared in *Hadis* that it is most repugnant to God and our Muslim society was so composed in the past that it never took place. During the last six years, ever since Pakistan came into being, because people have received accelerated promotions and easy money has been made in other ways the number of divorces has increased. Why is this so? Because the views acquired in the days of poverty are out of place in the days of plenty, and an old-fashioned wife does not fit in the new environments, with new radiogram, new frigidaire and new cars. The wives of the olden days do not fit, and as we become modern, and we do not like to practise polygamy, we divorce the first wife, do not provide for anything. Her children roam about in the street. But we are not polygamous. I would like to have the Divorce Law made so stringent that no man gets away with it so easily. But I know that I will not be allowed to do so.

The Muslim law of inheritance is the best in the world from the women's point of view. I agree, but this society has changed and certain amendments to it would make it still more profitable to women. As for instance, if there are only girls or a girl, she will not inherit her father's property fully, not all of it. The rest goes to her nearest relatives. I think since Islam gives women the right of property, it will be completely in keeping with the Islamic principles, so that women should be able to inherit all their father's properties and it should not go to collaterals. There is also a law which is known as *Mahrum-ul-Meeras* in respect of persons dying before their parents. It causes suffering to many children because the children—who are not provided for—of the young man or woman who dies before the father cannot inherit the property of their grandfather. These should attract the attention of the liberal elements amongst the Muslims to effect necessary reforms. I have been to women's organizations and I can tell you from experiences that these reforms are wanted by women and by deeply religious women. There is nothing irreligious about it, nothing anti-Islamic. It is only a question of interpreting and understanding the Islamic law, but I am not frightened by this clause, because I am hopeful that the time will come when Islamic laws will be understood and interpreted correctly and this clause will not militate against progress.

Then I come to the discussion on the separate electorate. As I was not present during the discussion, I do not want to say much about it, except that I want to point out this that the Muslim League themselves wanted separate electorate when they were in the position of a minority in the Indian subcontinent. So it is not a measure designed to make others politically ineffective, because this is what they wanted themselves. You say you would not have any voice in choosing a Member or Central Ministers. Well, in the direct election it would be so, but once you are elected, in the legislature you will have a very strong voice. As a solid bloc, you will be the deciding factor, because in the House of the future there will not be only one Muslim Party. There will, I hope, be more than one Muslim League Party and you will be able to align yourself, as is the practice in every democratic country, with every party and yours will be a decisive vote. You will certainly not be ineffective in a future House. Therefore, instead of asking that it should be reconsidered I would like you to go ahead and pass this Constitution, so that there may be elections as soon as possible and a House elected by means of direct election comes in—and a House with more than one Muslim Party.

Now I come to the formula—the formula has resolved the deadlock which was causing such desperation, universal despair and frustration among the people of Pakistan. I congratulate the new Prime Minister on this achievement of his. When I say 'congratulate', I think it should be of some value because I am not in the habit of congratulating Prime Ministers. As a matter of fact, in the last six years I think this is the first time I am saying in my speech that I congratulate a Prime Minister. I congratulate him not because I think that it is an ideal solution. No, but because it resolves the deadlock. It is not an ideal solution, for it makes legislation very cumbersome and so delays action and what is more, it perpetuates forever and crystallizes the feeling of provincialism which has grown in the last six years. It is unfortunate because when we set out to make Pakistan, there was none of it; there was none of this haggling over seats and so on; there was none of the mistrusts of one group against another, because if it had been so, Mr Liaquat Ali Khan, Mr Ghulam Muhammad and others of Western Pakistan, whose names I do not remember, would not have been elected from the East Bengal Legislature. Was there any distrust then? There was not. I am sorry to say this mistrust or distrust has been manufactured and encouraged to grow till it became such a cancer in our body politics that it looked that we would die of it. It was made to grow. It was encouraged, so that agreement should not be reached, so that a certain group or coterie of persons should continue in power. It was a very dangerous game to play and things had gone as far as they could. But we can brook no delay. The Constitution for Pakistan must be framed and framed as soon as possible, so that the people can be elected by direct election to a House which is representative of them.

I am not in agreement with Mian Sahib's proposal that this House should be dissolved and a new House elected to frame the constitution. I do not agree with him for the plain, simple and practical reason that unless we define and agree on franchise and on how many seats we are going to have, elections cannot be held. I am of the opinion that we should pass this Constitution and pass it quickly. Let us finish this work and let us resolve this deadlock which has made people desperate. Let us have courage to face the people. I know that we should not delay this matter any further. The passing of the Constitution of Pakistan should have been a historic moment. It should have been a moment of great exaltation, for such an occasion comes only once in the lifetime of a nation, but unfortunately by delays, bickerings and differences we have made it as dull as an oft-repeated story. There is very little exaltation left, there is very little enthusiasm left for it. But for goodness' sake even now go ahead and pass the constitution and do it before it is too late. The sands are running fast and each day that you delay is I think, one day lost, which is very, very dangerous. I do not want to take the time of the House any further, but I do entreat with all the earnestness at my command: Please do not delay the framing of the constitution any more. Go ahead with it and before you rise—and that does not mean that you sit for the next six years and not rise—finish this work. This work has gone on too long. People are restive. People are dissatisfied. It is a dangerous practice for a Parliament to continue sitting after there is clamour and demand for its dissolution. We have talked about Muslim League days. Have we forgotten our own sense of frustration under the Government of India, when they did not allow election or by-elections. People do not change, They are feeling just the same now. There is the same feeling of frustration and there is the same feeling of impatience. It is human nature! We have been here too long; let others have a chance. There is nothing fresh in our point of view. It is time that a new House was elected and other people came at the helm of affairs. And if you do not permit them to come constitutionally and democratically I warn they will come anyhow. *prophetic*

APPENDIX 4

BEGUM IKRAMULLAH'S RESIGNATION SPEECH

14 November 1953

Sir, I object to the adjournment of further consideration of the Basic Principles Committee Report. We solemnly pledged ourselves when we met this time that we were going to finish this BPC report. We said it over and over again that though we had adjourned several times before, this time we pledged we met to finish this report but I find that we are going to adjourn again. We adjourned for the first time for the sake of Punjab elections. Then for the second time so that Punjab and Bengal may agree about something. Then now I find that it is going to be adjourned for the third time because of Bengal elections. I feel that the constitution of Pakistan is more important than any elections. In fact it is more important than winning of seats for any particular party. I, therefore, object to this postponement and adjournment. I am, therefore, forced to record my objection with the greatest regret and very profound sorrow. I do this for I am going against the party decision today. I know I must leave the League and as I am one of those who had been with the Muslim League from the day of its inception. It is with a heavy heart that I do so. I had hoped—in fact I had hoped against hope—that I shall sign the constitution of Pakistan as a Muslim Leaguer. Time and again I have voted against the party in the party meeting and kept quiet or abstained and even voted with the party in the House because I wanted to remain a Muslim Leaguer but things have come to such a pass that today with great sorrow and deep regret I resign from the Muslim League because I cannot be a party to the fooling of the people over and over again like this. Every time we pass one or two clauses and make a lot of fuss about it and say that it is Islamic and then put the whole thing in cold storage. I therefore register my protest and resign from the Muslim League Party today.

APPENDIX 5

NEWS ITEM ABOUT BEGUM IKRAMULLAH'S SHOWDOWN WITH MENON AT THE UN, 1956

DAWN 7 December 1956
Bharat challenged to hold plebiscite
Heated UN debate on Kashmir
Begum Ikramullah corners Menon

United Nations, Dec 6: Bharat and Pakistan had a heated debate in the United Nations today over the status of Kashmir, and Pakistan challenged her neighbour to allow the UN to hold a free plebiscite in the territory 'To settle this question once and for all'.

The Bharati Minister of State, Mr V.K. Krishna Menon, touched off the exchange when, in the course of a major policy address to the General Assembly, he said the Kashmir item was still on the UN agenda because 'We came here with a complaint of aggression...we want to see an end to aggression everywhere and we want to see an end to aggression in Kashmir.'

Begum Shaista Ikramullah, the Pakistani delegate, replied that she would 'not go into details of who is the aggressor and who is not. I will not take time trying to prove that not Pakistan but Bharat is the aggressor...'

'But we say let the decision of the Security Council that has been pending for four and a half years be put into effect—that there be a free plebiscite in Kashmir...'

'All we ask for is that there should be an independent plebiscite under the auspices of the United Nations and that this question be decided once and for all...Bharat takes a noble stand on many questions in the world. They must settle the Kashmir problem if they really want to take this noble part in moral affairs of the world.'

Begum Ikramullah said there were two groups of nations in the UN—smaller nations who wanted UN authority strengthened for their protection and existence, and bigger nations 'who are not always in Europe or America.'

She said that Bharat has been willing to deal with persons it considered 'tyrants' in its efforts to take over states such as Hyderabad.

She received long applause when she concluded her remarks.

Mr Krishna Menon then asked for the floor to reply to the Begum. He told the Assembly he did not wish to go into a 'dress rehearsal' of what he might be called upon to debate before another UN body later.

He suggested that the Begum should 'read some of the papers on the Kashmir question in the Security Council.'

'The complaint of aggression is a Bharati complaint,' he said. Mr Krishna Menon contended it was Pakistan who first invaded Kashmir.

Explaining Bharat's relations with the former princely states, he said his Government had had to deal with their rulers because they were feudal states and because of arrangements made at the time the British withdrew from Bharat.

The Bharati delegate said he thought it a shame that Bharat and Pakistan had to 'wash their dirty linen' here. He also referred to the Pakistan military agreement with the United States, saying that some Pakistanis were using it as a means of arming themselves against Bharat.

'Aggression is on their (Pakistan's) side,' he said. 'This discussion is not really within the competence of the Assembly. Mis-statements have been made about our armed strength.'

'We hope that in spite of all this some day and sooner the better Pakistan will agree with us that there should be no war between us, whatever our difficulties.'

He noted at one point that Pakistan had for eight years been trying to frame a constitution.

Mr Krishna Menon brought up the subject because of Pakistan's statements that they would raise the Kashmir question for renewed debate in the Security Council next month.

When Begum Ikramullah spoke the first time, Prince Wan Waithayakon of Thailand, the Assembly President remarked that 'the lady will have the last word.'

Mr Krishna Menon later said he did not object to a lady's having the last word, but when it came to a delegate's having the last word, that was another matter. Nevertheless, he said he would yield to the obvious desire of the Assembly to go to lunch (it was almost 2 p.m.).

'I have yet to learn that a lady's words have the power of satisfying hunger,' he said.

Prince Wan corrected Mr Krishna Menon on one point. 'I did not say that a lady must have the last word...,' the President said. 'I said the lady has the last word and she has. The meeting is adjourned.'

GLOSSARY

Adaab	Greetings; salutation.
Afshan	Tinsel strips for bedecking face, hair etc.
Ahimsa	Respect for all living things and avoidance of violence towards others both in thought and deed.
Amma	Mother.
Apa	Elder sister.
Ayat	Koranic verse.
Bajaras	Small sailing boats.
Benarasi (cloth)	Brocade.
Bhabi	Elder brother's wife; sister-in-law.
Biasatin	Women who sell ribbons, buttons etc.
Chaat	A spicy eatable.
Chacha	Paternal uncle.
Chalia	Areca or betel nut.
Chaprasi	A peon.
Charpai	Bed; bedstead.
Chattaie	Mat.
Chamki	Glitter, spangle; sparkling object; tinsel.
Choki	A small, low, wooden platform.
Choori	Bangle.
Choori-wali	Female bangle-seller.
Chuga	Cloak; gown.
Daigchee	A pot; cauldron.
Dal	Pulse.
Deorhi	Threshold, outer entrance to zenana.
Derban	Doorkeeper.
Dupatta	A cloth thrown loosely over the head and shoulders by women.
Duree	A small carpet.
Ehsan	Favour.

GLOSSARY

Eid	A Muslim festival.
Farsh	Floor; carpet; a floor-cloth.
Ferangi	European.
Gaddi	Throne; seat of honour.
Ghata-toap	Curtain made to fit over the *doli*.
Gota	Gold or silver lace.
Gotay-wala	A salesman of gold or silver lace.
Halwa	A kind of sweet dish.
Ittar	Perfume.
Jahez	Dowry.
Jalebi	A kind of sweetmeat.
Jawab-e-shikwa	Answer to the complaint.
Jora	A suit (of clothes).
Kajal	Lamp black, soot applied to the eyes.
Kamkhab	Silk or satin worked with gold or silver
Karigar	Artisan.
Khala	Maternal aunt.
Khuda hafiz	God be your protector; Goodbye; farewell.
Karanti	Westernized.
Kurta	A tunic; a shirt.
Mali	A gardener.
Masnads	Richly embroidered velvet carpets.
Maulvi	Muslim priest.
Mogra	Double Jasmine.
Mohalla	A quarter or part of a town.
Mulla	Muslim priest.
Muz'afar	A sweet dish of rice, prepared with saffron.
Nani	Maternal grandmother.
Nehari	Beef stew.
Paan	Betel leaf.
Paan-daan	A box for storing ingredients eaten with betel leaf.
Pallu	Border of cloth.
Parathas	Bread made with butter or ghee, and of several layers, like pie-crust.
Phupi	Paternal aunt.
Pindal	A canopy under which a meeting is held.

Pughri	Turban.
Qawwal	Professional singer at saints' tombs.
Razai	Quilt.
Sajdah-e-shukar	To prostrate oneself with gratitude.
Satyagraha	Passive resistance.
Sehra	A garland which covers the face and is worn by the bride and the bridegroom at the marriage ceremony.
Shamiana	A marquee.
Shikwa	Complaint.
Silai-wali	Seamstress.
Surahi	A goblet; a long-necked flask.
Surmah	Collyrium: antimony reduced to fine powder for applying to the eyes.
Swaraj	Self-government; home rule.
Tasmiyah	Giving a name (to).
Teeka	A mark made on the forehead; an ornament of gold or silver worn on the forehead.
Thappa	Broad silver lace.
Thelaywalla	One who vends.
Zenana	The female apartment.

001 246-426 6215